TAKING THE SHORT BUS

Teacher I Need you

A novel by

BRUCE BERYL FISHER

SUBTITLE FROM THE SONG
by
Sir. ELTON JOHN
Based on real events

TAKING THE SHORT BUS

5830 E 2nd St, Ste 7000 #9983
Casper, WY 82609
USA

DEDICATION

To my mother and father and my Uncle Abe who understood too clearly the importance of education. Steve D. Feiner (History teacher). Every young person during adolescence progresses through the door of awareness. I was lucky you were at the threshold to greet me. The acknowledgment of your untimely passing before our chance of re-acquaintance will forever drive a wedge through my heart with despair. Diane S (English teacher). Your warm smile and compassion for reading. You introduced me to the worlds of Herman Raucher, Leon Uris, Robin Cook, Phillip Roth, James Michener, and Howard Fast, which led me to my own works. Diane V. and John S. (Principals). How in the world did you ever put up with me? I was a living hell. You were both saints beyond earthly define. Frank James (Talent Agent). Your strong moral support helped me bounce back from the brink of personal devastation. Thanks Frank, for getting me into New York. It changed my life for the best. And to my friend Sandy for sharing your experiences of Vietnam. Now I understand why I don't want to know.

Finally, to my wife Michele. You believed in me before I had tangible proof of success. Your blind faith leads me through relentless hours of hard work to achieve the impossible so I could present to you and our son the life that you both so richly deserve. And may I be the first to admit that you literally saved my life from despair. May all your Gods have a place in their hearts for all of you.

BBF

Austin:

"For without words, in friendship, all thoughts, all desires, all expectations are born and shared with joy that is unclaimed."

THE PROPHET
Kahlil Gibran

PREFACE

"Taking the Short Bus -Teacher, I need You" is not a self-help or a self-awareness book. It will not give advice on ADHD or a cure for any other learning disability. Taking place in and out of the city of Philadelphia between the years 1974–75, this historical/comedy/drama is about eighteen-year-old Eric Blum's trials and tribulations, and his anticipation of being his last year at a private school for special needs, if he can prove to the school authorities that he is academically, and emotionally capable to file back into society.

Philadelphia public schools in the mid-1960s-70s had failed to address learning disabilities in a time when learning disabilities and the knowledge of psychiatric care were detrimental to one's career. Today psychiatric therapy is socially acceptable. It sounds very chic to hear.

"I'm sorry, I must cancel our luncheon date. I made an appointment with my therapist,"

As for education presently, public schools had altered their way of teaching to become politically correct -a races, political movement based on fear, founded by guilt-, practicing Affirmative Action and Minority Quotas when the schools should be concentrating on getting back to the basic core of teaching reading, writing and arithmetic the way it should be taught for all students without discrimination or dumb sizing exams for the fear and guilt of leaving one child behind.

Although standardize testing to track and monitor the progress of student's academic progress is essential, financially awarding schools for high percentage of students who pass standardized testing should not be the criterion for allocating funds and grants to only those schools for their excellence. Personally, I would never dream of reallocating funds from any school, pass or fail. In my present adopted home state of Florida, when my son was attending grade school, students were forced to submit to the "FCAT" -Florida Comprehensive Assessment Test- or what my son used to call it, "The Florida Child Abusive Test". Since 2015 the FCAT had been replaced with -FSAT- the Florida Standards Assessment Test which sounds like the same difference. According to Wikipedia.com -not a reliable source for research, but a start-, the FCAT and other scholastic standardized testing originally designed to place students in their appropriate academic level had also been criticized by many students and teachers because the FCAT did not prepare students for the real world. FCAT scores were not accepted as application to any college that I know of. The parochial and private schools of excellence recognized under federal guidelines separately from state guidelines, and proclaimed as superior by the federal government, receive no public funds and are exempt from requiring their students to take the FCAT.

The FCAT test came under fire from education groups and parents for taking up three-quarters of the school year to teach students how to pass the test, rather than taking the time teaching students the fundamental material in the core subjects such as English, math, sciences, and the arts.

Another point of criticism on the FCAT was that all students of the same grade took the same test even though students were enrolled in different courses. To compensate for this in many Florida public schools, teachers were directed to cover FCAT skills regardless of what subject they were assigned to be covering. FCAT had nothing to do with a student's aptitude, scholastic progress, or achievements, but only to justify the allocation of funds.

The lower-class public schools that didn't do as well on the FCAT didn't get the appropriate funding needed to afford the implementations our property taxes and state lottery were supposed to be paying for.

Those schools were financially thrown by the wayside by the school board. The result was schools with excellent teachers in the lower-class neighborhoods were so frustrated from being academically and financially ignored, they simply babysat rowdy students who didn't care, or have the desire to conform to learn. Great teachers gave up teaching and merely collected paychecks and benefits. I know if I didn't send my son under the age of eighteen to school I would have been arrested as truant, unless I assured the department of education he was being homeschooled.

If it's severely frowned upon to be illiterate in this country, and if education is portrayed as a high priority, why is it that teachers and other educational curricula are first to be cut in a budget crunch? And why isn't there ever enough tax money for the public schools to run efficiently? I surely pay enough property, and local sales taxes, road tolls, and over-priced parking meters to accommodate any needs for my city's fire, police, and other utilities, let alone the school board. I even buy a lottery ticket every so often that was designed to be allocated for education.

A friend of mine pointed out a collage of over fifty taxes that people are accountable for daily. And this is just a small example:

Accounts receivable tax, building permit tax, cigarette tax, corporate income tax, dog license tax, unemployment tax, fishing license tax, hunting license tax, inheritance tax, inventory tax, IRS interest tax -*tax on top of tax*-, IRS penalties tax -*tax on top of tax*-, liquor license tax, luxury tax, marriage license tax, Medicare tax, real estate tax, service charge tax, and Social Security tax.

Then there was the phone bill. Telephone federal excise tax, telephone federal universal tax, service free tax, telephone federal, state and local surcharge tax, telephone minimum usage surcharge tax, telephone recurring and nonrecurring charges tax, utility tax. And of course, before you can drive… CDL license tax, road usage tax, recreational vehicle tax, gasoline tax, vehicle license registration tax, vehicle sales tax, watercraft registration tax. And if you want to eat, there's a food license tax and, well water permit tax. And let's not forget if you decide to get hurt on the job, worker's compensation tax. As I mentioned before this is just a small example daily.

Multiply all that by the population of the city -not including those under the age of taxation-, and you must ask, why isn't there ever enough money? The answer is simple. The local school boards, federal and local city controllers do not know how to prioritize and reallocate our tax funds unless it comes down to financing a sports stadium or arena. And there they find the money with little to no problem.

The two greatest resources this country has are our children and our senior citizens and presently our local and federal governments are not reinvesting wisely in those assets. Paolo Lionni, author of 'The Leipzig Connection', stated in 1993.

"One has only to read old debates in the Congressional Records or scan the books published in the 1800s to realize that our ancestors of over a century ago commanded a use of the language far superior to our own. Students learned how to read not comic books but the essays of Burke, Webster, Lincoln, Horace, Cicero. Their difficulties with grammar were overcome long before they graduated from school, and my review of a typical elementary school arithmetic textbook printed in 1910, shows dramatically that students were learning mathematical skills that few of our current public high school graduates know anything about".

Have you seen the new math that our public schools were forcing our children to learn -Common Core-?

The high school graduate of 1900 was an educated person, fluent in their language, history, and culture, possessing the skills needed to succeed."

Because I was enslaved by the late twentieth century politically correct, affirmative action, minority quota public educational system that seemed to be more concerned about their fiscal quarter than teaching our children of what was needed to survive academically in this global economy, I must admit, I don't fit the previous graduate educational criteria from 1900 myself.

The greatest generation this country has ever produced to date are from the twentieth century. Born during the 1920s, they survived the "Great Depression". Sacrificed rations for the war effort. Set us up industry for twenty-five to thirty-year jobs. Insured our savings so that the next generation could have a secure and comfortable way of life. And on the workings of a slide rule, sent twelve men to walk on the moon, and safely returned them back to earth. I assure you, not even one of those people from that "Great Generation" had ever taken or had to pass an FCAT.

In my unprofessional educational opinion, the only thing that the late twentieth and early twenty-first century American public education institutes produce with their "politically correct, affirmative action, minority quotas, and standardized testing", are children and teachers who are nervous, neurotic, and hyperactive, leading our psychiatric fathers to label children who happen to be psychologically or physically hyperactive "ADD and ADHD".

How was ADD and ADHD discovered? Peter Breggin, in his 1991 book '*Toxic Psychiatry*' relays,

"At first psychiatrists called hyperactivity a 'Brain Disease.' When no brain disease could be found, they changed it to 'Minimal Brain Disease' (MBD). When no minimal brain disease could be found, the profession transformed the concept into 'Minimal Brain Dysfunction.' When no MBD could be demonstrated, our children where labeled 'ADD' (attention deficit disorder) not because of a problem the children have; it's because some problems our psychiatric fathers and teachers who cannot tolerate active children have."

Not knowing how to correctly deal with this label, according to late author Jim Marrs in his book "*The Rise of the Fourth Reich*".

"Our psychiatric forefathers decided to drug our children to curb what they have concluded was ADD and ADHD with Anafranil, lithium, Xanax, Valium, Thorazine, Amitriptyline." And our psychiatric doctors' choice of pharmaceutical candy, Prozac and Ritalin while attending our public schools.

Let us not forget Columbine High in Colorado in 1999, when two high school students -Dylan Klebold and Eric Harris- gunned down and killed one teacher and twelve students, leaving twenty-one students wounded. Harris was once prescribed the antidepressant drug Zoloft. At the time of the massacre, he was on Luvox. And in 2012, twenty-year-old Adam Lanza fatally shot twenty children and six adult staff members at Sandy Hook Elementary in Newtown Connecticut. Lanza was pre-scribed Fanapt for his Autism. Not to say that those were the drugs that cause these psychotic, homicidal "over-medicated" deranged time bomb teenagers lurking through the hallways of our public schools to commit murder. But the list goes on of fervently medicating our children through the dawn of the twenty-first century.

Eric Blum had suffered from a learning disability -dyslexia- reading on a fourth-grade level while attending eighth grade in an overcrowded public school, falling through the academic cracks. Plus, an emotional break-down from the result of his brother killed in Vietnam.

With his learning disability, the public-school authorities passed him from grade to grade to fill-in the percentage of students needed to receive the funding for the following year. Eric Blum was lucky. His parents caught on to the public-school scam and had Eric transferred to a private school that had the patience, time, and funds to help Eric academically catch up.

Even though Taking the Short Bus-Teacher, I need You- takes place in the last part of the twentieth century, the pushing of func-tionally illiterate, incompetent students from one grade to the next to confirm funding for the following school year continues to be standard procedure for hundreds of American public schools at the dawn of the twenty-first century.

This story not only deals with the issues of learning disabilities. It deals with adolescence. Finding one's place and self. And coming of age.

I like to consider this book a time machine at the end of the Vietnam war, and at the dawn of disco music. A time spent with people who are no longer with us, and most places that no longer exist. A time when people were not afraid or ashamed to laugh at themselves. A time before political correctness.

If you are a person who is politically, sexually, and historically sensitive, do not read any farther, because this is my story, and I'm sticking with it.

Bruce Beryl Fisher

AUTHOR'S NOTE

The content of this story holds no bearing on my political affiliation, racial or personal religious beliefs. I am a storyteller and a witness from my time. Shakespeare once wrote, "The world is a stage." I was fortunate enough to have the front-row seat down stage in front of house by the center aisle.

Bruce Beryl Fisher

CHAPTER 1

CAROL SCHOR, AN attractive woman in her mid-twenties was the history teacher at Noah Webster Preparatory -a private junior and high school for children with special needs- was driving through the ritzy suburbs of Cheltenham Township, Pennsylvania outside the city of Philadelphia in a convertible 1967 light grey Volkswagen Beetle. The car had a warped exhaust manifold that could be heard from half a block away. The fumes from the car made Carol's eyes tear, threatening to ruin her mascara. To escape the fumes and to avoid the make-up malfunction, when the weather was admirable, Carol would drive with the windows and top down. The fall air was crisp and refreshing. She enjoyed driving in her bare feet. A squares of toilet paper squeezed between her toes kept her red freshly painted nail polish from smearing.

In a slight reverb, W.F.I.L- AM radio morning news reported by Chuck Stone on Carol's car radio announced Secretary of State Henry Kissinger indicating in Switzerland the Geneva Peace Talks were progressing, and the Vietnam War could possibly be ending early spring of next year. Although there had been some withdrawal, there was still well over one thousand American soldiers remaining in Southeast Asia.

President Ford said OPEC would enforce an oil embargo against the United States for supporting Israel militarily. Within the last two months gasoline prices soared from thirty-five cents a gallon to fifty cents.

Locally, Mayor Frank L. Rizzo of Philadelphia had stated that even though the Philadelphia teachers' strike had been over for the past week, details were still being hammered out over health and welfare.

After the news/sports/weather and the Arco Go Patrol helicopter traffic report from Walt McDonald, Who's That Lady by the Isley Brothers took over the airwaves. With her dark brown Farrah Fawcett feathered hair cut past her shoulders flowing in the breeze, Carol bobbed and sang along with the music playing loud enough to drown out the sound of the exhaust while she cruised through the burbs.

After finding a choice parking spot at the school, Carol turned off the engine, which instantly turned off the car radio. She opened her car door and dropped one of her two clogs on the ground. As she pulled the toilet paper from between her toes, sixteen-year-old student Tony Burns -who allegedly suffered from Tourette syndrome- walked up to the car and kicked the clog across the parking lot before Carol had a chance to slip into it. She strongly demanded he give it back. Tony laughed as he kicked it toward her. The shoe slid under the car. Carol had to indignantly bend down under the car to retrieve it. After collecting her school papers from the front seat, she slipped into her clogs, and proceeded to walk toward the school.

The building in which Noah Webster Preparatory was housed was a two-story English Tutor with a stone exterior and a black slate roof. It was originally built in 1840s as a residence for a local newspaper publisher who also had investments with the Reading Railroad Company. In the mid-1950s, his descendants sold the manor to a Calvary congregation.

In 1965 the congregation broke ground next door to build a bigger church with more adequate parking space and sold the manor to a nonprofit educational corporation catering to children with learning disabilities. In 1966 Noah Webster Preparatory was founded.

The studies and living spaces on the first floor of the old tutor were converted into classrooms. The eight bedrooms on the second floor were also converted into classrooms and had fireplaces that no longer worked except for the fireplace on the first-floor cafeteria. The interior of the cafeteria was enclosed in dark mahogany wood panels. The room was originally used as the ballroom for the manor, then the chapel for the church.

In 1974, Noah Webster Preparatory enrolled fifty-four students. The school had no less than four and no more than ten students in a class. Carol's classroom was on the first floor. Her small classroom was originally used as the kitchen for the manor. The only utility left was the double sinks under a pair of windows. The walls were painted pale yellow. A mounted four-by-eight-foot blackboard covered the front wall. Carol's desk was in front of the blackboard facing five students. Four were sitting by their desks. Student Tony Burns placed his desk against the right side of Carol's. Student Mark Stern whose desk was in front of Carol's was silently reading from a "Mad" magazine. Student Mick Maze was gazing into space sat to the left of Mark Stern, while Student Joey Pearlman, who suffered from autism swayed in his chair from behind his desk in the back of the room, all waiting for class to begin.

Carol stood behind her desk fixing her hair and make-up holding onto a hand-held pocket mirror. Realizing she had some time from her wristwatch before school began, Carol turned on the small transistor radio on top her desk and tuned in the disco song Rock the Boat by Hues Corporation.

Out on the parking lot following seven students, eighteen-year-old Eric Blum -carrying a paper lunch bag- reluctantly climbed out of the 1971 yellow Dodge window van disguised as a school bus with red and yellow warning lights on its roof. He was the last student to stroll into Carol's classroom. Hearing the music, Eric danced toward his desk next

3

to Joey in the back of the room. Unbeknown to Joey Pearlman, Eric mocked him by swaying with the rhythm of the music. Carol looked up from her desk and with wide eyes stared at Eric. "What?" Eric said to Carol as he slid over toward his desk and took his seat.

Eric opened the paper lunch bag and pulled out the double-decker peanut-butter and jelly sandwich his mother had made the night before and began to eat.

Attending the public school system in eighth grade, Eric Blum was failing academically. His parents had him tested by the children psychology department at Hahnemann Hospital in Philadelphia. Eric's parents were beside themselves when they found he was diagnosed with dyslexia, reading on a fourth-grade level. Plus, because of his brother's -Elliot- death in the Vietnam war in 1969, Eric had suffered from an emotional break-down.

The Philadelphia school system with its overcrowded classrooms and over-worked teachers did not have the time nor the funding to cater with children.

who had learning disabilities. By the summer of 1970, the Blum's founded Noah Webster Preparatory.

After four years and now a senior, with the help from psychological counseling at Webster, the school was observing Eric to make sure he was emotionally and academically stable to graduate and to reenter the real world. Eric felt he was ready to leave Webster and looking forward to moving on with his life.

Carol once again peered down at her wristwatch and saw it was time to conduct the next fifteen minutes of her advisory/history class and turned off the radio. She had started the school year off teaching the arrival of Christopher Columbus to the new world.

"Even though we have only fifteen minutes before your first periods, I want everybody to take out your history book and open to chapter seven." Carol announced.

While the students took out their history books from in their desks to chapter seven, Mark Stern placed his "Mad" magazine on top of the open history book page and continued to read to himself.

"Yesterday we were discussing Columbus's second voyage." Carol continued as she stared at Mark. "Who wants to read out-loud the first paragraph?"

"I will!" Tony called out as he raised his hand.

Carol glanced down at Tony with trepidation. She had suspicioned that Tony maybe taking advantage of his Tourette's syndrome by displaying inappropriate behavior during class, and occasionally losing verbal control as he would read.

"Ok. But just read what it says in the book, Tony. No additions." Said Carol.

Tony proceeded to read from the book as Carol returned her attention toward Mark Stern still reading from his magazine.

"'During the second voyage, Columbus sent a letter to the monarchs proposing to enslave some of the Americas' people, specifically from the Carib tribe, on the grounds of their independence-minded aggressiveness and their status as enemies of the Tai'no tribe...'"

As Tony read on, Mark Stern looked up from his magazine and saw Carol staring down at him wide eyed. Mark -unintimidated- licked his index finger then turned to the next page of his magazine and continued to read to himself.

"... Although his petition was refused by the crown," Tony continued reading. "In February 1495, Columbus disobeyed the Queen and took sixteen-hundred people from the Arawak tribe who were then taken by the Carib as captives and slaves.'... That's right! Don't listen that bitch! She ain't there to see!"

"Tony!" Carol called out.

"That Wop whore! Who does she think she is, the Queen of England?"

"Tony!" Carol yelled as the class laughed on. "Queen Isabella wasn't Italian! She was Queen of Spain! And didn't I tell you to just read from the book? I don't want to hear anything else from you but what's in the book! Now continue!"

Tony continued to read as Carol stared back at Mark... 'No room was available for about four hundred of the kidnapped Arawak leading to their release. The long-term consequence for the Arawak's of contact with Europeans was that thousands of people were almost entirely exterminated by disease... "those no good fuck'en dirty diseased wop rat bastards!"

"Tony! Columbus's men were not Italian! Now, that's it! You're done reading!"

"*Skinny bitch.*" Tony said under his tongue.

Carol held her breath the way Tony addressed her. She had been instructed by school authorities and the school psychologist to maintain a tolerant posture for his 'Tourette's syndrome'.

Carol continued with the rest of her lesson plan as Tony began to repeatedly drop his desktop.

"On his first arrival, the native tribes (drop) never saw a ship or (drop) even men like Columbus before and (drop) treated... (drop)... him and his men like gods. And because of that (drop) Columbus and his crew had the run of (drop) the island."

Carol turned her attention toward Mark Stern who was still reading from his "MAD" Magazine within the open page of his history book.

"Mark! What are you up to?" She asked.

"Spy Versus Spy." Mark replied as he continued to read.

"Okay, Stern! Since you're so interested in that magazine, why did the Pilgrims settle in Massachusetts?"

"The Pilgrims settled in Massachusetts because they knew they would not get the religious freedom that they had set out for in Virginia, since the earlier settlers already in Virginia were loyalist to the King."

Mark Stern didn't even look up from his comic book when he delivered that answer.

"Now you may go back to your magazine," Carol humbly announced. Mark licked his index finger and for the second time nonchalantly turned to the next page.

Once again, Tony began to repeatedly drop his desktop down onto the desk.

"What are you doing?" Carol yelled.

"Nothing!" Tony yelled back.

"Well then cut it out!" Tony dropped the top once again. Carol was getting madder than ever and felt like a pressure cooker ready to explode. Instructed or not, for the past three years she just about had it with Tony's verbal abuse and exploitations.

"Now you listen to me," Carol advised waving her finger toward Tony. "This may be your third year here, and the other teachers may have to tolerate your alleged Tourette's syndrome, but this year I'm not taking any more of your crap! I'm telling you now! If you don't begin to straighten up, I'm going to kick your ass right out of this classroom!"

Swearing and corporal punishment from staff was not encouraged at this institution, but not by any means was Noah Webster Preparatory a normal school.

Tony dropped the desktop as a challenge to her threat.

"You've been kicked out of every suburban school from Abington to Glenside." Carol continued. "And if you think you're so tough, I'll see that you're sent to a school in Philly!"

"They'll make me tougher, babe!" Tony called out with a smile on his face hiding behind his right hand that was holding up his head at his desk. Carol glared at him for a moment with a look that could stop a charging bull.

Tony could never be sent to a school outside his district. Especially from suburbia. It was a hollow threat.

Tony Burns: sixteen-years-old that had worn the same pair of denim pants, flannel shirt, and leather motorcycle jacket every day for the past two years. Besides his clothes being dirty, it smelled of motor oil.

At home, Tony was rebuilding a 1967, 289-cubic-inch Ford Mustang engine. In fact, from under the carport he had taken the entire engine out of the car piece by piece and carried it off to his bedroom on the second floor of his split-level up-scale suburban house in Jenkintown. When completed, how he was expected to carry a five-hundred pound fully assembled car engine from his bedroom down a flight of stairs and out the front door was anybody's guess.

Despite his Tourette's syndrome, Tony had one of the highest IQ in the school accompanied by an uncontrollable fowl mouth. Even his parents couldn't control him.

Tony's parents were wealthy, prominent, and well respected in their community. They had three children, an eighteen-year-old son, a fourteen-year-old daughter, and sixteen-year-old Tony. The Burns and the school psychologist agreed to let Tony do whatever he wanted to do, just as-long-as he didn't hurt himself or anybody else. Tony wasn't a bully toward any of the other students at school, but he did spend a lot of energy trying to intimidate Carol.

"Speaking about slaves," Eric interrupted in a cheerful voice from the back of the room between chews of his double-decker peanut-butter and jelly sandwich. "Did I tell you that I joined the Bishop McDevitt track team?"

"What does that have to do with slavery? And stop eating in my class." Carol demanded.

"You see, a week ago after school I went to Bishop McDevitt High school to watch my cousin Opie join the school football team. As I waited for my cousin by the field, this big husky coach approached me and asked if I would like to join. Out on the field I saw kids being carried off, and this was just the practice, so I turned to this coach and said jokingly, 'No, but I'll join your track team.' He asked me for my homeroom teacher's name." Eric took another bite from his sandwich.

Noah Webster Prep. was an academic institution. They had a gym class only to qualify as a school under Pennsylvania state law. There was no track or football, but there was an unofficial basketball team that played against other private schools in the area. Eric was a fast runner, perhaps the fastest at Webster. Out of fifty-four students, that wasn't much. Eric wanted to join a track team and saw an opportunity at his cousin's Catholic school just about a mile down the road from Webster.

Cousin Opie was an eighteen-year-old Coca-Cola addict. He would travel with a case of eight-ounce glass bottles of Coca-Cola in the back seat of his car. Opie thought it was 'the real thing.' It was the caffeine Cousin Opie was addicted to.

When Eric told Carol, he used the name of his homeroom teacher to get on Bishop McDevitt's track team, she became a bit suspicious.

"What homeroom teacher?" Carol asked him. "You mean to tell me that you gave another school my name? And stop eating in my class!"

"No," Eric replied. "I didn't give them your name. I gave them, Sister Mary!" Eric claimed as he took another bite from his sandwich.

"Who in the hell is Sister Mary? And one more bite from that sandwich, I'm going to bite your head off!"

"Ah! The praying mantis in you comes out!" Tony belts out toward Carol.

"Well, I figured that every catholic school has a sister Mary." said Eric as he chewed.

The rest of the class laughed. Even Mark Stern closed his magazine and turned to face Eric.

"Did you give them your real name?" asked Mark.

"I wasn't going to at first," Eric replied. "I was thinking of going under the name, Mick Maze."

"Hey, that's my name!" Maze called out.

Mick Maze was a chubby young man of sixteen years who wore thick-black-rimmed glasses and was known as the school sadist. Mick lived with his mother and younger sister somewhere in Abington Township. His parents had divorced years before. Outside of school, without the proper parental guidance, Mick attached himself to the wrong crowd.

"Last night, me and my buddies saw this cat walking across the street, you know!" Mick said with a smile only a sadist could wear.

"Oh no, no, no!" Carol said to herself as she covered her face with her right hand anticipating what she was about to hear. Other students patiently listened with dead pan expressions.

"So, I chased him, picked him up, and threw him in the back seat of my buddy's car, you know! The cat began to scratch and scream, so I punched it in the mouth to give it something to scream about."

Carol peeked at Mick through her fingers in horror.

"When the car was speeding about seventy miles an hour," Mick continued. "I rolled down my window, you know! I grabbed the cat by the back of its neck, and I hung him out over the highway. I saw this Mack truck coming in the opposite direction. I let the cat go, and before it hit the ground, SPLAT! Me and my buddies were so proud of ourselves... that we got off the next exit and headed back to watch-it-suffa!"

There was an absolute dead silence in the classroom. Eric glanced down to find his double-decker peanut-butter and jelly sandwich squeezed between his fingers representing cat guts. Carol was lost for words. If Tony had dropped his desk-top it would have been a welcome sound, but the most abrupt and ill-behaved child in school missed his only welcome cue. A helicopter flew by, and Joey Pearlman bolted out of his seat, ran behind Eric toward the nearest window over the double sinks to watch it fly by.

Joey Pearlman: A lanky seventeen-year-old which in a few years be diagnosed with Asperger. Mathematically brilliant, he would hardly talk and would sway for hours on end in his seat. When he heard a helicopter,

Joey would jump out of his chair to the nearest window to watch it fly over. He was fascinated by helicopters.

The entire class jumped out of their seats when the period bell rang out.

"Everybody out! Get to your next class, and I'll see you all Monday morning." Carol called out. "And Tony, you better be cool!" She added. Tony left the classroom with a hideous laugh.

As all the students exited the classroom, Eric slid the uneaten portion of the sandwich back into its paper bag and dropped it into his desk. He peeled himself out from his chair and walked toward Carol's desk as she continued to collect her lesson plan for the next period.

"So, tell me, whose leg I gotta fuck this year to get the hell out of this retarded house?"

"Eric! Watch your language! Who do you think you're talking to? You know what you must do. You must prove yourself mentally and academically! And stop calling this place a 'retarded house'! And stop eating in my class!"

"No matter what I do, the staff here doesn't feel that I'm good or ready enough leave!" Eric countered.

"Just do what you're told and stay cool."

"Now look, Carol! I've been cool these past two years."

When it came to liberal policies, Noah Webster Preparatory authorities turned a deaf ear when students addressed their instructors by their first name.

"Convincing the fattest student in school to dress up as Santa Claus, then trying to force him down the cafeteria chimney is not the school's idea of 'being cool'," Carol pointed out.

"Well, I didn't know that the fireplace was lit!" Eric pleaded defensively.

"Didn't you notice the smoke coming out from the chimney, Eric?"

"No! I don't remember. It wasn't important to me at the time. I have had enough of this place! I don't feel I belong here anymore!"

"I don't know what to tell you, Eric," Carol said as she continued collecting her things together at her desk. "This year has just started. I'm sure if you play your cards right, this could very well be your last year."

"You know what I think? I think you want to purposely keep me here so when I get a little older, you could grab me for yourself." Eric smiled flashing his eyes raising his eyebrows.

Carol stopped what she was doing at her desk, leaned in closer looking straight into Eric's hazel eyes and with a grin said, "Why don't you get a life, kid?"

Eric leaned even closer and replied softly, "I'd love to, but this school and my parents won't let me go without a diploma!"

CHAPTER 2

DON'T ASK ALICE

IT WAS LATE afternoon after school in front of a single two-story stoneface house in the Northeast Oxford Circle section of Philadelphia. Mark Stern pulled over to the curb in his mother's 1972 canary yellow Ford Torino. Eric slid out from the front passenger side. "Thanks Mark. I'll see you Monday."

As the Torino slipped away from the curb, Eric paused for a moment to glance at the house. He then proceeded to walk around to the side. Through the kitchen door window, Eric watched his girlfriend seventeen-year-old Alice Cappadonna slide a whole chicken out from the open oven to be basted.

Alice was a beautiful slim Italian with long straight jet-black hair that hung loose toward the center of her back. Eric knocked on the kitchen door. Alice slid the chicken back into the oven, closing the oven door then turned to give Eric a slight smile as she let him into the house. They kissed on the lips for a moment. Eric unzipped and peeled off his navy-blue windbreaker and handed it off to Alice. On her return to the oven, she tossed the jacket toward one of the four chairs surrounding the 1950's style four-by-four foot yellow and red metal kitchen table but missed. She continued stirring the pot of rice on top of the stove with no intention of picking the jacket up.

Eric picked the jacket up and carelessly hung it over the back of one of the kitchen chairs, then sat down to observe Alice preparing dinner.

"That chicken smells mighty good!" said Eric.

"Thanks. You got here early. I didn't expect you for at least another hour."

"Yeah, well, Stern had his mother's car with him today. He gave me a lift from school. When is your mother getting home from work?"

"Soon."

Eric's eyes followed Alice around the kitchen till they contacted a couple unopened envelopes of mail and a small unmarked brown tinted plastic bottle on the kitchen countertop. He reached from his chair to pick up the bottle. Eric popped off the white plastic cap to peer inside. The bottle was quarter filled with Quaaludes, better known at this time as 714s. He replaced the lid and the bottle on top of the counter. Eric watched Alice for a moment before saying a word.

"I wish you would stop using this shit!"

Alice didn't have to turn to see what Eric was indicating. It was the same old story.

"I wish you would get off my back about it!" Alice snapped.

Many times, in the past Alice promised Eric that she would stop taking the drugs and just as many times she had broken her promise.

"Why do you need this stuff?" asked Eric.

"Would you rather have me snort from a bottle of ammonia?"

"It clears my sinuses," Eric confessed.

Eric a had a sinus condition and found just a snort of ammonia cleared his nasal passages.

"… And I had a rough day today!" Alice declared. "And that's just school! And now, I have to cook and clean the house. I'm old enough to make my own decisions, Eric! I've been taking care of myself since I was nine. Don't start with me now!"

Alice's parents had been divorced for several years. Her father remarried and lived elsewhere in the city. With a daughter and a son to support, Alice's mom worked two jobs to make ends meet.

Along with Alice's household chores and academic responsibilities, having to take on the tasks of a young adult robbed her of her childhood. Quaaludes, alcohol, and weed were her own little recess from reality. Now, at the age of seventeen, she was weary of school and playing house.

"I think we have to talk, Alice." Eric was feeling philosophical this evening.

"I think we have to split-up, Eric!"

Eric was speechless. He never expected Alice to think such a thing, let alone suggest it. It was the emotional blow of all blows.

"No. I don't think so," Eric replied.

"Well, you better think again!"

Alice was quick and stern with her reply. She stirred the rice in the pot over the stove with the metal ladle for two revolutions which gave her enough time to compose. Alice glanced in the corner of her eye to find Eric sitting on the kitchen chair staring solemnly at the floor. She replaced the ladle on top of the stove, walked toward Eric, and squatted down in front. Eric gazed down into her almond eyes looking up at him. She spoke softly and gentle.

"Eric, I don't feel that we're making it anymore. I feel that we're splitting apart, going in different directions. Look, you never even smoked pot. Don't knock it unless you try it."

"But Alice!" pleaded Eric. "I love you. I don't want to see you get hurt."

Alice looked down onto the floor as she mumbled to herself." I knew this wasn't going to be easy. I practiced all day for this." She looked up into Eric's painful face. "Eric, I know the way you feel about me, and that's why you don't see that it's not working out between us anymore."

"Is there somebody else?" asked Eric.

15

Alice slapped her thigh in disgust as she stood up and stormed back toward the stove. "Does it always have to be 'somebody else'? Eric…"

Alice abruptly stopped in mid-sentence as her mother unlocked the kitchen door from the outside and walked into the kitchen. Before Mrs. Cappadonna got herself focused, Eric reached over to the countertop for the vial of ludes and shoved it in his pants pocket. Alice saw the plastic bottle was missing. Eric offered her a nod of acknowledgment that the bottle was safely out of sight. Alice faced her mother with relief.

"Hi, mom, Eric's here!" she said as she kissed her mother on the cheek with a forced grin.

Mrs. Cappadonna took off her jacket and placed it over Eric's jacket on the back of the kitchen chair.

"Hi, Eric. How are you?"

"I'm fine. How are you, Mrs. Cappadonna?"

"Tired." Mrs. Cappadonna replied with a frown.

Eric had assumed if you ever wanted to know what your girlfriend will look like in twenty years, look at the mother. Mrs. Cappadonna was an attractive lady in her early forties with shoulder-length dark hair, and for somebody who was not a member of a gym had kept her figure in good shape.

"What time are you going home tonight?" Alice asked Eric. After a day of school, babysitting, and making dinner, Alice was not in the mood for company. Especially entertaining a boyfriend, she no longer wanted to be with.

"I was planning on leaving around ten," replied Eric.

"I didn't notice your car here," Mrs. Cappadonna inquired as she picked up the two unopened envelopes of mail on the countertop and glanced down at their addresses.

"No. I got a lift from school. My car is at home. I still have to fix it."

"Well, I'm going up to take a nap. If I wake up before you leave, I'll give you a ride home." Mrs. Cappadonna offered as she dropped the two envelopes back onto the counter and continued to walk into the living room.

"Thank you," said Eric.

"Mom, I just cooked a chicken," announced Alice.

"Thanks honey. Just save me a piece for when I wake up." Mrs. Cappadonna said from the living room as she climbed up the stairs to her bedroom for her nap. Alice was hoping that her mother wouldn't nap too long to give Eric a lift home.

"Well," said Alice to Eric. "Do you want to join us?"

"Why, are you falling apart?" joked Eric in the voice of Groucho Marx miming holding a cigar. Alice either didn't get the joke, or maybe didn't hear it. She was too busy getting the chicken out of the oven. "Yeah, uh," Eric continued, "I'll have a breast or two."

Alice shared a smirk and shook her head, getting the pun of Eric's last remark as she placed the chicken in its pan on top the kitchen counter, then walked to the bottom step in the living room to call her younger brother down for dinner.

In the dining room, Eric, Alice, and Alice's brother -eleven-year-old Nicky- sat at a long rectangle wooden dining room table that seated eight, covered with a white lace tablecloth. It was a silent meal. Not once did Alice look up at Eric while she ate. Eric was feeling uncomfortable sitting across from Alice and her brother.

"I don't want us to split up," Eric commented out of the blue.

"Uh oh," Nicky mumbled between chews feeling an argument brewing. Nicky kept his head lower than normal in case of any incoming debris. He had been observing Alice and Eric arguing off and on for the past week.

"I don't want to talk about it now!" Alice said.

"When?" asked Eric, pushing for a definite deadline.

"When I'm good and ready!" She snapped back.

Alice threw a piece of a chicken leg back onto her plate with some of the white rice splattering on the white laced tablecloth. She stood up pushing away from the table, stormed out of the dining room and into the living room pushing aside the 8-tracks and cassette tapes on the coffee table searching for the album Living in The Past by Jethro Tull. With album in hand, Alice turned on the Panasonic combine eight-track FM/AM stereo/turntable on top of the coffee table. She placed the vinyl on the turntable. The flute introduction of Living in The Past fluttered out.

Eric got out of his chair and followed Alice into the living room holding her by the shoulders from behind. "I'm sorry." He spoke.

Nicky watched from the dining room table. *"This could be better than Saturday Night Wrestling,"* he thought.

Alice looked up at the clock hanging on the wall over the fireplace mantel and noticed that it was seven-thirty. She pulled away and turned to face Eric, giving him a less subtle hint that was time for him to go.

"I don't think my mom will be up in time to give you a lift home. Maybe you should go now."

"Alice, listen…"

"Look, Eric," Alice said in defeat, "I'm supposed to meet a couple of my girlfriends at the grocery store.

"Can I come along?"

Alice took a deep sigh "I guess it's all right to tag along. But just keep your mouth shut, okay?"

The night autumn air was brisk and refreshing. The brown leaves on the cement pavement crackled under Alice's and Eric's feet as they walked silently side by side down the dark street. Some of the homes had fireplaces and Eric could smell the warm aroma of burning wood.

Inside Mister Grocer grocery store, Eric was standing by the magazine section reading the latest issue of Popular Science magazine with a steam powered car on the front cover. Just a few feet away Alice flirted with the checkout boy. The relationship building between Alice and the checkout boy was getting too friendly for Eric to concentrate on the article.

If there was any chance of saving this relationship, any jealous reaction on his behalf could jeopardize that opportunity. So, from behind his magazine, Eric had to grin and bear it.

"I'll just take his pack of gum," Alice said with a frown.

"Alice," the checkout boy scolded with a broad flirtatious smile. "Don't you know that chewing gum is bad for your teeth? Is that all you want?"

"This is all the money I have with me," Alice smiled back.

"Awww, that's too bad," mocked the checkout boy rubbing Alice on the head as one would scratch a cat between the ears.

Eric jumped out from the magazine section with a cheery manner and said, "I have some money, Alice. What else do you want?"

"Nothing," replied Alice, disheartened. "I don't want anything else."

"Is this your brother?" asked the checkout boy.

"No."

"Oh, then he's your boyfriend?"

"Oh, no… well… yeah. He is." Alice didn't know what to make of Eric.

"I'll wait for you outside, Alice," Eric said as he made his way toward the exit.

"Why? Is the smoke too much for you in here?" she teased.

"Yeah," Eric snapped. "In fact, it's beginning to stink."

Eric finally realized he was no longer her boyfriend but rather a shadow, a leach. But he couldn't just walk away being emotionally attached to her. Eric waited outside the grocery store for Alice as a dog would wait for its master when no pets were allowed.

As Alice walked out of the store, two of her girlfriends appeared out from the dark parking lot. Eric had never met them before and without introduction the four walked on. Before exiting the parking lot, Alice stopped and turned to face Eric.

"Look, I don't think my mother is up from her nap yet. Maybe you should get the bus or something, Eric."

"Yeah, perhaps you're right," Eric agreed reluctantly. It was obvious that he had overstayed his welcome. "Walk with me to Five Points where I can get the bus?"

"That's too far of a walk for us," said Alice.

"How about halfway?" Eric didn't want to let go so easily. Alice hesitated.

"Okay. Halfway, but could you walk behind us please? I want to talk to my friends in private."

Eric reluctantly stepped back a couple of paces as the four proceeded to walk. He could still hear the conversation before him.

"Well, did you get it?" asked one of the girls.

"No, but I could get it soon," replied Alice.

"How soon?" asked the second girl.

"Probably by Wednesday."

"So, where can we do it?"

"How about next Friday night at my house?" Alice volunteered. "My mother will be in New York visiting her boyfriend that weekend. And I have to babysit Nicky. So, we could do it then." Alice stopped short to face Eric who was still walking a couple of paces behind. "Can you hear us?"

"I really wasn't… uh…" Eric was caught off guard.

"Do you know what we're talking about?"

"I have a frightful idea," said Eric.

"You really have no idea!" Alice replied.

"Micro-Dots!" Said the second girl. "A good hit is enough to get you stoned for the next six to eight hours."

"Damn drugs," mumbled Eric.

"What?" asked Alice.

"Never mind."

"Look!" said Alice. "If you're going to say something, you might as well say it out loud!"

"Well, the nerve of that little bitch", Eric thought to himself. *"Here she is asking me to walk behind so she could talk to her friends in private, and the minute I say something under my breath, it becomes a federal offence."*

At the halfway point to Five Points, Alice once again stopped to face Eric.

"Well, Eric." She announced. "I have to get back home. I don't know if my mother is still asleep, and I don't want Nicky to roam the house unattended." Eric looked concerned. "Don't worry about me, Eric." Alice continued. "I'll be all right. Really. It's okay." Eric frowned then kissed her on the lips. "Goodbye, Eric."

Alice and the two girls proceeded to walk away. Eric began to jog toward the direction of Five Points. After a couple of blocks, he stopped and turned to look back. Eric could barely make out the image of Alice and her two friends disappearing down the street into darkness. For some reason Eric felt this would be the last time he would ever see or hear from Alice again. Her "*goodbye*" sounded too final.

·····················

Five Points is a retail section in Northeast Philadelphia where five major streets come together: Cottman Avenue, Veree Road, Township Line, Rising Sun Avenue and Oxford Avenue.

The intersection hosted a transmission shop, bridal shop, a bar and grill, a coinvent store and the Burholmes Baptist Church. At the conjunction of Five Points in the center, a cement monument dedicated to fallen veterans of World War I. One could find a bus and end up in any part of the city from this location. During the day, Five Points is one of the busiest shopping districts in the area. By ten at night-when Ma and Pop shops close, it becomes a ghost town.

Eric had been dating Alice for almost a year and although he usually drove to Alice's house from his neighborhood in Mt. Airy which is in the Northwest section of the city, he was still getting familiar with the Northeast.

Before Eric had received his driver's license, he had taken public transportation a few times to this location. He knew he could get the S bus at Five Points that would leave him off around the corner from his home.

At this time of evening the S bus ran every half hour on the hour. The bus stop was not properly illuminated. Eric was more worried about losing Alice than paying attention to his surroundings. Three boys approached him, and one asked for the time. As Eric looked down at his wristwatch, another boy punched him in the stomach. Eric doubled over in nauseating pain as the third clubbed him on the back of the head with his fist. Eric wanted to fight back, but it happened so fast, and the three assailants were overwhelmed, Eric had no time to react. The boys held him down onto the ground then dragged him from view of the deserted street, picked him up, then dropped him against a shadowed brick wall of a closed storefront. As Eric was helplessly thrown back onto the ground, the three boys ripped at his windbreaker and his pants pockets looking for money and other valuable items. One of the boys found Eric's wallet and emptied its contents.

"Man, don't lose the draft card!" Eric wheezed.

Another boy plucked the draft card off the ground and peered at it.

"Draft card? Why do you need a draft card? The draft is over!"

"I keep it as a memento," Eric coughed out. Eric, being the last surviving sibling in his immediate family, and with his history of psychological problems, his parents would have had no problem keeping him out of the armed forces. But the draft ended a year after Eric received the card and kept it for ID and as a memento from a more politically turbulent time.

The second hoodlum grabbed the draft card from the first and pulled out a BIC lighter from his front pocket.

"I'll show you a memento. This is how I remember the draft!"

The boy lit the card and tossed it, letting it disintegrate onto the pavement.

Disappointed only to find a ten-dollar bill, the third boy threw the wallet to the ground toward Eric. Some coins fell out and rolled in the darkness. Another boy ripped off Eric's wristwatch as a consolation prize. The third boy plucked out of Eric's pocket the plastic vial that Eric forgot to give back to Alice. After popping off the white lid, the boy patted the contents into the palm of his left hand.

"Hey!" the boy said to his pals. "Lemons! We could sell them, man!"

"Yeah!" said the second boy. "We got us here a junkie!"

The three boys continued to kick and punch. Eric lay motionless in a fetal position when the thugs ran off.

It was chilly, but still warm enough for the last of the Indian summer flies to swarm over Eric's bleeding nose. With one eye open, he saw the S bus approaching. Too weak and too much pain to run for it, Eric let the bus go. He slowly crawled on his belly to retrieve his wallet that was lying on the ground just four feet in front of him. Eric peeled up slowly from the ground to his feet using the wall behind as a crutch. All his personal papers and ID were beginning to whisk away with the night breeze. The ashes from his draft card had already blown onto heaven. Eric retrieved his empty wallet, driver's license, and house keys. With no money for the bus, he decided to walk home. It was a good five miles, and he knew by the time he would reach his house in Mt. Airy; it would be way past eleven-thirty PM. Expected to be home by ten, Eric knew his parents would be worried sick. Since his brother's death, Mr. and Mrs. Blum had become overprotected with their last son.

Walking through shadowy neighborhoods was Eric's number one concern. Going back to Alice's house crossed his mind. Chances were, she wasn't home, and even if Alice was, she probably wouldn't open the door for him no matter what time or condition he was in. He thought of calling his teacher–Carol-, but she lived in the suburbs of Holland, Bucks-county. Besides, Eric didn't have enough change to call long distance. Calling the cops was a free call. But in Philly, kids who get jumped or mugged usually never get the law involved. There was Mark Stern who lived a couple of blocks away. Most likely he was on a date driving his mother's car.

Eric used the inside of his torn windbreaker to wipe the blood from his nose. His stomach had a sharp pain every time he twisted his torso.

It was a fifteen-block walk south on Rising Sun Avenue keeping a low profile from the few pedestrians who happened to pass by.

At Rising Sun and Sanger Street across from a movie theater, was the K-Diner.

Uneasy about walking into the restaurant for help in his current condition, he spotted a truck driver about to enter. "Excuse me, sir! Do you know how I could get to Broad Street?" If Eric could get too Broad, he'd be halfway home.

"No, I'm sorry. I don't know this area too well," replied the driver as he retreated into the restaurant.

Walking another half of a block, Eric could smell the bread being baked from the Bond Bread bakery. He spotted another man about to enter his car at the Bond Bread bakery parking lot.

"Excuse me, I'm trying to get to Broad Street," Eric called out.

"The closest to Broad that I'm going is Sears Department Store on Roosevelt Boulevard. You can walk south from there. Need a lift?"

At first, Eric was hesitant. Suppose this man was a psycho serial killer? And the way this evening was progressing, he wouldn't be surprised. Eric jumped into the front seat of the stranger's car. It was dark enough that the man hadn't notice Eric was in any physical altercation within the hour. Besides, Eric wasn't in the mood for explanations. He would have to save his strength to explain to his parents why he was late coming home from Alice's house.

At the Sears Department Store at Roosevelt Boulevard, the man let Eric out of the car. Eric continued to walk south on Roosevelt Boulevard. At Broad Street and the boulevard, Eric squinted to make out the time on the City Hall tower which was located fourteen miles away in center city. Too far to see, he estimated it to be close to ten o'clock. Hurt, cold with a slight limp, Eric commenced walking north on Broad. After a couple of minutes Eric saw a C bus coming in his direction. The C bus would let him off just a few blocks from home. Acting on a hunch, he dipped into what was left of his right pants pocket and pulled out a dollar bill that the thieves had overlooked. The bus cost thirty-five cents. SEPTA -Southeastern Pennsylvania Transportation Authority- accepted exact change only. There were usually no stores open at this time of night that would give Eric the correct change needed to board the bus. He let the bus go.

Walking two more blocks north he spotted and entered an all-night supermarket called Food Fair. A lone young lady pushing a shopping cart around the aisles caught Eric's attention.

"Excuse me," said Eric, trying not to startle her with his appearance. "Would you happen to have change from a dollar?"

"Sure," replied the lady not paying attention to Eric's condition as she pulled her handbag from the shopping cart and brought out three quarters, two dimes, and a nickel.

Eric gave the lady his last dollar bill. There was nothing else for him to do but to wait on Broad Street for the next C bus on a dark, unfamiliar corner in an unfamiliar neighborhood. Without letting down his guard, Eric let his mind drift about the evening's activities. *'Will I ever see Alice again? Why does Alice hate me? How do I explain to my parents why I am so late getting home? Why did I go all through all this tonight?'* Looking south toward City Hall, Eric saw another C bus approaching in his direction. Eric paid the fare and grinned at everyone as he walked down the bus's center aisle to grab an empty seat next to an old man who was half asleep. He was so relieved to board the bus, Eric didn't care about his beat-up appearance.

At about eleven-fifteen before unlocking the front door of the Mt. Airy row house, Eric tucked in all the rips and tears on his pants pockets to conceal as much damage as he could. Inside the house, sitting on a worn dark green cloth sofa in a dimly lit living room, his parents waiting impatiently watching the evening news with NBC local anchor Vince Leonard on television. His mother was almost in tears.

"Where were you all night?" Mrs. Blum asked. "We were worried! And look at your face! It's blotchy! What happened to you?"

"It's a long story, mom. I'm okay. I tripped and fell running for the bus on the way home from Alice's." Eric tried to play-down the incident. His parents had been through enough losing their eldest son to war. Eric didn't want to worry them about him roaming unfamiliar streets at night. But Mrs. Blum would not let up.

"Where?" she asked.

"At Five Points in the Northeast. I'm all right. Just a little bruised, and my nose hurts."

"Well, let's go into the kitchen, and I'll wipe your face down. Maybe we should get an Ice-Pac for your nose." said Mrs. Blum.

Eric preferred to go to bed and forget the whole incident. But this was not the time to argue with his mother. He followed his parents into the kitchen without protest.

"You know, I called Alice to see if you had left from there." continued Mrs. Blum as she pulled an Ice-Pac out from the top freezer of the Frigidaire. Eric sat at the kitchen table across from his father and tolerated his mother patting his nose and face. "She told me you had left. This was about ten-thirty. So, I asked her to walk up to Five Points to see if you were still there waiting for the bus. She said she would look for you, but she never called back. I got this sneaky suspicion she didn't go. Did you two have another fight?"

"No, mom."

"Well, he's home now, and he's okay. That's all that matters," announced Mr. Blum.

Eric's father was a thin, quiet calm man in his late forties who was laid back and would rather let matters take their own course, whereas Mrs. Blum -a frumpy-women- a couple years younger than her husband was the family matriarch and would rather take the bull by the horns and fight for truth and justice.

Mr. and Mrs. Blum were from that "great generation". Born in the 1920s. The hard-working lower middle class. Elevated out of childhood from the 'great depression' right into adulthood with the rations of World War Two.

"Well," Mrs. Blum said leaving Eric holding the Ice-Pac. "We'll talk about this tomorrow." Satisfied, her son was home and safe, she walked out of the kitchen to go to bed. Mr. Blum had noticed the rips and tears on Eric's pants that Eric tried to conceal.

"Must have been one hell of a fall, son." Mr. Blum remarked, not convinced by Eric's story. "Did they take anything worthwhile?"

Eric got up from his chair, walked to the refrigerator to replace the Ice-Pac in the freezer. "There were three of them, dad. Held me down. Ten dollars. My watch. Burned my draft card. That's about it. Can't fight a gang, you know."

"Burned your draft card? Eric, I want to say something."

"Sure, dad, what is it?"

"Eric, I don't think I have to remind you that since your brother's death, things haven't been the same around here. And they never will for as long as your mother and I are alive. God, willing you have your entire life ahead of you. Your mother and I are trying very hard to make sure that nobody and nothing cheats you out of your life as did your brother. So please, bear with your mother and me when we become too protective or inquisitive. We really don't mean to… but we do if you get my drift."

"I do, daddy. I know exactly what you mean. I really do. I'll be more careful from now on."

"Good! You're the only son we have," continued Mr. Blum. "There ain't no more after you. So next time, if you get in any type of trouble, call the police or if you expect to come home late for any reason, give us a call."

Eric walked over from the refrigerator to his father, bent down over the kitchen table to kiss him on the forehead. "I will, daddy. Goodnight."

Eric and his father did not have a close relationship. Since Eric was born, Mr. Blum was diagnosed with diabetes that contributed to a bad heart, phlebitis, and poor circulation in the legs. Too weak to enjoy the fruits of youth through his son. Eric was too young and carefree for the tolerance of middle age, and ill health. Still, there were moments in time when they reached out to share each other's concerns.

CHAPTER 3

THE WORLD IS A STAGE
SATURDAY MORNING

THE NEIGHBORHOOD OF Mt. Airy, Philadelphia bordered the suburbs of Cheltenham Township, Montgomery County. Eric lived within
a line of seventy-five houses bricked together called 'row homes' built by
the Korman construction company in the 1950's.

The neighborhood was 98.6 percent white till the late 1960's when
the Philadelphia school board began bussing in black students from
surrounding black neighborhoods to attend the predominantly white
Jewish Mt. Airy schools. White Mt. Airy residents failed to organize
resistant blockbusting, panic selling, and redlining especially during
the early 1970s when those practices were prevalent. By 1974 less than
20 percent of the residences were white. But Mt. Airy became worldly
known as a racially diverse and harmony balanced neighborhood.

In the one-car garage below the kitchen sat Mr. Blum's 1965 dull
colored aquamarine four-door Chevy Bel-Air. Eric pushed the car out
from the garage and onto the driveway behind the row house. He was the
only one in the family who drove. Mrs. Blum never went for her driver's

license, and since his heart ailment she prohibited her husband from getting behind the wheel.

Eric was under the hood fiddling with the carburetor. He didn't know as much about automobiles as he pretended, but thanks to the automotive knowledge of Tony Burns from school, Eric learned enough about his car to troubleshoot most of the mechanical problems that had arisen. After adjusting the carburetor and spraying it with starter fluid, Eric climbed into the car and turned the ignition key. The car started. Now he was satisfied to have transportation that would at least take him to school without the use of that short yellow school bus, to work, and out of the neighborhood of Mt. Airy.

· ·

The school psychologists suggested it would be better for Eric to regain his confidence and self-esteem through a job that brought forth the taste of money combined with light responsibility. In 1973, Noah Webster Preparatory with agreement within local businesses found Eric a job as an usher at a movie theater.

The Cheltenham movie theater was located outside Philadelphia in an outdoor strip mall called Cheltenham Mall. The theater was a modern contemporary design built in 1961. Although the building was owned by the mall, the theater was managed by RKO. The single screen raked seated theater could seat close to 1,500 people in one showing. The twin Norelco 35/70mm projectors stood about seven feet tall in their own projection booth behind and above the audience.

Eric worked Saturday nights and Sunday afternoons. A uniform was required. Black polyester pants and a white button-down shirt -both which he bought- and a black jacket supplied by RKO. The initials RKO were embroidered with gold color thread on the chest pocket topped off with an outdated thin nylon black tie supplied by Cousin Opie's father's funeral parlor.

A flashlight was issued to each of the three ushers by RKO: Eric, a puggy sixteen-year-old boy named Bob, and Cousin Opie O'Neil.

During the showing of the film Serpico starring Al Pacino, Bob was standing by Opie's post, which was one of the four entrances from the lobby to the theater.

"I wonder what's been bothering Eric tonight?" pondered Bob.

"Why?" asked Opie.

"Cause earlier I tried to talk to him, and he seemed to be in a bad mood. He hasn't moved from his post all night. He just stands there watching the movie. How many times can one person see Serpico?"

"How many times have you seen it, Bob?"

"Seventy-five."

"Well, I have an idea," Opie suggested. "I know how to get him out of a bad mood."

Opie chased Bob down his aisle toward the front of the theater, on stage, behind the screen, back out and up Eric's aisle. Eric, along with the rest of the patrons, watched the live event that was unfolding before them. As Bob and Opie ran up Eric's aisle, Eric backed out of the theater into the lobby closing the double doors behind him waiting for Bob to pop out from the other side. When the theater doors opened, Eric leaped forward to prance on Bob. However, an old lady came out of the theater startled at the sight of Eric in flight just inches from her. From the shock of seeing the lady, Eric froze in mid-leap with his mouth and eyes wide open.

"What are you trying to do, give me a heart attack?" the lady said. "You boys better stop it! Scared me half to death!" The lady proclaimed as she walked on toward the candy counter in the lobby.

Bob walked out of the theater from behind the lady laughing while Eric was still in leaping position. The chase continued back into the theater. Eric and Bob ran down the aisle while people were trying to watch the movie. Eric caught up with Bob on the stage and by his tie dragged him behind the screen. Al Pacino's face became distorted as the boys wrestled out of view.

After a few moments, the screen was still. All the patrons glared with an evil eye as Eric came out alone from behind the screen straightening his tie and dusting himself off as he walked up the aisle toward the double doors in the back of the theater. Bob followed a few paces behind with his hair messed up and his black tie in knots. Eric thrust open the double doors to the lobby. Opie -in the lobby- stood by laughing as Eric quickly turned to grab Bob's tie, yanking it causing Bob's head on the other side to knock against the closing double doors. Eric let the tie go. The tie hung limp between the split of the double doors.

"I think we killed him, Opie," Eric said with fear in his voice. "It's not moving. I mean, the tie. The tie is not moving."

"Then open the doors."

"No! You open the doors."

"I'm not opening the doors. You're the one who did this to him," declared Opie.

"You started by chasing him in the first place!" Eric gave in and slowly opened the double theater doors. Then, with a quick jerk, Bob's head popped out.

"Hello!" said Bob in a Mickey Mouse voice accompanied with a smile.

Opie and Eric chased Bob back into the theater. Once again down the aisle ending up in front of a thin man sitting next to a heavyset woman who was eating popcorn out a medium-sized cardboard cup.

"Will you guys please get the hell out of here?" the thin man called out.

"Oh, shut up!" Eric snapped back as he waved his hand accidentally contacting the man's toupee sliding onto the woman's lap. Eric was so scared; he ran out of the theater into the theater's dressing room behind the lobby to hide for the duration of the show.

Eric was nonviolent and non-confrontational. It was that damn Cousin Opie who knew how to get him wild up!

Between shows as the new audience was settling in, Opie walked back into the dressing room where he found Eric sitting on a wooden folding chair by a four-by-four-foot card table.

"I got scared when that wig slid off," proclaimed Eric. "But I never laughed so hard in my entire life. Are they still here?"

"They're gone," Opie said with a laugh. "But before they left the theater, they went over to the office and demanded to see the manager to report us. But the Ghost Lady wasn't there. So, they threatened to write a letter to RKO."

'The Ghost Lady': that was the nickname the ushers had given Ethel the theater manager/boss. She was a tall husky woman in her mid-fifties with grayish blonde hair in the same style of all three Andrews Sisters. Ethel was a chain-smoker and had a hideous hack of a cough. Ethel smoked so much in her tiny ten-by-fifteen-foot office that whenever she walked or move, the smoke would seem to take form of an apparition of fingers and try to grab hold of her body hence the nickname, 'The Ghost Lady'. Ethel was probably the best boss that anybody would want to work for. She treated her employees with respect and always backed them up in any patron confrontation. Ethel loved her ushers, and they loved her in return. But there was usually a three-week turn around for cashiers at the ticket booth adjacent to her office. Not even the best of the hardcore smokers could endure Ethel's extreme nicotine exhaust.

In the back hallway, before Eric and Opie returned to their post at the theater, Opie opened the door to the janitor's closet where he kept a case of twenty-four coca-colas in eight-ounce glass bottles. He pulled out a bottle opener from his jacket pocket, popped off the top of one of the bottles, and jugged the soda down while Eric sniffed from a gallon jug of ammonia.

"OY! I do see God... Do you want a snort, Op?"

"No, Eric! I got my own problem here as you can see," replied Opie as he finished off the coke.

Eric and Opie walked back to their posts in the theater to wait for the show to begin. A perspiring old man wandered up from his seat. "Hey, usher!" the old man rudely announced. "Is the air conditioner on?"

"Yeah!" Eric replied with his own brand of nasty. "But it has to warm up!" Eric turned and left the theater for the lobby leaving the man bewildered.

The lights in the theater dimmed. All three ushers closed the theater doors and met out in the lobby. When all was settled, Eric slid a water pistol out from his jacket pocket. The three ushers scurried back into the theater and sat in the last row that was void of people. As Eric shot the pistol in the air, water dripped onto the patrons. The patrons gazed up at the ceiling to inspect. Eric and the two ushers laughed silently from their unobstructed point of view.

Opie slid a marble from his pants pocket and rolled it on the raked cement floor under the chairs. Once again, the ushers silently laughed watching the row of heads of patron's bob up and down like dominoes in sequence as the marble knocked past the metal feet of their chairs towards the screen.

From the lobby the office door was heard slamming closed accompanied by a horrifying hacking cough. The ushers ran to their prospective individual posts before Ethel walked into the theater. She opened one of the theater doors and saw Cousin Opie standing at attention at his post. Ethel was also aware of Opie's mischievous reputation. With a slight grin, she saw through the 'perfect usher' act.

"What are you up to?" she asked.

"Nothing. I'm just standing here."

"Where's Eric?" Opie pointed toward the next exit door across the theater. Ethel walked out of the theater and back into her smoke-filled tomb.

Once the office door was heard slamming closed and the grayish ectoplasm seemed to have dissipated, the three ushers conjured out into the lobby.

The candy lady -aka Crank- behind the glass candy counter at the concession stand in the lobby was in a perpetual bad mood-hence the nickname. Crank was in her early seventies, or-so she claimed. Ethel theorized that Crank was in her early eighties. Eric once offered to hacksaw off one of Crank's legs so he could count the rings to terminate the dispute. On this night, Old Crank was rude toward one of the patrons who asked for extra napkins with her popcorn. The three ushers stood nearby in the lobby to witness the action as the small argument progressed.

"Enough for whom? I'm sharing this popcorn with five other people!" claimed the woman.

"I gave you enough for five!" said Crank. "These napkins are accounted for!"

"That's the most ridiculous thing I have ever heard! cups, maybe! But who counts napkins?" asked the woman.

"RKO!" replied Crank. "Look, just take the napkins!" Crank surrendered regretfully. The patron grabbed a pinch of napkins from the dispenser on the glass candy countertop then walked away. When no other customer was at hand, Crank turned and faced the back counter to count the money from the evening's sales.

"She's not one of us," said Opie.

"Follow me," announced Eric.

Bob and Opie followed Eric toward the glass candy counter. As Crank counted money still with her back facing the boy's, Eric took out his water pistol from his jacket pocket and squirted the glass countertop. Then moved the water pistol back into his pocket. Crank with a fist full of bills turned and closely inspected the glass countertop. Opie and Bob tried to suppress their laughter.

"What's all this water doing here?" she asked.

"It's from the lights," replied Eric being as seriously informative as he could.

Opie and Bob laughed as they walked behind the wall that separated the concession stand from the lobby. The old doorman, who really was in his seventies and hard of hearing, was standing nearby turned away trying not to show any mirth.

"What lights?" asked Crank.

"Well, you see, these lights over the candy counter are water cooled," explained Eric. "Now, when they start to go bad, they begin to leak. That's why they're called 'floodlights'."

It was hard for Eric to keep a straight face, but he was on a roll. Crank put the money in the pocket of her baby-blue smock, walked from behind the candy counter, across the lobby, and knocked on Ethel's office door. Eric tried to wipe the glass countertop with the sleeve of his jacket to alleviate any evidence of foul play. But the polyester material would not absorb all-if any-of the moisture, and left water beads.

"Who is it?" Ethel hacked out from in her office.

"It's me!" replied Crank.

Ethel held her office door ajar and peeked out. A gasp of white smoke bellowed out as fingers tried to close the office door. "What is it?"

"Your lights are leaking!" Crank announced.

That was it. Eric couldn't hold it in any longer. He and the doorman barreled into the theater joining Opie and Bob in hysterics.

"My, who are what?" Ethel yelled out.

"Your lights are leaking! Follow me. I'll show you."

The Ghost Lady and Crank crossed the lobby floor toward the glass candy counter. A path of white smoke following halfway formed as fingers fruitlessly trying to grab hold of Ethel's neck. Eric, Bob, Opie, and the doorman peeked out through two circular windows on the double theater doors. All four had tears in their eyes from the silent laughter as Ethel inspected the countertop, then the lights overhead.

"Who told you that the lights are leaking?… Never mind! I have an idea who it was."

Ethel walked over to one of the theater doors and opened it to find Eric standing at an attention. The other two ushers were already at their posts as the doorman slipped by Ethel through another exit and stood by his ticket stand out in the lobby.

"What are you doing to that old fart?"

"Nothing," replied Eric. "What's up?"

Ethel didn't know whether to believe Eric. She just shook her head, walked out of the theater, and hacked back into her smoked filled office.

It was toward the end of the evening. The three ushers rallied together in the lobby. A man and his date walked over to the doorman and handed him the tickets. Opie ushered the couple into the theater, yet they did not thank him or seem to acknowledge that Opie provided a service.

"Not even a 'thank you.'" Opie announced to Eric and Bob, who were standing in the lobby. "It's like the ushers are invisible. If I pulled down my zipper, let my schlong hang out, how many people do you think would notice when I usher them into the theater? Watch!" Opie pulled down his zipper to expose himself. When he jerked his body forward, then, and only then for a split second would 'it' peek out from between the opening of his jacket. Bob and Eric glanced at each other as though Opie was completely mad, but both broke into laughter. The doorman peeked around the wall and pointed toward Eric.

"Ghost Lady wants you."

Eric walked up to Ethel's office and knocked on the door.

"Come in!" Ethel coughed from within. Eric could hardly breathe when he pulled himself into the office that resembled a London fog. Ethel sat behind her desk with a lit cigarette in the ash tray and a 75-watt light bulb on her desk amidst her paperwork. Thick cigarette smoke draped around Ethel's neck resembled a hangman's noose.

"A light bulb burned out in the lobby. Will you please replace it?"

"Sure, Ethel." Eric retrieved the light bulb from Ethels' desk and walked out into the lobby with a trail of smoky fingers trying to nab him from behind.

In the lobby Eric past by Opie while Opie was conversing with the old doorman who hadn't noticed that Opie's schlong was pointing at him. Bob was behind the wall by the candy counter silently laughing with Eric who proceeded to walk to the dressing room to retrieve a twelve-foot wooden "A" frame ladder. But before reentering the lobby, Eric went into the janitor's closet to take another whiff of ammonia from the gallon jug. "Oh! There you are God!"

Back in the lobby, Opie saw Eric getting set to climb the ladder under the spent light."

"I'll do that for you, Eric," Opie volunteered.

Eric and Bob held the ladder as Opie climbed up to the top. A young man popped out of the theater and proceeded toward the ushers.

"Excuse me. Where can I find the bathroom?" he asked.

"On the second floor." Opie said from the top of the ladder. The man looked up to see where Opie was pointing not noticing the compass needle pointing south between Opie's legs.

"Thank you," said the man as he walked off.

All the ushers gazed at each other in disbelief. Could Opie have been right? Could the ushers be 'transparent?' Opie climbed down from the ladder and handed Bob the spent bulb as Bob took the ladder back into the dressing room.

Another young man and his date walked into the building to surrender their tickets to the doorman. Opie opened the theater door making a slight hoop-de-doo jerking motion with his body making sure his private peeked out from behind his jacket.

The man and his date walked into the theater unaware of what Opie was trying to show them.

Eric walked over to Opie and shook his hand for a job well done. As the two boys laughed on, Opie progressively surrendered a forlorn expression.

"What's wrong Op?"

"I can't move!" Opie replied as his face began to show more signs of stress. "I got hair caught in the zipper of my pants."

Eric escorted his cousin to the dressing room. Opie slowly and carefully took off his black jacket trying not to twist his torso in such a manner that would pull on the pubic hairs caught in his pants zipper. With his legs spread wide open, and his private hanging out, Opie slowly sat down on the wooden folding chair.

"What am I gonna do?" Opie cried out.

"Don't panic, Opie. I'll get scissors from the office and cut you out of this!"

"No, wait Eric!" Eric stopped at mid gate. "What if the Ghost Lady should get suspicious and wants to know what you need the scissors for? What if she comes back here to investigate? Now picture this, Eric. Here's the scenario. I'm sitting here with my legs spread wide open, and my schlong hanging out. And you're hovering over me with a pair of scissors. What would you say then, 'No Ethel, this is not what it looks like!'" Opie stops to think. "Damn! I don't think I can drive in this position. I'm just going to have to walk home like this and pick up my car tomorrow!"

"Ethel is collecting our jackets tonight for the laundry. How are you going to walk home through the neighborhood with your schlong hanging out with no jacket?"

"Walking home is not the problem. I could always take the secondary streets. Nobody will see me. How am I going to get into my house without my parents noticing?"

"Well, if it makes you feel any better, I was jumped in Northeast last night coming home from Alice's' house." Eric conceded.

"I was wondering why you were in a bad mood earlier. And your face looks a little blotchy. Are you okay?"

"I'm fine, they just took some money and my watch. Alice and I broke up."

"Again?"

"I think this time, it's for good."

"That's too bad. I'm running low on pot."

"Opie! I was trying to get her off that stuff!"

"Well, I got a little confession to make myself. I didn't make the football team at McDevitt. So, I signed up for track. Oh, and by-the-way, Bishop McDevitt high school is having a school dance this Friday night. If you want to stay on our track team, I suggest you be there to show face."

Eric helped smuggle Opie out of the building by the back-alley exit. Since Opie drove, he didn't bring a jacket or a sweater, so there was no way to hide his genitals. What Opie did bring with him for the mile walk home were two eight-ounce bottles of coke. From the alley door, Eric laughed as he watched his cousin discreetly and carefully walk across the huge empty parking lot bowlegged and exposed.

With the pressure of wanting to leave Webster by the end of the school year, and the frustration from the break-up with Alice, Eric decided he needed a change in his life. He knocked on the office door and walked into Ethel's smoky tomb.

"Ethel?"

"Yes, Eric?" she said as she coughed, and paused from writing her nightly report.

"Ethel, I wish to make this my last night here at the theater… can I open the door or something? I can hardly see you."

"I have money sitting around, but sure Eric. Leave it ajar."

Ajar was not what Eric had in mind. More like blown off its hinges would have been appropriate. The ticket girl who was no more than ten feet away sitting on a stool in her own little booth adjacent to Ethel's office, resembled a tear gas victim with red watery eyes and a pink bandanna over her nose and mouth.

"I know I should have given you at least two weeks' notice but", said Eric. "I have been here for over a year now. I'm looking for something with more of a challenge. Something I can prove to my school that I'm mentally capable enough to find a job on my own."

"Does your school know that you're leaving us?"

"No. I made this decision tonight."

"I see. Do you want some time to think about it? Do you want some time off?"

"No, no I really don't know what I want. But I know this isn't it."

"Well, I can't keep you here. I do advise you to tell your school authorities about your decision. They did get you this job."

"I will."

"I'm going to miss you." Said Ethel.

"I'll miss you, too, Ethel. I want to thank you for not telling anybody how I got this job, or about my retarded school."

"It's not a retarded school." grinned Ethel. "I don't hire retards."

"You hired my cousin, Opie."

"If there is anything I can do for you, please give me a call. And if you should need a job... please give me a call."

"I will, Ethel. You're the greatest. I guess that's it."

"Good. Because this is the longest, I've been going without a cigarette. And I'm dying," claimed Ethel with a hack.

After inhaling a percentage of the smoke in the Ghost Lady's office, and before leaving the theater, Eric ran back into the janitor's closet for one more whiff of ammonia from the gallon jug. "Wow! God is in all colors!"

Out in the parking lot, Eric slid into his car and turned on the ignition. At the other end of the parking lot, he noticed the silhouette of Opie against the parking lot lights still carefully walking slowly bowlegged. Eric rolled down his window to yell out, "Bye-bye, Opie!" Opie slowly turned to face Eric with half a smile and raised a bottle of Coca-Cola as a salute. Eric turned the old Chevy in the direction of Mt. Airy and peeled away laughing.

CHAPTER 4

THE DAWN OF DISCO

"SOME OF YOU (drop)… may not recall what we were discussing (drop)… in Friday's class." Announced Carol "So, I'll try (drop)… to refresh your memories (drop, drop)."

Carol tried to recap last weeks' class over Tony's dropping of his desktop. She stopped cold and stared at him. With a smile, Tony lifted his right leg and passed wind. Carol kept a straight face as the class laughed on. Tony did it a second time and joined in laughing with his classmates as he dropped his desktop once again. Carol looked down at her desk silently hoping that the rest of the class would observe that she was not amused. From his pants pocket, Tony pulled out a BIC lighter and clicked it, placing the open flame against his rectum. He passed wind for the third time. A small blue flame jetted out from the lighter. The entire class was raving with laughter.

"Get out!" Carol yelled. "Get out of this classroom!"

"No!" Tony yelled back with a grin.

Carol's face turned crimson. She tried to calm herself down before taking savage action against him. "I'm going to count to three," she said calmly. "And if you're not out of this classroom by then, in front of everybody, I'm going to kick the living shit out of you! One!..." Tony sat behind his desk resting his head on his right hand over his mouth, smiling as a challenge to her threat. "Two!..." The class became fervent. Joey Pearlman was beaming as he rocked in his chair from the back of the room pointing toward Tony's feet.

"Tony! Your pants are on fire!" Mick Maze called out.

Tony looked down to find his right pants leg smoldering. As he jumped out of his seat patting out the ember while laughing, Carol watched in silence not knowing whether to laugh or cry.

Tony figured this would be a good time to leave the classroom. He knew he was in enough trouble as it was. Burning down the school was not another blemish he wanted added to his soiled academic reputation. The class was still howling with laughter as Tony laughed his way out of the classroom.

"Well," said Carol. "I can see that this class will never get back to normal today. Class dismissed. Oh, and Eric. I want to see you."

As the class emptied out, Mark and Mick looked back to wink at Eric. Eric slid out of his chair, shuffled to the threshold of the classroom door, and hung his head staring down at the floor looking melancholy.

"Hello," Carol said. "Are you okay?"

"I don't know. Am I?" Replied Eric.

"I haven't heard from you all morning. You want to walk back into my classroom and talk about it?"

Eric shrugged as Carol walked over to put her arm around his shoulders. They both moved back into the classroom. Eric sat in Mark Stern's seat as Carol stood behind her desk to prepare for her next period.

"I hope you got a good laugh out of Tony this morning." Said Carol.

"Yeah. He's quite amusing when it gets boring in class." answered Eric.

"I'll ignore that remark and accept your apology," Carol replied with a slight grin. "How's Alice?"

"I lost Alice. We broke up on Friday night. I wrote her a letter last night saying that if she wanted to see me again, she should give me a call. And if she doesn't, I'll understand."

"So now, you're going to have to wait."

"Yeah, but it's that 'waiting' that's so damn hard. It's like that feeling you get when you wait up late at night for *Warren* to get home."

"I don't live with Warren," Carol said with a laugh. "Besides, my home life is none of your business anyway. That little creep. She doesn't deserve you."

"I know. I need an older woman. Someone with more experience." Eric raised his eyebrows and flashed his eyes. Carol gave him a smirk as she clicked her tongue. "Is there any news about my release from this retarded house? And please don't tell me this year has just started!"

"Release?" Carol replied. "It's up to Principal Swanson and the school psychologist. They determine who's ready to leave. The moment I find out, I'll let you know. I promise. And stop calling this place a 'retarded house'!"

"You're right. I'm sorry. Tomorrow, I'll borrow a BIC lighter from Tony and light my butt on fire... No, better yet! I'll just sit silently at my desk swaying back and forth until the next helicopter flies over! I just want to get out of here already! Four years is enough for this place. I'm okay! I'm reading at my grade level. I pass all my classes and exams." Carol stopped fiddling at her desk and endowed Eric with a foolish grin.

"Alright, most of my classes and some of my exams... not all." Eric recoiled.

With a pout, Eric lifted out of his seat and headed toward the door. Carol reached over before he walked through the threshold. She knew something else was bothering him. She gently grabbed him by the arm and pulled him back into the classroom. He stood in front of her glaring at the floor.

"I quit my job last night." He announced.

"I see. Does Principal Swanson know?"

"No. I haven't told anybody yet except for you and my parents. My mother just about went through the roof."

"Why did you quit? The school got you that job. That job could have been your ticket out this year."

"Oh, come on, Carol! An usher at a movie theater? There are better jobs that I could get on my own to prove to the school that I'm mentally and emotionally stable to conquer the world. I was bored at the theater. Look at you! You have a job. You have your own apartment in the suburbs. Where do I live? In a closed-in, stuffy, dust-infested tomb where I have to huff every so often from a bottle of ammonia to clear my sinuses. I have a father who's a sick, beat old man. A mother who's a nut case. And both are waiting for a dead man to walk through the front door! I lost Alice. You have *Warren*! Life is getting very complicated. "

Carol grinned at Eric's sarcasm at the way he articulated her boyfriend's name. "You know, Eric? When life gets complicated for any young man, it's a sign of him growing up.

"I just don't know what to do anymore... I just don't know." Conceded Eric.

"Life is a big mystery for me too." Admitted Carol. "I ain't all together myself you know. If everybody knew what was expected in life, what would be the purpose for living? If we all knew what was waiting for us around the corner, why should we move on?"

"I think I need somebody to talk to." Eric proclaimed.

"You can talk to me anytime, Eric. You know that."

"I know, Carol, but... maybe I need a shrink."

"I'll set you up an appointment for counseling."

"No! Don't send me to that resident nut case psychologist we have here. Because he's the one that keeps analyzing me, and then tells the school and my parents that I'm not ready to leave this retarded house. After four years, I deserve an independent second opinion!"

"I'll talk to principal Swanson about recommendation for independent counseling. In the meantime, cheer up, cause the school smiles with you."

It was mandatory that all students seek in-house counseling at Webster. But after four years of therapy from the same therapist, Eric was warranted for a second independent opinion.

Eric surrendered a slight grin and stared at Carol for a moment. "Carol?"

"Yes, Eric?"

"Thanks. Thanks for being here."

"That's what teachers are for." She replied.

"Yeah, 'teacher'. Look, Carol." Carol shook her head. She knew where this was leading too. "I can't help to think, I just want to know. Just saying. How we get along. You and me."

"Eric," She abrupt. "No! I explained to you last year about this 'you' and 'me' routine. There is no 'you' or 'me' here or any other place or time. I am not attracted to you in that way. I'm your teacher. You are my student. Outside of school, we're friends. Now you're stepping out of bounds. I think you had better get to your next class. It's almost time."

Carol understood and sympathized with the pressures Eric was facing. It wasn't long ago she was his age and had teenage crushes on teachers from school. Besides, school was understandably boring for any student who had spent eleven to twelve years in a classroom. The outside world is much more inviting. Eric couldn't quit school like he did his job at the movie theater. His parents were very strict on education. And they had spent most -if not all- their life savings getting him the education he needed to catch up with his peers. With school, Eric just had to hang in there. With Carol, he had to know his boundaries.

Besides being the history teacher, Carol was also the unofficial school vice principal, the keeper of school records and student council adviser. For four straight years, Eric was elected school student body president. It was believed that Carol fixed the elections to get Eric reelected. The truth of the matter, with a little help from Tony Burns and some of his school goons, Eric allegedly won his elections on his own.

....

The following Friday night the parochial high school 'Bishop McDevitt' located in Jenkintown, had their first dance of the school year. The dance was held at the school's gymnasium.

Eric went with his cousin Opie to be seen and hobnob with the students. It was the way to remain on the school's track team without seeming peculiar as an outsider to McDevitt's authorities.

Once inside the gym, Opie and Eric danced their way pass students to the music of Eddy Kendricks' Boogie Down hosted by two disc-jockeys stationed at one end of the room queuing records.

Opie mingled with the students he knew on the notion Eric could fend on his own. Eric was becoming a familiar face at Bishop McDevitt, even though the school staff and students couldn't nail him down to any one class.

Not since the British music invasion of 1964, had Philadelphia enjoyed top billing producing number one rhythm and blues soul singers and bands in the music industry. Artists such as The Tramps, Sister Sledge, Patty Labelle, The Stylistics, Harold Melvin & the Blue Notes and Hall & Oats had dominated the top dance soul and crossover white Billboard charts. Opie and Eric were getting caught up in the new disco craze. They knew many of the new dances and even made up a few dance routines of their own.

One of the two disc-jockeys had put on the 45 vinyl, Express by B T Express. Eric and Opie found each other through the crowd and inaugurated a dance routine. Many of the students stopped dancing to encircle the two boys. Then all the students followed along and danced. Even the nuns who stood-by as chaperones were swaying to the funky beat. One of the two disc-jockeys -Lou- walked over from the disc-jockey table to where Opie and Eric were dancing and watching. When the record was over, Opie strolled over to the soda bar and ordered five coca-colas for himself as Eric wandered off toward the men's room. Lou caught up with Eric before he entered and introduced himself.

"Hey! I'm Lou one of the disc-jockeys." Eric shook Lou's hand. "You dance pretty good."

"Yeah. I like disco. I'm Eric Blum."

"We work for PD," declared Lou.

"Who's PD?"

"Oh, you know. Everybody knows PD! How could you not know him?" Eric shrugged, not familiar with the initials. "Pete D'Angelo? He has that dance show every Saturday morning following Jerry Blavat's dance show. It's like a Bandstand!"

"Oh, yeah! I know who he is!" Eric remembered. "He's on UHF, right? I watch him whenever I get a chance."

"Yeah! Right now, we're in reruns. We're trying to pick up new sponsors to get back on the air next season. This is really Pete's dance. He's a disc-jockey over at WCAM in Camden, New Jersey. He's on the air right now. Peter hires me and Steve -the other disk jockey- to work on his dances when he can't make it. We're looking for another disc jockey. Would you be interested?"

"Yeah! But I wouldn't know what to do."

"There's nothing to it. I'll show you everything. Follow me! I'll introduce you to Steve."

Eric followed Lou to the front of the gym where two turntables, a couple of speakers, three record boxes and loose records scattered about over the top of two four-by-eight-foot folding tables. Steve was queuing a disc.

"Steve!" Lou yelled over the music. "I want you to meet, uh, Eric Blum. He wants to join us."

Eric shook Steve's hand, but Steve was too busy queuing to chitchat.

"Boy, you guys have a lot of records here," announced Eric. "How do I get in touch with you, Lou?"

"Just leave me your name and number, and I'll give you a call tomorrow. Maybe tomorrow night we'll meet Pete at his nightclub in South Philly."

"I'm underage." Eric admitted.

"It's a soda bar. An under twenty-one club. Where do you live? I'll pick you up."

"Mt. Airy."

"Ah, that's nigger town, man!"

"My neighbors are cool."

"All right, well, wear something hip."

....

The next night, the two boys rolled out of Lou's brand new red 1974 two-door fully loaded hard top Pontiac Grand Prix parked in a parking space off Broad and Snyder in South Philly. Lou wore a light brown sport jacket and printed shirt with the collar overlapping the lapels of his jacket. The shirt was unbuttoned down toward the center of his hairless chest with a couple of layers of gold chains, no socks, and his tawny baggy pants hung over his brown clogs. Lou's hair was curly, light brown, hanging shoulder length like Eric's. Eric wore the same style clothes with platform tie shoes. The two boys looked like brothers. The only difference, Lou was a couple years older and thin as a rail.

Eric could tell by the way Lou carried himself that Lou was part of the 'in-crowd'. Eric heard rumors that in-crowd guys didn't wear underwear. Not taking any chances, Eric shed his underpants before he got dressed for the evening. At first it was uncomfortable to walk about without any gonadal support, but he quickly got used to it. It was also uncool to wear an overcoat even though the temperature was at least in the low forties. Maxi coats were in style for men, but they were too long, cumbersome, and heavy to carry around. With just a thin sport jacket and an open shirt, Eric was hip, but freezing.

The two boys strolled up to the front of Pete's underage nightclub called, "PD's". Taking care of Business by BTO was heard muffled outside the club from behind the thick black wooden door that opened every few seconds to let young people in or out.

"Pete's car isn't here," Lou said. "He usually parks on the sidewalk in front of the club."

Looking North, Eric observed the clock on the city hall tower. "It's almost ten. Let's go in. I'm freezing standing out here."

"Well, don't you want to wait for Pete?' asked Lou. "We'll make a great entrance!"

"Of course. But how long do you want to wait? He might not show up tonight."

"Yeah, maybe you're right." When Lou opened the front door, Taking Care of Business seemed clearer and ten times louder. The boys were faced by two bouncers in the middle of conversation.

"… I'm telling you!" Bruce the bouncer told his partner Charles over the music. "The car radios can't be traced. Just be a mule and deliver them to South Carolina. We'll get you a different car on the return trip."

The two bouncers abruptly stopped talking when realized that Lou and Eric were standing before them.

"This is Charles Gammer," Lou announced. "Charlie, I want you to meet my new friend, Eric Blum. Eric will be working with us."

Eric shook Charles's hand. Charles Gammer was a tall, husky Irish man about five to seven years older than Eric.

"And this is Bruce Fisher." Bruce had wavy long light brown hair past his shoulders and was about Eric's age and size. Bruce was reluctant at first to extend his hand out to greet Eric. The two bouncers let the boys in without a cover charge after which Bruce continued his conversation with Charles.

"… So, don't worry about it. You're covered, and it's a piece of cake. By the time you get back to Philly, those radios will be in Miami on a light freighter on their way to Haiti…"

The interior of the club was painted black, surrounded by strobe lights. The soda bar was two-deep with teenagers. Steve swam through the crowd to meet up with the two boys.

"Hi guys!" Steve shouted out at the music and the crowd. "I reserved a booth!"

Steve, Eric, and Lou fought their way through the crowd to a reserved booth on the other side of the club.

When Taking care of Business was over, the crowd settled down and drew their attention toward the dance floor in the middle of the room. Two black male dancers were dancing a choreograph to the song Jungle Boogie by Kool and the Gang.

"Pete won't be here tonight!" Steve shouted out.

"Why?" asked Lou.

"He was called into Camden to do a fill-in at WCAM. He's on the air."

Eric watched the dancers on the floor for a moment while Lou slid out of the booth and walked over to the soda bar. Eric diverted his attention onto Lou trying to pick up a girl.

Eric had met Alice, who was his first serious girlfriend at a resort in the Catskills. But living in a neighborhood away from his own peer group, and attending a school that was predominantly male, Eric lacked the experience needed to address the opposite sex. With his new-found socially adaptable friends, Eric thought that he could finally learn the tricks of the trade in meeting women.

•••••••••••••••••••••••

The following Monday afternoon at Noah Webster, Eric wouldn't have missed much in Carol's last period homeroom advisory class. She marked him present so he could run over to meet his cousin Opie at Bishop McDevitt High for track practice.

51

In one of the two bathrooms at Webster, Eric changed into a white button-down shirt, red tie, and a navy-blue Bishop McDevitt blazer that Cousin Opie had lent him. He wasn't concerned that he was wearing dungarees or white high-top converse sneakers. In a knapsack he carried his track clothes.

Eric jogged the mile to Bishop McDevitt. The school let out early and the hallways were vacant of students. The classroom on the second floor where he was to meet Opie was empty. Eric hustled down to the first floor and out of the building onto the track field waiting for his cousin to show up. Opie came running toward him from the school.

"Come on, Eric. We're gonna be late!" he said as he grabbed Eric by the jacket collar and tugged him along.

"Where were you?" Eric asked. "I went to your classroom, and nobody was there! What are we going to be late for?" Eric tried to keep up with his cousin as they both reentered the building.

"Sorry about that!" replied Opie. "My class was canceled. We're late for class pictures!"

"What class pictures?"

"Yearbook, Eric! They're taking the track team pictures."

"But Opie…"

Opie dragged Eric into a classroom set up with two rows of bleachers, track coach, the team, and a photographer. Before Eric could take a breath, Opie pushed him onto the second-row bleacher where the two boys blended in with the rest of the track team and their coach.

"Say, Cheesus!" The photographer called out. Eric accidentally shouted "OY" as a flash of light from the camera temporarily blinded him.

"You're in our yearbook, buddy!" Opie announced to Eric.

"But Opie. I don't even go to this school!"

As the other teammates began to disperse the classroom, coach Ryan called out. "Eric Blum!"

"Yes, sir?" Still blinded by the flash, Eric missed his first step off the bleacher. Opie caught him in time.

"Eric, when I was asked to gather up the team for this photo session, I couldn't find you on file. I think we had better go down to the office to have this cleared up before the secretaries go home for the night. Who's your homeroom teacher?"

The two boys glanced at each other. Eric could only make out a blue dot where Opie's head was assumed to be.

"Carol Schor?" Eric timidly replied.

"Who?" asked the coach.

"Um, coach Ryan?..."

Eric could sense that it was getting complicated being on this track team. And although it wasn't his faith, Eric couldn't lie in a school of God. It was time for confession.

"There's something I have to tell you, sir," conceded Eric.

"What's that?"

"I don't belong to this school."

"You what?" asked the coach.

"I don't go to this school."

Coach Ryan turned toward Opie. "Do you know this guy?"

Since Opie was a legal attendance, he wanted to save his own neck. "No. This is the first time that I have spoken to him. Now, if you two gentlemen will excuse me, I must use the bathroom."

"Bastard!" Eric said softly as Opie walked off leaving him alone with the Coach.

"What do you mean you don't go to this school?" asked Ryan.

"I don't belong here."

"You've been on this team for about a couple of weeks now! Say, didn't I see you at the school dance last Friday night?"

"Yes."

"Well, where do you belong?"

"Noah Webster Preparatory."

"Weber?"

"No. Webster."

"Wester?"

"No. Weber… I mean…" Eric was getting so nervous that he was tongue-tied to the point where he couldn't pronounce the name of his own school. "Oh, forget it."

Coach Ryan tried again. "Webster?"

"Right!… No… yeah! That's it!"

"Well, how did you get on this school's track team?"

"I was waiting on the field for my cousin who wanted to join the football team and one of your coaches asked if I wanted to join. I told him I like to join the track team."

"Which one of my coaches?"

"I don't know. He was a football coach."

"Didn't he know that you didn't belong here?"

"I guess not. He didn't ask."

"Well, I'm sorry. I'm going to have to kick you off. Regulations you know. Suppose you fall or get hurt? Whose fault would that be? Where's the liability?"

"Yes. That's very true," Eric acknowledged respectfully.

"Besides that, you're an outsider. Do you know what could happen if you ran with us in a competition against another school, and somebody found out you didn't belong? We could be disqualified by the archdiocese of all sports and scholarship funds. Not only for this year, but perhaps forever. This school depends on its sports. Sports is our moral and there are kids who come here on sport scholarships. They intend to get into college on those scholarships. Otherwise, they would never be able to afford the higher education without it. If we lost all those funds and benefits because of you, think about how many other deserving kids would have lost out! Just by being here you have put this school's reputation and athletic future in grave danger my friend!"

"I'm sorry, coach Ryan. I never thought about it that way. You see, my school doesn't have a track team…"

"... That's not my problem!" the coach snapped, then paused to think. "Look, I do hate to let you go. We need a runner like you. So why don't you get Weber to transfer you over here?"

"No... it's Webster... and besides, that would be impossible."

"Why? What kind of school is this Webter?"

Eric closed his eyes trying to ignore the stupidity of the mispronunciation of his school's name.

"No! no, it's Web... it's a private school."

"So are we. You can still get a transfer."

"No. I've been going there for four years. And I'm supposed to be graduating this spring..."

"... Well, do you want me to call Wester?"

"No, sir. I just can't go here. You see, among other complications... I'm Jewish."

"We could get that transferred... You're what?" Eric nodded his head. "Well, that's not too surprising. We have a couple of 'them' here also."

"Oh! How 'white' of you," Eric replied under his breath. "Thanks anyway."

Opie caught up with Eric who was walking across the football field. "What happened, buddy?"

"Buddy?" repeated Eric. "I don't think we know each other. I've been kicked off the team!"

"Yeah, well. At least you made our yearbook."

"Great! Years from now you'll help me explain to my kids how their Jewish father's picture got into a catholic high school yearbook. Let's go home Benedict Arnold!"

....

The following Friday night, Eric was gazing out the window of Lou's Grand Prix as it drove over the Walt Whitman Bridge passing a billboard on the way to the South Jersey coast reading, 'ZABERERS RESTAURANT! JUST MINUTES AWAY!'

Zaberers was a popular restaurant located in Ocean County, New Jersey off the Black Horse pike just a few miles inland west of Atlantic City. Zaberers kept their customers waiting for a table in their lobby for a half hour to forty-five-minutes exposed to the free appetizer. The high in sodium hors d'oeuvres would conjure up a thirst for the bar where Zaberers probably made most of their money. No matter where you were in South Jersey, the billboards read… ZABERERS RESTAURANT! JUST MINUTES AWAY!

"Well, I don't know," Eric confessed to Lou. "I waited for Steve for about an hour, and he never showed up at my house. I called his sister, and she told me that Steve left a couple of hours before."

"I wouldn't worry about it," Lou said casually as he drove. "He's not very punctual. It's his loss."

"Where are we going anyway?" asked Eric.

"We're going to a night club called 'Dio's'. The Stylistics and Harold Melvin & the Blue Notes are going be there tonight."

'Dio's Supper Club' was a popular nightclub in Pennsauken New Jersey that featured local rock bands and top-40 pop/soul groups in the early 1970s. Eric knew he would have no problem getting into Dio's since the drinking age in New Jersey at this time was eighteen.

Pete D'Angelo used to push Harold Melvin & the Blue Notes records on his radio show at WCAM before they made it big when payola was in-form.

························

It was ten-forty-five Saturday morning when the phone on the night table beside Eric's bed rang. Eric jolted out of bed to pick up on the second ring.

"Hello?" Eric uttered groggily.

"Eric, Steve!"

"Steve!" Eric snapped wide-awake. "What happened to you last night? I called your house, and your sister told me you left already. But you never showed up!"

"I was in jail."

"Jail?"

"I was on the subway heading to your house till this nigglet came over to me with a knife and demanded all my money. I kicked him in the stomach, and we started fighting. Some of the passengers who got off at the next station called for Rizzo's boys. When the cops came, I was on top of the nigglet. The cops, -who were nigglets themselves-, thought I started the fight. They threw me in jail and let the nigglet go. Every time I tried to tell my end of the story, the cops would lay this telephone book over my head, then whack the book with their nightsticks. I had one phone call to make. I dared not call my father. So, I called Pete D'Angelo to bail me out of jail. As we were walking out from the roundhouse downtown, Pete asked if this was my first time arrested. I said, "Yeah!" He laughed and kissed me on the forehead. I spent the rest of the night barhopping with him."

"I heard that Pete's a fag."

"Eric!"

"Sorry. Well, the next time the three of us go out together, Lou or I will pick you up from your house."

"So, how was 'Dio's'?" asked Steve.

"Man, great! 'Harold Melvin & The Blue Notes', followed by Billy Paul!"

"Damn!"

"So, how do you feel?" asked Eric.

"I got a headache like you wouldn't believe." replied Steve.

That night Lou picked Steve up from his house in South Philly and Eric in Mt. Airy, then proceeded to drive to the Marriott Motor Lodge on City Line and Belmont Avenue in Bala Cynwyd.

The three boys waited out in the cold on the parking lot in front of the Kona Kai. The Hawaiian theme bar and restaurant that was related to the hotel. The tiki torches outside the bar burned bright as a brand new 1975 bronze, two-door Cadillac coupe De Ville slinked up. What impressed Eric about the car were the square headlights. Steve and Eric hopped in the back seat while Lou took his place in the front next to Pete D'Angelo.

"If you guys in the back have any sharp objects in your pockets like a knife, a comb, or keys, take them out. This is a brand-new car, and I don't want anything to puncture my upholstery," Pete said over the loud disco music pumping out from the car radio.

Pete D'Angelo was a tall Italian man in his mid-thirties. Big cars and money came easy for Pete. He owned an underaged teen soda bar in South Philly. He had his own local dance show on a UHF channel every Saturday morning which was now in hiatus airing on reruns, plus his own radio show on WCAM-AM, a medium market radio station competing with a major market. Located on the eighteenth floor of Camden New Jersey's city hall facing Philadelphia a couple of blocks from the Ben Franklin Bridge.

It had been said that Pete was connected to the Philadelphia Bruno family, and the teen nightclub in South Philly was a purported front for racketeering. Pete had been married, but since his divorce several years ago, rumor had it in the business that Pete and Lou spent so much time together, they were part-time lovers. But this was all hearsay.

The Caddy seemed to float off the Marriott's parking lot in the direction of the Schuylkill Expressway heading east toward the city of Philadelphia.

"Pete! This is Eric Blum. The kid I was telling you about," announced Lou. "Great dancer!"

"Oh yeah?" remarked Pete.

Driving on the expressway at sixty miles an hour, Pete leaned over toward Lou, rotating his body to face the back seat. Eric didn't know what to make of this idiosyncratic driving technique.

"We want to start a new dance show next season," Pete announced. "We're looking for dancers. Lou tells me you're into the disco scene."

"Yeah. I really dig it. Especially the sounds that are coming out of Philadelphia." Replied Eric, anxious about the way Pete was driving.

"Yeah, I know," answered Pete twisting his body back around to face the road ahead. "It's about time. Since those freaks from England took over ten years ago, nobody wanted to dance anymore. Well, that's one thing I have in common with my rival dance show host, Jerry Blavat. We both hate the Beatles!"

Jerry Blavat was also a local disc jockey with his own TV dance show called Discophonic Scene, plus a radio show at WCAU-FM, a major market radio station in Philadelphia. Blavat was also known as the Geator with the Heater, and The Big Boss with the Hot Sause. He owned a popular over twenty-one-night club called Memories in Margate, south of Atlantic city, New Jersey.

In the early 1960's, with his media connection, Blavat had broken-in acts such as The Four Seasons and the Isley Brothers. With better financial backing than Pete D'Angelo, Blavat's' radio and TV dance show had more legs and influence in Philadelphia.

Pete's bronze caddy entered downtown Philadelphia by the Ben Franklin Parkway. The car turned right on 17th Street to Walnut, then another right. The beautiful people were blending in beautifully with all the characters of the evening along the streets and sidewalks of Rittenhouse Square Park. Men in their tightly permed or shagged haircuts wearing their long Maxi coats, and platformed shoes accompanied by women darning lose flared bellbottom slacks, shag and feathered back hair.

As 'The Sound of Philadelphia' by MFSB -Mothers Fathers Sisters Brothers-blasted from the car's stereo, a faint male but feminine voice was heard calling out from the pavement through Lou's ajar window.

"Pete! Pete!"

Pete stopped the Caddy while cars behind sounded their horns. All four heads in the Caddy turned to see who was running up from the pavement behind. It was three young gay men waving Pete down. Lou lowered his window as one man stuck his head through.

"Pete! Oh Pete! You must give us a lift," cried the man.

Eric didn't know how to react at first. This had been the first time he knowingly had contact with a gay man.

"Well, I have no room!" said Pete.

"We're only going to 20th and Walnut," pleaded the man.

"Okay. Pile in," Pete said reluctantly.

The man who poked his head into Lou's window jumped into the front seat basically sitting on Lou's lap. The other two squeezed into the back seat beside Eric and Steve. The men were dressed highly fashionable for the time, but feminine. Their cologne was sweet and over-bearing.

As the Caddy floated off to 20th and Walnut, the man next to Eric had his arm around his lover. Eric turned toward Steve and surrendered a slight seductive wink and an air kiss. Steve turned to face out the window shrouding the laughter.

It took only a few minutes for the car to reach three blocks.

"Well, we're here!" Pete shouted out.

"Thanks Pete," said the men next to Lou as the three peeled out of the car. "You're a real doll." Then pinched Lou in the cheek. "And he's a real cutie."

The man closed the car door as the three walked on and Pete and his entourage laughed headed toward their next destination.

"Eric! How would you like to be part of my staff?" offered Pete. "Lou here is our fashion coordinator. Steve is our music director; you could be dancing director."

"Sure!" Eric replied excitedly.

The Caddy waffled to a stop in the middle of a dark secondary street somewhere in Center City. Double parking a car leaving enough space for a vehicle to squeeze by seemed to be the normal thing to do if you were a true South Philadelphian.

The three boys piled out of the car and followed Pete into a dark alley. At the end of the alley was a gay bar. The name A's was hanging like a shopkeeper's shingle over the doorway. Heavy palpitating music could barely be heard leaking out from inside the club behind a thick black wooden door.

"There's somebody I have to meet in here for business," said Pete. "Now you'll probably see some weird things. Just pay it no mind."

A robust gay bouncer dressed in leather counting cover money guarded the door.

"Are you for real, D'Angelo?" The bouncer stated as the small entourage approached.

"They're cool, they're with me!" Pete declared.

"I don't care if they brought their mothers with them and a doctor's note! Among other obvious reasons, they're underage. Get them out of here!"

Although the drinking age in New Jersey was eighteen, Pennsylvania was still twenty-one.

"Is Billy, -the owner- here?"

"Yeah! But I'm sure he's busy."

"Maybe so. But not for me. Tell him Pete D'Angelo is here with a couple guests."

"Just wait here," declared the hissy bouncer clicking his tongue against his teeth as he stepped into the club letting the palpitating music gladly spill out onto the alley before the thick black door closed behind.

"I've never been to a fag bar before!" Eric proclaimed.

"Don't get too aroused, poster boy!" Pete replied. "You still may not get the chance. And the word is 'Gay'."

"Sorry."

Eric wasn't sure if Peter was gay or not. But with a local TV show in-sight he was starry-eyed and didn't care.

Within a few moments, the bouncer came out from behind the black door.

"Okay. Billy told me to let you in, but they stay away from the bar and drink soda! You hear me? Soda! And they keep a very, very low profile."

"Okay, okay!" responded Pete as he and the three boys slipped past into the bar.

The interior of the bar was a dive, intimate, decadent, and dark. Accompanied by bright strobe lights. It was easy to understand how anybody of any gender could get aroused in this place. Without the support of underwear, the deep heavy pulsating, vibrating beat from the bass in the loud funky music made Eric's penis palpitate within the lining of his pants. As the three boys walked in, some of the men at the bar glared with inquisitive lust.

"Alright, guys. I'm going to meet somebody at that table toward the center of the room. Just hang out here by the corner and don't make any eye contact. Keep to yourselves. I'll order cokes for you." Said Pete as he slid his right palm into his right pants pocket. "Now, here's a quarter. Play Pong."

Lou took a quarter from Pete and he and Steve played the arcade video game by Atri. Traveling around with D'Angelo, Lou and Steve were used to this environment. Eric found it difficult not to gaze. This was a whole new experience for him. In his own naive world, Eric was shocked to see the abundance of men on men and women on women holding, dancing, and kissing each other acting as though this was a party for the last day of the planet.

The male bartender with feminine attributes who otherwise would be known as 'flaming', wearing tight Daisy Dukes, and a printed Hawaiian shirt unbutton and tied around his torso exposing his navel, swooshed over to the boys with three cokes on a tray. Eric looked up to receive his drink and was astonished to find a tall ravishing full-bodied, long-haired blonde woman in a black pencil dress walking over toward D' Angelo's table. The Jane Mansfield wannabe took the empty chair in front of Pete. The boys were told to keep to themselves, but Eric was infatuated by this Veronica Lake. '*How could she be gay?*' he thought. In between the music and the loud patrons, Eric picked up tidbits of the conversation between Pete and Barbara Stanwyck.

"Please, Pete! Talk to him!" pleaded the woman. "My club opens in two weeks. If I don't pay back any of my seed money, I'm dead. They're going to take over and rip my club apart before I get a chance to open. Why is he doing this to me?"

"I don't know, Mary," Pete replied acting blasé as he sipped his Jack and Coke.

"Will you please ask him and let me know? I'm using up my own savings to open this place. That was money for my Scandinavian trip. Pete, please! Help me. I'm dead. I'm going to literally be a dead girl if he pulls his backing, and I can't pay it back before time!"

"I'll see what I can do, Mary. I'll talk to him Monday morning."

"Please, Pete!" The woman kissed Pete's hand. "Thank you! I don't know why he's doing this to me! This is not the time to pull out! I'm a dead girl, Pete! I'm dead!"

"Okay, Mary. Just calm down. I'll see him Monday morning, and I'll give you a call."

"Pete, I just don't know how to thank you!"

"Don't thank me yet, Mary. I still have to talk to him."

Pete and the woman stood up from the table. The woman walked pass the three boys by Pong. Eric followed her with his eyes as she exited through the black door.

"I don't think she's your type, son," laughed a gay man at the bar along with a couple of his buddies.

"Come on guys," said Pete as he walked by. "Let's get out of here and call it a night."

In the dark alley on the way to the Caddy, Eric had to know. "Pete? If you don't mind me asking, who was that woman you were talking with?"

"That was no woman," said Lou.

"That was Tommy," Steve added. "Tommy Lorenzo."

"Tommy?" asked Eric.

"Yeah. That's his real name," laughed Pete. "He goes under the stage name of Mary Nolan."

"You mean to tell me…" asked Eric.

"That's right," continued Pete, with a smile and a laugh. "He's a transvestite. He took the name Mary Nolan from a 1929 film star. It's the name of his new club on Market and 20th Street, Nolan's, if he can clear his finances with my boss on time."

"May I ask who your boss is?

"No!" Pete replied sternly.

....

The following Friday night, Pete was contracted to DJ a teen dance hosted by the AZA (Aleph Zadik Aleph for young men), and BBG (B'nai B'rith for girls) at the Shaare Shamayin synagogue in Northeast Philly. Unfortunately, Pete had a radio show at WCAM at the same time and had his three boys fill in at the dance for him. Eric was behind a turntable spinning discs as Steve stood by the dance floor with a microphone and stand acting as M.C. Lou tried his hardest to do the least amount of work. He mingled within the crowd, being rudely obnoxious unsuccess-fully trying to pick up girls.

Between queuing records, Eric looked up for a moment and noticed a familiar face dancing on the dimly lit floor. It was Renée, a tenth grader and one of the four girls who attended Noah Webster. Renée stopped dancing after spotting Eric behind the record players at the disk-jockey table and walked toward him.

Standing only five-foot-four inches, at sixteen-years-old, Renée had a medium build that just fit well in her tight jeans. Her button-down blouse revealing just a hint of cleavage. Renee's dark brown hair fell just below her shoulders. At school, she was somewhat loud and obnoxious and was known as the school brat. No boy at Webster wanted to be associated with her in a serious relationship. But no doubt every boy at Webster wanted to explore into her pants.

"Hi," said Renée. "Are you working with these guys?"

"Yeah," replied Eric. "I'm working for Pete D'Angelo."

"Where's Pete tonight?"

"He's in Camden doing his radio show. So, we fill in for him when he can't make it."

"How long have you been doing this?"

"Oh, about a few weeks. I got rid of that ushering job." Eric put Rock Me Baby by George McCrae on the turntable. "How are you doing in school?" He asked just to keep an awkward conversation moving.

"Fine. And you?"

"Well, Carol Schor's been calling me a small ass because I'm a little behind." Eric said chuckling at his own joke.

"Oh," replied Renée, not getting the pun. "Can you take a walk? It's kind of hot in here."

"Sure. I have some time."

Eric walked over to Steve by the microphone on the dance floor to ask him if he would hold down the turntables until he returned from walking with Renée. Steve looked back at Renée and gave a slight smile of approval.

As George McCrae serenaded the room, Eric and Renée walked across the dance floor toward the exit. Lou watched from the other side of the room with envy. The goal of naive Eric picking up a girl before he did didn't sit well with his ego.

Outside of the building on a cold concrete step in a dark corner, Eric and Renée sat alone. The muffled music of Rock Me Baby from the dance could still be heard.

"Are you going to college next year?" Renée asked.

"If they let me out of that retard school."

"What do you want to take up in college?"

"I would like to study American history."

"Influenced by the one and only, the great Carol Schor." Renée said resentfully.

Renée fell into believing that there may be something going on between Eric and Carol. But mostly, Renée was intimidated because the boys at school were paying more attention toward Carol Schor than her.

"Hey! She did a lot for me!" defended Eric.

"Like?"

"Well… when I first came to Webster, I was in eighth grade reading on a fourth-grade level with dyslexia. Plus, I suffered from an emotional breakdown. Carol pointed out to me famous people who had problems similar to mine who overcame and made a difference in the world. She showed me a whole new universe. She gave me back my confidence and self-esteem."

"Eric?" Renée was hesitant to ask her next question. "Do you tell people that you have a problem?"

"First of all, I *had* a problem. I don't have one anymore. That's why I want out of that crazy place. And second…" There was a long pause before he gave in. "No, I learned a long time ago not to disclose my past. Some people think I take the short yellow school bus because I'm retarded. I learned to keep my mouth shut. People don't seem to understand. Do you?"

"No," Renée responded quietly. "I don't know how to deal with people who don't know how to deal with it themselves."

"What was your problem?" Eric asked.

"Unlike you, I still have a learning disability," admitted Renée. "I can't comprehend what I read, dyslexia. Why did you have a breakdown?"

"I had a brother who was killed in Vietnam. My parents are still having a hard time coping with the loss. I live in a house of remorse."

Eric and Renée gazed into each other's eyes until their heads became one and their lips met.

Eric felt safe kissing the school brat. Nobody back at Webster would ever know. Lou appeared interrupting by clearing his throat.

"Oh, there you are!" announced Lou. "I was beginning to think you didn't have it in you, Eric. It's time for you to take over the turntables."

Eric donned an unfavorable look toward Lou as he stood up and offered his hand to help Renée off the cold cement step.

Back in the dance hall, Eric took his place behind the turntables. Renée grabbed a chair and sat beside him.

"Are you ready?" Steve asked Eric from the dance floor.

"Yeah, I'm all set." As Rock Me Baby ended, Eric segued Love's theme by Love Unlimited Orchestra.

As the instrumental took over, Steve walked behind the turntables and peered over Eric's shoulder for a couple of records. Lou stood next to Steve.

"Eric's got a girlfriend; Eric's got a girlfriend!" Lou chanted. Eric and Renée looked back and gave Lou a dirty look. Lou bent down and whispered into Renée's ear.

"Want to dance?"

"Drop dead, faggot!" Renée said over the music. Lou backed off.

"Eric! Get ready to put on Year of Decision by The Three Degrees," Steve called out as he walked back to the stand-up mic on the dance floor. Eric took a flashlight from the tool chest, dipped into the 45 case, and pulled out The Three Degrees. He laid the disc on an unused turntable. Steve pointed to Eric. Sweet angelic voices from three girls in perfect harmony filled the dance hall. Steve looked back toward Eric. "This is not Year of Decision."

"No?" Questioned Eric from behind the turntables.

"Idiot!" said Lou. Lou was beginning to get verbally abusive toward Eric.

"No," Steve yelled back over the music. "Well, I don't know what you have on, but keep it. It sounds great!"

For the second time, Eric retrieved the flashlight from the tool chest and tried to read the rotating disc.

"When-Will-I-See-You-Again ", Eric called toward Steve.

"That's side B!" announced Steve.

A young girl walked over to Steve by the mic. "What's the name of this song?" she asked.

"'When Will I See You Again', by The Three Degrees."

"Can I get it in the store?"

"Sure. It's on the flip side of Year of Decision."

Over the course of the evening, a few more young people walked up to Steve asking about the song. Steve yelled over toward Eric, "We have to tell Pete about this record! I think we might have a hit on our hands!"

The dance ended about eleven. As Steve and Eric packed all the records and equipment, Lou continued to be obnoxious trying a fruitless last attempt to pick up girls.

"What's his problem tonight?" Eric asked Steve.

"Lou has no problems. He never gets his hands dirty. He just takes the credit."

Out in the parking lot while teenagers were dispersing, Eric who was carrying a case of 45's headed toward Lou's Pontiac loaded from trunk to back seat with disc-jockey equipment. Renée walked beside. Lou followed close behind.

"My parents aren't coming home tonight. They're away for the weekend," Renée offered as a hint. "Would you like to come over?"

"I would like to, but I must see Pete in Camden, New Jersey. But I'll see you in school Monday morning." Said Eric.

"Eric, you're such a jerk-off!" Lou pointed out. "Can't you see that she wants to get porked? Go for it!"

"Lou!" Eric cried out.

"Here's my number," Renée said as she retrieved a pen and a match-book cover from her handbag and proceeded to write her number down.

Lou tried to peer over Renée's shoulder to read the number. "Give me a call tomorrow."

Lou and Steve were in the loaded Grand Prix when Eric was a few yards away on the parking lot with Renee.

"Come on, Eric! We're in a hurry!" Lou shouted out from behind the steering wheel.

"Okay, I'll be there in a sec!" Eric called back as he turned toward Renée. "Now listen Renée. In school, don't blab around that we were together tonight."

"Okay, sure," Renée responded with puzzlement.

"Come on, Eric!" Lou called out.

"Why don't you want me to say anything, Eric?" Renée asked.

"Well, I want out of that place, and I'm trying to keep a low profile this year."

"Come on, Eric! We're in a hurry!" Yelled Steve.

"Yeah, yeah. I'm coming, damn it!" Eric shouted back. "Well, I have to go to Jersey. I'll see you Monday at school."

Eric kissed Renée on the lips, then ran toward the waiting Grand Prix. Steve stepped out of the car so Eric could squeeze into a small space in the loaded compacted back seat.

"Will you call me tomorrow?" Renée shouted out.

"I'll try," Eric yelled out from the back seat. "But I can't promise."

Steve slipped back into the front seat and closed the car door as Lou stepped on the accelerator. Renée watched the red car spin off the parking lot down the dark street with Lou screaming out from his window from the Wizard of Oz. "Auntie Em... Auntie Em... You'll never get to see your Auntie Em! Hahaha!"

....

It was just after midnight as the Pontiac crossed over the Ben Franklin Bridge into Camden, New Jersey heading in the direction of Zaberers!

Just minutes away! Disco music from Pete's show at WCAM was blasting from the car radio.

"Are you going to go out with her?" Steve asked.

"I don't know," said Eric as he gazed out the window over the black Delaware River.

"I was dancing with her tonight," Lou added as he drove.

"Was that before or after she told you to 'Drop dead, faggot'?" asked Eric.

"I think we have a smash record here," declared Steve trying to avoid a growing argument between Lou and Eric.

"Yeah, well, remember, it was me who put the wrong side of the disc on the turntable." boasted Eric.

The Pontiac turned onto the nearly deserted parking lot of Camden City Hall. It was after business hours and WCAM's door on the eighteenth floor was unlocked when the three boys barged in. Luckily Pete was not on the air at the time sitting behind the analog console in a sound-proof studio.

"Pete! Pete!" Steve said excitedly as he ran into the studio.

"What's up? Did something go wrong tonight?" Pete asked anxiously as he pulled his muff headset off from around his ears.

"Better!" said Steve. "Eric put on side 'B' of Year of Decision by The Three Degrees, and we heard this." Steve handed Pete the disc.

"What is it?" asked Pete as he placed the disc on an unused turntable.

"When Will I See You Again. The kids loved it!" Eric said. "We must have played it about five times!"

As the preceding record on the turntable was about to end, Pete raised his hand for the three boys to calm down before he went live on the air. He replaced his headset back around his head, turn the pod up on the board.

"You're listening to PD right here at WCAM, 1310, Camden, New Jersey. It's twelve-thirty on a Sunday morning, and I was just handed a brand-new release by The Three Degrees-if you please-, and When Will

I See You Again. Why don't you give Uncle Pete a call here at the hotline, 609-555-3545 and tell me what you think?"

The song took over the airwave as Pete clicked off the on-air toggle switch at the console, slid the headset off from around his head.

"It was amazing, Pete," Steve continued. "The kids kept requesting it!"

"And Eric met a girl tonight at the dance!" Lou heckled.

"Is this true, Eric?" Pete inquired with a foolish grin.

"Oh, she's just a girl from school who was at the dance."

"Well, I hate to do this to you guys," said Pete "but I'm afraid you can't hang around. The management frowns upon parties while I'm on the air."

"Okay, Pete." said Steve. "Just tell us how the record holds out.

....

It was about two-thirty Sunday morning when Eric returned home. On the second floor he could hear his parents snoring from their bedroom down the hall. Not wanting to wake them, he quietly pranced into his bedroom and flipped on the light switch from the wall. Eric got himself undressed, slipped on a pair of underwear. He laid on top of his bed finding next to him the local newspaper -The Leader- left by his mother with an article about the problem with teens, drug, and alcohol. The article stated two-weeks prior to a fatal accident involving Alice Cappadonna jaywalking against the traffic crossing Roosevelt Boulevard -a twelve lane main artery- in Northeast Philadelphia. She was struck by a car on the southbound lane followed by four more vehicles that could not slow down or stop fast enough to avoid her. The police report speculated that a fifth car dragged Alice's lifeless body approximately seventy-five yards before stopping. An autopsy on her remains revealed that drugs and alcohol were saturated throughout her system.

The news immediately hit Eric hard in the stomach. As he began to shake from shock, a lump had formed in his throat and a tear dripped down his cheek. His heart felt like a cold lead weight. He had been so busy the previous weeks getting his own life together, that he didn't have time to think about the deep embedded feelings he still had for his first girlfriend.

Eric reflected to when he tried to convince Alice to stop the drinking and the drugs. Now, it was that spiral feeling of never seeing her again. Never having the chance to reconcile. It was the realization of the world never getting to know her, or her children, or her grandchildren. And the man who would have one day married her will now walk-through life unaware the woman he did marry was because Alice wasn't there. Perhaps the butterfly theory is a fact.

....

Monday morning as Eric drove the old Chevy to school, When Will I See You Again was blasting from the car radio. He softly sang along as he pulled onto Noah Webster's parking lot. Students Aaron and Sam approached the aquamarine car and waited for Eric to open his door.

"We hear that you're going out with Renée," announced Aaron.

"Who told you that?" asked Eric as he exited his car grabbing his brown paper lunch bag.

"It's not even nine o'clock in the morning and the entire school knows." Said Sam. "Renée told everybody."

"What did Renée say?" asked Eric.

"That you met her at a dance Saturday night and now you two are seeing each other. Renée would have told Webster himself if she knew where he was buried." Said Aaron.

With lunch bag in hand, Eric marched up the stone steps to the school patio, through the French doors and into the cafeteria where Renée was conversing with a couple of the students. She rushed over and gave Eric a bear hug and a peck on the cheek. The students in the room watched on.

"Why didn't you call me?" she asked.

"I didn't think you were serious."

"I was serious. I wanted you to stay over my house Saturday night."

Eric looked around to find the students were paying more attention to his intimate conversation than their own business.

"What do you think this is?" Eric charged the eavesdropping students. "E.F. Hutton?"

Eric aggressively grabbed Renée by the arm, and just about dragged her out of the building onto the stone patio.

"Why did you tell everybody?"

Renée was getting upset as Eric held her right arm too tight for comfort.

"I didn't. I just told a couple of people!"

Eric calmed down, lightened up his grip on her arm and with a slight grin gently held her by the shoulders. "Oh, I guess it really doesn't matter."

"What's your problem, Eric? Are you embarrassed of me?"

He paused for a moment before answering. Eric did feel uneasy to be associated with the school brat.

"No… It isn't that. It's… well, I just broke up with a girl, and I guess I'm being cautious about jumping into another relationship. I'm sorry."

The first period bell rang out, Eric smiled at Renée and gave her a soft tug on her chin.

Eric entered Carol's first period class and walked straight to his desk toward the back of the room next to rocking Joey Pearlman. As he placed his brown paper lunch bag in his desk, Mark Stern chuckled while glaring at his Playboy magazine. Even Mick Maze and Tony Burns were grinning.

"So!" Carol announced standing by her desk as she was straightening up her papers for the day's lesson. "I hear that you're going out with Renée." She had to give Eric a jab after all the times he jabbed her about Warren.

Eric looked up from behind his desktop opening his brown paper lunch bag with the double-decker peanut-butter and jelly sandwich. "Does the whole world know?" he asked as he took a bite from his sandwich.

"No. Just the entire school," replied Mark raising the Playboy magazine over his head letting gravity unfurl the centerfold. The entire class gathered around Mark Stern, including Carol and Joey Pearlman swaying behind Eric's right shoulder to examine Bebe Buell, Miss November 1974. Stern slowly looked up to find himself surrounded by students and teacher. "Who am I, E.F. Hutton?"

"Oh, how disgusting!" Carol said as she glared at the centerfold. Tony Burns laughed in her face.

....

After school, Eric drove the old Chevy to Alice's house in Oxford Circle section of the city to find out for himself if it was true. Standing on the sidewalk, in front of the stone front house, he felt an aura of grief. The house itself looked subdued and quiet. The atmosphere was chilled. Even the birds singing in the trees sounded in mourning. And although winter was gradually approaching, the trees surrounding the house appeared bearer than usual for this time of year. Fatality was in the air.

Eric pulled open the aluminum screen storm door, then knocked on the thick wooden white door. He stood back letting the screen door slowly close on its own hydraulics. After a moment of stillness, Mrs. Cappadonna pulled open the white door to see who had come to visit. She pushed the screen door open glaring down at Eric with no intention of invitation. Although it had been within a couple weeks since the last time, he had seen her, Mrs. Cappadonna looked twenty years older and withdrawn. The dark circles under her eyes that weren't there weeks prior appeared swollen from the result of lack of sleep and sorrow.

"She's not here! She's been gone for close to two weeks Eric! And now you show up?"

"Mrs. Cappadonna. I just found out. I'm so sorry." Alice's mother persisted in gawking at Eric without a word of acknowledgment. "I don't know what to say." Eric continued. "I loved your daughter. I wasn't the one that broke up. I didn't want to break up. There were many times that I tried to talk her out of drinking and the drugs, but she wouldn't listen to me. I wanted to be her best friend, if not her boyfriend."

"Were you, Eric?" Mrs. Cappadonna barked out. "Were you Alice's best friend?"

"I tried, Mrs. Cappadonna."

"Then where were you when she was crying for help?"

"I don't understand."

"Why didn't you tell me that Alice had drug, and alcohol problems?" Mrs. Cappadonna lashed out. "Why are parents always the last ones to know? Can't the newspapers ever get anything straight? Can't they? I'm a single parent! Alice's father never gave me enough alimony to support our children. I work two jobs to keep a roof over our heads, food in their stomachs, and clothes on their backs! I can't watch them all the time! And kids don't tell their parents everything! Did you really love Alice, Eric? Then why didn't you come to me when she was having problems at school? Or when she was too intoxicated to baby-sit for her brother? How much love did you have for Alice that you didn't want to become a snitch and tell me, so that I could have had the opportunity to save my only daughter?"

Mrs. Cappadonna backed into the house and slammed the wooden door close producing a sound of finality. The aluminum screen storm door slowly followed suit as to signify not just closure, but reflection. Eric was left standing on the bottom step alone in the chilled air completely speechless. And even through the thick stone walls of the house, Eric could hear Mrs. Cappadonna sobbing.

Eric did try to help Alice. But she was her own worst enemy. Some people fall so far off the edge with their vices, that all the friends and lovers in the world cannot retrieve them. But on the other hand, Eric thought, Mrs. Cappadonna might have been right to notified her about her daughter's behavior. Perhaps he should never have placed the Quaaludes in his pocket so Mrs. Cappadonna would had found them on the kitchen countertop.

And even if Alice didn't want to be associated with him for being a snitch, at least she might still be alive to tell him so. Maybe in years to come, perhaps they will meet again and laughed about it. Or at least cursed the ground he walked on. Now, there was no chance of either of that ever coming.

· ·

Friday night, Steve, Lou, and Eric met Pete D'Angelo in the lobby of Camden radio WCAM. Pete told the boys that every top-40 radio station in Philly was airing When Will I See You Again. Steve and Eric were a bit disappointed but not surprised when Pete handed off the credit toward Lou. Lou accepted the credit with a wide smile.

· ·

Monday morning before class, Carol stood behind her desk getting her assignments ready for the day's lesson while Tony was intermittingly dropping his desktop. Mick Maze gazed into space. Mark was reading another one of his magazines. Eric was sitting behind his open desk eating his double-decker peanut butter and jelly sandwich as he observed Joey Pearlman walking in chaotic small circles behind him.

"Eric," Carol called out as Tony continued to drop his desktop. "Remember when you requested to see a counselor?"

"Um, yeah?"

"You still interested?"

"Yeah, sure."

"His name is Dr. Goldman. He should be here this morning."

The door to the classroom opened, and Renée walked in. "Can I sit in?" she asked with a squeaky-clean voice.

"Don't you have class?" Carol asked.

"No! Nice tits, yip! Renée has no class at all!" Tony called out then dropped his desktop. The students laughed on. "Sorry, Eric."

Eric smiled as he chewed his sandwich. Renée smirked at Tony and continued to walk toward the back of the classroom.

"The English teacher isn't here today." Renée reported. "So, the rest of the class went to art, but I would rather be here."

"Yeah, round butt, so she could be with Eric!" Tony once again called out.

"That's not true!" Renée defended as she pulled an empty seat next to Eric. She glanced over toward Joey who was showing a flirtatious grin as he swayed over her. Renée surrendered an uncertain grin, then shuffled her chair closer toward Eric who was still chewing on his sandwich.

"Hi, Eric."

"Hi, Renée."

Tony continued to drop his desktop as the phone on the wall by the blackboard rang. Carol walked over to pick up the receiver, trying to hear.

"Hello? Okay… fine." Carol hung up the phone and walked back to her desk. "Eric, Doctor Goldman is here. He's in one of the empty rooms on the second floor."

"I bet ya that Renée leaves!" Tony yelled out.

"That's not true!" said Renée. "Carol, I'm going to art class."

"Goodbye Renée!" Carol mocked as Renée got out of her seat and walked toward the classroom door.

....

Walking down the second-floor hallway, Eric heard his name being called as he pasted an open door to a small unused classroom.

"In here!" said the voice. "Come in."

Eric turned back to peek into the dimly lit room. The only natural light protruding came from the space between the vertical venation blinds hanging over the two windows behind Dr. Goldman's desk.

Sitting behind the executive oak wood desk accompanied by a box of Kleenex, an open manila folder, legal size tablet, a pen, a cigarette lighter, ashtray and a dimly lit desk lamp was Dr Goldman. In front of the desk was a dark brown leather armchair.

Dr. Goldman was in his late thirties, wearing a three-piece gray suit, wired rimmed glasses, a beard, mustache, and smoked a pipe. A stereotypical psychologist for that time. When it came to looks, if it wasn't for the New York accent, Goldman could have passed for Dr. Sigmund Freud himself.

"Dr. Goldman, I presume?" asked Eric.

"Have a seat," Goldman offered as he blew smoke out from his pipe and mouth. Eric sat down in the leather chair in front of the doctor's desk.

"What a dark room you have here," mentioned Eric.

"Better to concentrate in." Goldman picked up the pen and began to jot notes on the yellow legal-sized lined tablet. "I've been told that you were seeking independent counsel. Perhaps I can be of some service?"

"Perhaps. The school's paying for you, right?"

"No. Your parents' insurance company is footing the bill. I was recommended by the school." Goldman said as he continued to write.

"I'm going to ask you a straight-up and forward question." Said Eric. "Since the school recommended you, am I going to get a fair evaluation?"

Goldman stopped writing, took the pipe out of his mouth, and laid it on the desk. "You can rest assured my evaluation will be independently straightforward and professionally honest. But to do that, we first must learn to be open and trust one another for the sessions to be successful, and a goal to be obtained. So, this is how we start: I ask you, 'What seems to be the problem?' And you reply... ?"

Goldman picked the pipe up from the desk, put it back into his mouth, and continued writing on the tablet as smoke billowed out from both sides of his lips.

"Well... um... There are a lot of problems. I really don't know where to begin." Said Eric.

"Well, let's start with school. Are you planning on continuing your education when you get out of here?"

"Well, there lies the problem. Am I getting out of here? They've been telling me for the past two years 'this could be your last year'. I feel I don't belong here anymore."

"Well, we'll have to see."

"Yeah, I've heard that for the past two years too. And please don't tell me that the school year has just started. Because if I hear that from you, you could just take out that pipe, and drop your pen right now because I'm walking right out of this room! My parents don't have to pay higher insurance premiums they can't afford for a shrink to tell me something I have already been told for free!"

Goldman looked up at Eric taken back by his feistiness. "I'll keep that in mind." He said as he continued to write. "So! That's what they've been telling you? 'Next year'?"

"That's what they've been telling me every year... 'Next year!'"

"Then let's just talk about next year. If we were to get you into a college, what would you like to study?" asked Goldman as he continued to write.

"History, I think."

"You think?"

"I'm not too sure, now. I hear that the teaching field is overcrowded."

"Well, if you should happen to change your mind about history or even college, what do you like to do for the rest of your life?"

"That's another big problem. My parents keep asking me that same question: 'What do I want to do for the rest of my life?' They're constantly on my back about it! Hell, I haven't been around long enough to know what I want to do. Besides the suburbs and the Jersey shore, I have never been out of Philadelphia. How do they expect me to know?"

"Do you get along with your parents?"

"Yeah, usually. But lately I've been hanging away from the house as much as possible."

"Why?" asked Goldman as he continued to jot on his tablet.

"Well, I guess I'm getting more independent. And most of the people I hang out with are from outside the neighborhood." Eric paused to think for a moment as Goldman continued to write. "There's another reason. I guess from reading my files you know I had a brother who was killed in Vietnam a few years back. My parents are still mourning his death. The house is just too depressing."

"Miss your brother?"

"That's a silly question, Doc."

"Maybe. But there are some people who resent the fact that kin had died. Some of these people substitute mourning with anger. You could be angry at your parents for letting him go."

"Angry at my parents because my brother was drafted and killed in Nam? No. I don't know where you get the anger from. I'm not angry. My brother didn't volunteer. He was drafted. My brother is dead. No matter how much I mourn, it's not going to bring him back. My parents subconsciously think he's still coming home. I just want to move on. Now that I have come to think about it, to be honest, I don't know if I do miss my brother. I guess that sounds kind of cold. My parents won't give me a chance to miss him. They're constantly comparing me with Elliot."

"Ah-ha, I see." Said Goldman as he continued to write. "So, staying out of the house is an escape?"

"Yeah. I guess you can say that."

"So, is that what caused you to have an emotional breakdown? Your brother's death? How did you pull through?" asked Goldman as he continued to write.

Eric paused to watch Goldman write his notes, "The shrinks here helped. A lot of therapy"

"Do you have a lot of friends, Eric?

"One good one. My cousin, Opie. He goes to the catholic school-Bishop McDevitt in Jenkintown. He lives in the Logan section of town. My other friends moved out of the neighborhood."

"Why did they move?"

"Well at first, Mt. Airy where I live was mostly white, Jewish. Then a few years back, the Philadelphia school board began busing blacks into the neighborhood schools. The Jews got scared, packed up, and moved out of the school district. The more Jews moved out, the faster the blacks moved in."

"Why didn't your parents move?"

"They couldn't afford to. Besides, I was going to this retard house at that time. So, I wasn't affected by the Philly school system."

"I see," said Goldman as he continued to write. "Do you like black people, Eric?"

"I got nothing against them. I can remember when my parents bought their first color television set. When taking it home, the bus driver won't let us sit in the front of the bus. The worst part, we had to bring it in from the back of the house." Goldman looked up from his desk unamused to see Eric smile with a slight chuckle. "I was only kidding, man!" recanted Eric. Goldman continued to write. "I have nothing against the blacks. At least they treat me better than my old white neighbors."

"Do you associate with any of the black children in your neighborhood?"

"No. Mt. Airy turned into a young, black professional neighborhood. Most of the kids are five to ten years younger than me."

"Do you have a girlfriend?"

"Yeah... I guess," Eric smirked.

"Where does she live?"

"She lives in Greater Northeast Philly. She's enrolled here. She's in tenth grade."

"Ah-ha, I see."

There was a brief silence as Eric observed Goldman jotting down more information on his tablet and the smoke billowing out from his pipe and mouth.

"I had a girlfriend before this one." Eric added. Goldman continued to write as though he was not paying attention. "Her name was Alice. She was my first girlfriend."

"Ah-ha."

"Yeah… she was killed about couple weeks ago." Goldman stopped writing and looked up at Eric. "She was run over by a car… Well, several."

"I'm sorry."

"That's all right. We broke up before it happened."

"Still, you must have some feelings for her."

"Yeah. She was the first girlfriend I ever had. She was self-destructive. Drinking and partying. It was reported that she was high when she stepped off the curb and onto the highway."

"Wow, man. I'm really sorry for your lost." Goldman put down the pen and held his pipe with his right hand against his lips paying more attention to Eric. "Do you take any drugs or alcohol, Eric?"

"No. Should I tell you if I did?"

"Uh… that's totally up to you, if you think it will help in our progress."

"I see you write everything down. I feel a liability in our confidentiality," said Eric.

"Did your other psychologist write anything down?"

"Not as much as you. He would just sit there and watch me. Staring, analyzing. Already concluding that I'm not ready to leave this retarded house. But he did smoke a pipe. I guess that comes with being a psychologist. So, tell me Doc, do they hand out that suck stick with your diploma?"

Goldman chuckled. "Well, you have a sense of humor, I must say that. You're right, I write things down. But I do it only so that I can review our sessions later to mark our progress. But you don't have to worry about your security. You're under doctor-patient confidentiality. Nobody can see these files unless I get subpoenaed."

"Well then, I was afraid to tell you that I feel in some way responsible for Alice's death."

"In what way is that?"

"Well, partially. I mean, there were the drug pushers and the people who supplied her with alcohol, and then there was me. I could have told her mother that she was self-destructive. Maybe if her mother knew earlier, Alice would be alive today."

"That's hindsight."

"What do you mean, hindsight?"

"Who knows, Eric. Her mother might have kicked her out of the house. She could have died out on the street."

"She did die out on the street. I don't know. That sounds odd coming from a shrink."

"Yeah, I call it shock therapy. That's when you wake up people before it's too late and show them the value of life. The reality is Eric, you can't blame yourself for something you couldn't have foreseen. Look, I'm supposed to be a man of science, right? But I believe in fate. Perhaps it was her time."

"I suspected her time would have been in her seventies or eighties. Not seventeen." Replied Eric.

"Hmm, maybe so. But then again there are the stillborn. Those who never get a chance at life. You know, everybody remembers their first love, Eric. I still recall mine. I was in third grade."

"Puppy love?" Eric jested.

"I don't know about puppy love, Eric. I remember having the same feelings of adoration for this girl in third grade that I had when I first met my wife years later in college. You'll always have strong feelings for Alice.

Especially now that you two didn't get a chance to reconcile." Eric's eyes filled up with tears as Goldman continued. "It's part of life. It's part of the master plan." Goldman took the pipe out of his mouth and observed Eric for a moment till Eric got himself composed. "Do you want a tissue?" Gesturing toward the tissue box on the desk.

"No," replied Eric as he wiped the tears with his arms.

"Do you work?" Goldman asked as he placed the pipe back into his mouth and continued to write.

"Well, I work part-time with a local disc-jockey spinning records. I'm hoping it will lead into something."

"Where do you want it to lead?"

"I don't know. I just want to get out of here."

"Where is 'here'? You mentioned 'here' before."

"'Here'!" replied Eric. "'Here', as in this stupid retard school. 'Here', as in Philly altogether!"

"Where do you want to go?"

"I don't know. I just want to start anew. I'm just so confused."

"Aren't we all?"

"You, Doc, confused? I would think not. Above all, you're a shrink. You're not supposed to be confused."

"Just because I'm a psychologist doesn't mean I'm immune from being confused. I'm only human. I have bills to pay. Two children to feed. A wife, home, cars. Things aren't given to me Eric because I'm a shrink. I earned them. I have troubles and worries like you and your parents. I still have life decisions to make."

"Are you from Philly?" asked Eric.

"No, New York. I was born in Manhattan."

"Rich?"

"My parents were working lower-middle-class."

"And now?"

"They're dead."

"Sorry."

"They died a long time ago."

"Brothers, sisters?"

"An older sister, still in New York."

"Your education?"

"New York public school system. Received my BA and MA in abnormal behavior at Cornell University. Transferred to the University of South Florida for my pre-med *Go Gators*! Received my doctorate in child psychology at the University of Pennsylvania."

"Why so many schools?"

"Because of the electives that were offered, the grants, scholarships, the free beer, and the women. You see, my parents couldn't financially afford to help me through college. They were poor Romanian immigrants. They could hardly speak English. And at that time there weren't as many governmental grants for education to be handed out as there are today. I had to study hard to make it on my own."

"My cousin Opie doesn't have to study. He passes all his tests. Did you go to any other school?"

"Well, I received my second doctorate in learning disorders, and a fellowship at Temple University, where I still lecture and teach as an assistant professor."

"After all that education you're just an assistant professor? Man, you've been duped. One more question."

"Shoot."

"With all this experience, what in hell are you doing taking a job at this one-horse retard school?"

Goldman pulled the pipe out of his mouth and grinned. "Well, that's where I'm confused. Perhaps by the end of this school year, you'll help me find that answer."

....

It was toward the end of the period when Eric walked back to his desk in Carol's class. Nothing seemed to have changed in the last forty minutes. Carol stood by her desk staring at Tony as he continued to drop his desktop.

"We have a detention after school," Carol told Tony. "Just you and me."

"Yep." Said Tony with a wide grin. "I knew that day would come."

Carol stared at him for a moment. "You're an asshole."

....

That afternoon after school as Eric walked out onto the stone patio to the parking lot, he found Cousin Opie with another boy leaning against his dull powder blue four door 1969 Oldsmobile Cutlass Supreme.

"Opie! I haven't heard from you in a while! Where have you been hiding?"

"Well, I know you're going to find this hard to believe but, I've been grounded by my parents."

"Tell me what you did this time, and I'll try to act surprised," said Eric.

"It's a long story, I can't get into. All I can say is that I been kicked out of Bishop McDevitt. Now I attend Central High School in Philly, which happens to be all boys. My parents made me quit the movie theater because I didn't make enough money to pay them back for this year's tuition from McDevitt. They wanted me to work it out with them at the funeral parlor. It's bad enough that I live with the stench of formaldehyde and embalming fluids throughout the house all the time. So, I got a job as a busboy at the Steak 'n Brew restaurant at the Cheltenham Mall next to the Cheltenham movie theater. The money isn't any better, but the tips are great. And because of the hours, I don't have to stay at home as much. This is my first cousin on my father's side from New Orleans

John, this is my first cousin from my mother's side—Eric." Eric walked down the steps from the stone patio to shake John's hand.

Eighteen-year-old John O'Neal stood a lean six feet, four inches tall. He wore an open denim jacket that exposed a T-shirt with the logo of the New Orleans Saints football team.

"Got your car here?" inquired Opie.

"Yeah? What's wrong with this piece of shit?" asked Eric pointing at the Olds.

"I don't have much gas. I'll put a couple of cokes in your back seat, then we'll go to Pauline and Eddie's for dinner."

....

Meanwhile, back at Webster, Carol sat behind her desk in her classroom reading a recipe from a Redbook magazine as Tony tackled a written assignment for detention. He was repeatedly tapping his foot against her desk. It was an annoying hyperactive reaction from being forced to keep that toilet mouth shut, and to sit still for an extended period. She told him to cut it out.

"Cut what?"

"Stop kicking my desk."

"I ain't kicking your desk!"

But the kicking continued. "Tony!"

"What?"

"Stop kicking my desk!"

Tony gave a good hard swift kick that spilled droplets of coffee from Carol's coffee cup onto her magazine. With one swift movement, Carol rolled the magazine, stood up from her chair, and swung the magazine toward Tony aiming to miss. Out of reflex Tony lifted his arm in self-defense. Carol's fingertips and Tony's arm made contact. Carol looked down to find one of her flawless shiny red fingernails cracked.

"You broke my nail, you bastard!" Carol said softly.

Enraged without thinking, she dropped the magazine onto her desk and slugged Tony across the face with the back of her hand. Tony in shock just about fell off his chair.

"You fuck'en hit me, you ugly son-of-a-bitch!" Tony yelled out holding his jowl. "You fuck'en hit me, you ugly whore you!"

The sound of him addressing her as a whore made Carol's entire body shutter. She slugged him a second time twice as hard, forcing Tony to slide off his chair onto the floor beside his desk. She was over his lame body with both fists clenched ready for that third shot if he should open that filthy trash mouth of his one more time. Tony stared straight up at her distorted face as he sobbed in horror holding his jaw with his right hand and his left arm blocking a potential third blow.

....

The busy diner style restaurant named Pauline and Eddie's was in a strip mall on Cheltenham Avenue in Cheltenham township down the street and west of Philadelphia's city park named, Tookany Creek. Inside the diner, Opie, Eric, and John settled into a booth. The menus and silverware were previously placed on the table. Opie sat across from John and Eric. A frumpy middle-aged waitress adorned with a pale-yellow dress and a white apron walked over to the table with pad and pen.

"Okay, boys. What will it be?" she asked looking down at her pad.

"I'll have the chopped birds' feet," Eric requested with a straight face staring at the menu. The waitress looked down at Eric with less than an amused grin. "I'm only kidding. I'll have a cheese steak hoagie, witd provolone, mayo, raw onions, lettuce. No peppers, no tomatoes, and French fries, well done." Eric leaned in closer toward the waitress and spoke discreetly. "I've heard you serve coke in a liquid form. I'd like to try that please. I can still get it with a straw, right?"

The waitress, unamused, looked over toward John. "I'll have a cheeseburger, French fries, and a coke," John requested in a thick southern drawl as he peered down at the menu.

"Do you have grilled chicken breast?" Opie asked the waitress.

"Yes, we do," said the waitress.

"Does it come with or without the brassier?" Opie looked up from the menu and could see that the waitress had no sense of humor. "Well then, I'll just have a bowl of vanilla ice cream and five glasses of Coca-Cola. I want all the cokes out at the same time."

"Is he serious?" asked the waitress.

"Very!" Eric and John both verified with a candid face.

The waitress shook her head as she took the menus off the table and walked back toward the kitchen.

"So, tell me, Opie. Living at home has been hell?" Eric asked.

"Oh, you know. Same old shit since I was kicked out of McDevitt. They're on my case about my future. They want me to take over the family business. I don't have the stomach for it, man. How 'bout you?"

"Yeah. My parents are on my back about my future too". Said Eric. "And I'm hoping I can graduate from that retard school of mine by June. Gee, I wonder why my mother never told me what was going on with you? What happened?"

"My mother told your mother not to say anything," replied Opie. "But a couple of buddies and I hid all the toilet paper that was in the school bathrooms. Then we melted down a laxative with a portable burner. We planned to inject the school's milk when we were caught by the school authorities as we were breaking into the cafeteria."

"Holy moly!" said Eric as John snorted from laughter. "Poor Ghost Lady." Added Eric. "Did she get anybody to replace you?"

"Not since I left. Bob is still there. You interested?" Opie asked with a laugh.

"No, I don't think I could handle that place anymore." replied Eric. "Besides, I have a new job now."

"I know. My mother told me you hooked up with Pete D'Angelo. Hey, is he really a fag?" asked Opie.

"I don't know. He never made a pass at me, but he did manage to get me into a gay bar."

"You want a steady paying job?" asked Opie.

"Yeah, where?"

"At the restaurant where I work."

"No, thank you. I don't think I can deal with a restaurant."

"Well, just thought I'd ask. How 'bout you, John?" Opie asked his cousin. "Are your parents on your back about your future?"

"Nah. My daddy's been pretty cool. He knows I'm still in high school."

"What does your dad do?" asked Eric.

"My daddy's a consultant for Getty Oil. I like what he does. Makes a ton of money. Goes to the oil fields out in the Gulf of Mexico weeks on end."

"Are you sure you don't want me to get you a job, Eric?" Opie asked again. "The restaurant has an opening."

The waitress returned with seven cokes on a tray, placed them down on the table then walked away.

"Yeah. I'm sure," replied Eric.

"Are you making enough money with Pete?" Opie asked Eric.

"Well, he pays me whenever I work on his dances. Mostly I've been eating off the fat of the land. My parents give me money when I need it."

"Is D'Angelo really related to the mob?"

"I don't know, Opie! You keep asking me these questions. He never made a pass at me, and I've never seen him with a gun!"

"Hey! I'm sorry about Alice, man." Said Opie.

"Yeah, thanks," Eric replied solemnly.

"Who's Alice?" asked John.

"His old girlfriend," answered Opie. "Run over by a car... a few cars actually."

"Okay, Opie! Thank you," Eric intervened.

"Have to admit. Must have been one hell of a mess."

"Okay Opie, enough!"

"Maybe not! There probably wasn't much of her left to make a mess." Opie thought.

"Opie, stop!" Eric yelled back.

"Are you seeing anybody else?" Opie asked.

"Yeah, this girl from school."

"Are you serious with her?"

Eric had to think about that one. "Yeah, I guess."

The waitress returned with an armful of food. One by one, the proper plates are placed in front of the right person. Eric dove into his cheese steak hoagie and French fries as the waitress left the table.

"Does she have any girlfriends?" asked Opie.

"No, she has leprosy! Of course, she has girlfriends!"

"Well then, why don't you introduce me to a couple of her friends?"

The waitress returned with a bowl of vanilla ice cream, then left.

"Introduce you?" Eric stopped eating and looked up at Opie with a straight face, then turned toward John. "I'll tell you about a time Opie set me up with a girl. One day, last year, Opie and a mutual friend of ours, -Carl-, picked up these two bimbos who were hitchhiking. So, this weekend, Carl's parents were out of town. Carl and Opie planned on spending the night with these two broads. Opie needed a ride to Carl's house since he didn't have a car at this time. So, he gives me a call and says he has an extra girl for me, and I should pick him up. Now, being that I am a typical horny American male, young, dumb, and full of cum, I agreed. The girl that Opie had for me was Carl's younger sister." Opie began to break up in laughter almost under the table. "The girl was six years younger than me," Eric continued with his version of the story, "... and ugly."

"How ugly was she?" asked John with a smile and a quarter of the burger in his mouth.

"She was so ugly that when she was born, the doctor didn't know which end to smack first."

Opie laughed a little harder trying to hold his head above the table with one arm on the bench seat.

"And fat!" continued Eric.

"How fat was she?" John asked.

"She blocked out the light when she walked toward me. At first, I thought it was an eclipse. In gym class at school, she was the only student that could do eighteen pull ups, and never go over the same chin twice! When Carl's sister went to order fried chicken at KFC, the girl at the register asked what size bucket. And Carl's sister pointed up and said, 'The one on the roof'. I mean, look, thank God this girl was not interested in me. But this was not the worst part. The worst part was that Carl had two Great Danes that attacked me with kisses the minute I walked into the house."

Opie was laughing loud enough to be a slight nuisance to other people around him.

"Toward the end of the evening, Carl and Opie go off to bed with these two bimbos." Eric continued. "Where was I? I tried to fall asleep on the living room couch watching a Marx Brothers film on television with two Great Danes. One's licking my balls, while the other's farting in my face." Eric turned toward Opie who was trying to catch his breath from laughing so hard. "Find you a girl? You should drop dead!"

Opie laughed as he looked down at his bowl of ice cream. "Yeah, I remember that night. That was a couple of days after Jim Croce was killed."

Two booths in front of Opie sat four teenage girls. They were sharing some gossip and giggling. Opie piled ice cream onto his spoon.

"Opie, please don't do this" begged Eric. "Opie, I'm asking you not to do this."

"This one is for Jim Croce. For all the great songs and good stories." Said Opie as he flung the ice cream off his spoon, over and between Eric and John, where it hit the back of the head of one of the four girls. The girl reached to touch the back of her head. She felt the ice cream dripping down her hair into the collar of her blouse.

The girls gave the boys a dirty look. Opie repeated the action. The second spoonful hit the girl seated next to his first target.

"Oh, damn Opie!" Eric said.

The second girl turned and threw a piece of her hamburger and ice from her soda at the boys. Eric, John, and Opie responded by lofting some of their own food.

The waitress walked out of the kitchen with an armful of plates of food finding the entire dining area in an uproar of flying provisions and screaming people. She ran back toward the kitchen yelling for the cook.

"Eddie! Eddie!"

"What is it, Pauline?" The cook stormed out of the kitchen waving a cleaver knife. Opie, John, and Eric darted out from the restaurant.

"Well, at least we didn't have to pay the bill," remarked Opie as he ran toward the parking lot.

"Damn, Opie!" said Eric chasing close behind.

On the parking lot, the neighborhood hoodlums known as The Road, which consisted of seven boys-were-leaning or sitting on top of their two cars.

The Road was a gang of hoodlums who were established in in Mt. Airy in the early to mid-1960s. The associates were Irish or WASPs who attended the parochial schools in the area. They received their commission by hanging out at a strip mall on Vernon Road located across from Temple Stadium where the Temple Owls played football.

After the Jews moved out of Mt. Airy, The Road and their families were the last holdouts except for the Blum's. The gang tried to fight for their turf, but it was a losing battle since more black families were moving into the neighborhood faster than The Road could enlist white gang members. Eventually, The Road retreated their turf into the surrounding suburbs. They still wore their leather motorcycle jackets with The Road stitched or painted on the back.

One gang member noticed the graphics on John's T-shirt under his open denim jacket as John ran by.

"The New Orleans Saints blows!" The gang member announced.

John stopped dead in his tracks and turned to face the gang. "What did you just say?" asked John.

"Now, John," Eric said nervously as he stepped back to drag him along, "We don't do any southern redneck action here. When somebody says something to you, you just keep walking'. Besides, it's just a fuck'en' football team!"

The gang slid off their cars toward John and Eric. "Oh shit!" said Eric, as he continued to run toward the old Chevy still dragging John behind.

Opie was already by the Chevy. Eric unlocked his door, jumped into the car, and reached over to unlock the passenger side as he thumbed for the keys to start the engine. Opie opened his door then unlocked the back door holding onto John who was continuing to challenge the gang. "I'm dead." Eric said to himself as he cranked over the engine of the old Chevy.

Opie finally pushed John into the back seat of the car, while the gang drew closer. John rolled down his back window to continue calling out to the gang. Some of the gang members ran back to get to their own cars.

Eric drove off the parking lot down Cheltenham Avenue toward Wyndmoor, a community that bordered Philadelphia and Cheltenham Township. Spinning left off onto Ivy Hill Road, Eric drove onto a soccer field with The Road in two cars in hot pursuit. Eric broke up the soccer game by driving across the field making a complete circle chasing soccer players hoping the two cars behind would chicken out. In his rearview mirror, he saw the two cars were still behind with gang members hanging out their car windows holding pipes and rattling chains. John caught a soccer ball that was thrown at him and threw it toward the goal and scored as the car drove by. Eric drove off the field and back onto the streets of Wyndmoor.

The chase continued through the Wissahickon section of the city recklessly cruising through traffic lights and stop signs.

John still had his head hanging out the back window cursing at the two cars hot on the scent. Members of The Road with their heads hanging out their windows vocally challenging John resembling barking dogs who were enjoying the force of the wind. Eight-ounce glass Coke bottles in the back of Eric's seat knocking against John's ankles. Opie spotted a place to hide. It was a dark driveway between two parked cars.

"Turn here!" Opie yelled. Eric turned into the driveway before The Road turned onto the dark street. "Duck!" Opie yelled out. The two boys butted heads as they hid under the dashboard. John was still cursing. Opie jumped up to reach John's jacket collar to pull him down between the front and the rear seat. The two pursuing cars passed the parked old Chevy without notice. John continued to mumble.

"How do we calm the big guy down?" asked Eric.

"Beer." replied Opie.

"What?"

"Beer. When John gets mad, beer calms him down."

"Well, I have a fake ID that D'Angelo handed me," announced Eric.

"You don't need it. We look old enough. And I know a place that will serve us without ID."

Opie took the boys to a working-class bar somewhere in East Oak Lane. The interior had no distinguishing features that pertain to any time, but old and not well maintained. Some of the paint on the ceiling was peeling off. This was the type of neighborhood bar that only welcomed the locals. A football game was being televised from a television mounted eight feet above the back bar on a smudgy, clouded mirrored wall.

A few customers wallowing in their drinks either at the bar or at tables. Three tanked construction workers dressed in their faded jeans and flannel shirt with their hardhats laid on top of the bar were drinking beer and eating tuna fish sandwiches.

Eric, Opie, and John sat at an around table in the center of the room. Eric gazed around while Opie and John had drawn their attention toward the football game for a moment before snapping back to reality.

"What do you guys want?" asked Opie.

"Bud!" said John.

"Well, I'll get a pitcher." Eric ordered a vodka Collins. "What are you a faggot? Is that what D'Angelo turned you into?" asked Opie.

"No," laughed Eric. "You're going to order a pitch of Bud. So, I figured if nobody else is drinking beer, why should I?" replied Eric.

Opie walked over to a crusty looking bartender who was behind the bar rubbing a glass with a damp white towel. The three construction workers looked Opie over.

"I'd like to have one pitcher of Bud, two frosty glass mugs, one vodka Collins, and three glasses of Coca-Cola without ice."

"Sorry," said the bartender as he continued to dry the glass. "No Coke. Shasta."

"You gotta have Coke, man. Suppose I wanted a rum and coke, then what?"

"Then it's rum and Shasta! You want Coke? There's a Coke machine across the street at the closed gas station, but you drink it outside."

"Okay, okay. I'll have three glasses of Shasta. Make that four. No ice."

As the bartender filled the order, the three construction workers turned their attention from Opie and laughed among themselves. Opie returned to the round table with one pitcher of beer and two frosty glass mugs. The three construction workers continued to chuckle at Opie as he returned to the bar to pick up the small round tray with four Shastas and a vodka Collins.

At the table, as all three watched the football game, John slurped his beer calmly. Opie downed two glasses of Shasta, then half a glass of beer. Eric sipped his vodka Collins.

The three construction workers turned to face the boys with their backs leaning against the bar.

"Do you know what I think about the youth of today?" asked one of the construction workers loud enough for the boys at their table to hear.

"No, what?" asked his two buddies with a grin.

"I think it stinks!"

Eric held on to his drink with both hands-which seemed to be vibrating in the glass. Opie and John remained calm watching the television.

"And another thing," the worker continued. "I don't think that twenty-one is a good legal age to start drinking. Thirty is more like it!" The worker pointed toward the boys' table. "Now let's take these three boys here. I bet they protested the war..."

"What did he mean by 'Let's take these three boys here?'" Eric asked himself.

One of the construction workers threw an olive onto the boys' table. Eric, along with Opie and John, paid closer attention to the game on television.

"Tell me boys. Does mommy know you're out drinking with the men tonight?"

"My mommy doesn't know anything right now," Eric thought to himself. *"If my mommy knew that I was about to be murdered by three buffoons, she'd kill me!"*

The third construction worker flicked a piece of his tuna fish sandwich that stuck onto Opie's cheek. Opie had enough. He and John slowly stood up from their chairs to face the three workers at the bar who were dumbfounded and quickly sobered up seeing the actual strength and size of John showing off his six-foot, four-inch frame picking up the round table with one arm. Glasses rolled off and smashed onto the floor. Eric remained seated waiting to hear the theme song from the film The Good, the Bad, and the Ugly. His legs shaking with his glass in hand. The bartender pulled out a sawed-off 12-gauge Remington shotgun fondling the trigger just about out of sight from behind the bar.

"Okay, fellas!" said the bartender. "Just calm down, now!"

A couple of patrons ran out of the building. Others sat by their tables or stood by the bar like statues observing. Opie slowly walked toward the three construction workers.

"Oh shit!" Eric said under his breath. "I'm going to die tonight."

The three workers weren't sure if they should rush Opie or not. John made up their minds to stay put by lifting the table higher over his head, threatening to loft. Opie strolled over to the construction worker who had instigated the situation and picked up his pitcher of beer from the bar.

"I'd love to buy you this round of beer. But I'm afraid you're not going to like it. You see, people are going to laugh at you."

"And why is that?" asked the worker with half a smile.

"Well, I think you're going to look awfully funny walking around in life with part of this glass jug protruding permanently out of your ass."

"Opie?" Eric said timidly. "Let's make like an alligator and drag our asses out of here."

"Just a minute, Eric."

Opie raised the pitcher of beer over the construction worker's head, then slowly proceeded to pour. The other two construction workers took a step toward Opie.

"I wouldn't!" Opie suggested.

The two workers took another quick look at John who was ready to loft the table. John lifted the table higher, and Opie continued to pour the beer over the worker's head. The other two workers stepped back. Eric recited the mourners' kaddish in Yiddish for himself. Everybody in the bar was silent with anticipation. The bartender was still fondling the trigger out of sight from behind the bar. After the last drop of beer, Opie calmly placed the pitcher back onto the bar. Then, slowly walked backwards toward John and Eric. Eric was still sitting with nothing in front of him but holding onto an unfinished glass of vodka Collins.

"Now!" Opie yelled.

Out of reflex, the bartender shot off a round into the air. Plaster and dust floated down from the ceiling onto the construction workers. At the same time, John threw the table toward the workers and followed Opie running out of the bar. Eric tossed his glass, flipped over in his chair, and followed the two boys out the door as fast as his legs would carry him.

The boys ended up back at Webster's parking lot. Street Fighting Man by The Rolling Stones sang out from the Cutlass radio. John was stretched out in the back seat while Opie smoked a joint behind the steering wheel.

"Wanna toke?"

"No Opie," Eric replied, standing beside the driver side car door.

"So, I guess we had an exciting night, eh?" asked Opie.

"You know, Op? I'll be honest. Besides the fact that you're my cousin, my parents like you. You put on a good innocent act in front of them. But if they ever found out what you're really like…"

Opie laughed with a snort. "So, does that mean you're going to the Steak 'n Brew tomorrow and apply for the job?"

"No! And don't tell my mother. The last thing I need is for her to be on my back about a job I don't want. It's bad enough that I'm your first cousin for life. I don't have to work with you all the time."

"Amen!" John yelled out from lying in the back seat of the car.

....

It was about nine-thirty that night when Eric returned home. His mother and father were lounging on the sofa in the dimly lit living room watching a detective show on television called Harry-O starring David Janssen. Eric proceeded to climb the stairs to his bedroom.

"Carol Schor called you," Mrs. Blum announced.

"She did?" Stopping halfway up the stairs.

"Yeah. She said you could call her up until eleven."

"Oh, I wonder what she wants?" Eric continued to climb.

"Did you do something in school I should know about?"

"No, mom."

"Should I worry?"

"No, mom. Everything is cool."

Eric raced up to his bedroom, closed the door, lay on his bed, reached for the phone receiver on the night table, and dialed.

"Carol Schor! And to what do I owe this great, unexpected pleasure of your phone call this evening my dear? Please tell me you dumped the geek."

"No, Eric. I did not 'dump' Warren. I'm in big trouble," Carol said.

"Trouble? What type of trouble? It is *Warren*, isn't it? That asshole! Don't you guys' use protection?"

"No, no, it's not that type of trouble, you jackass! I slapped Tony this afternoon."

"You what?"

"I decked Tony! Not once, but twice! I had him for detention. I gave him a written assignment. He kept kicking my desk. I asked him to stop several times, but he refused. I raised my magazine over his head just to scare him, and he broke one of my fingernails."

"OY!"

"Yeah! Big time! So, I just snapped and slugged him. He called me a bitch and a whore, so I slugged him again. If he had said another word, I swear I would have beat him till he stopped breathing."

"Wow! I wish I could have been there to see that. Well, you know he's been asking for it."

"Yeah, I know!"

"So, now what? You think you're fired?"

"I don't know, man. I have a meeting tomorrow morning with Tony and his parents in Principal's Swanson's office. I'm going through the want ads tonight just in case."

"Where's *Warren*?" Eric teased.

"He's at his apartment."

"Well… I'll support you however I can, Carol."

"Thanks, Eric. I thought I'd let you know before the rumor mill got started. At least now, I have one student I can count on who knows the truth and won't badger me."

....

The next morning Mr. and Mrs. Burns, their son Tony, and Carol sat in Principal Jim Swanson's tiny office. The office on the second floor was once part of a bigger room, perhaps originally another bedroom that was squared off at fifteen-by-twelve feet when the school was taken over from the church. Principal Swanson had been promised a bigger office for the past year and a half, but the maintenance people at the school had been dragging their feet in preparations. The larger room Dr. Goldman was occupying was suggested to be Swanson's office but had always been slighted to be an extra classroom in the future. Mr. and Mrs. Burns and Carol's knees were just about scraping against the front of Swanson's industrial office desk.

Principal Swanson was an attractive man in his mid-fifties with a thick full head of silver hair. He spoke in a soft, soothing, sensual settling voice.

"As you know it's not Webster's policy to enforce capital punishment on any of its students," Mr. Swanson announced commencing the conference. "Now, Miss. Schor has been with Noah Webster Preparatory for the past four years, and never during any of that time have I heard her raise her voice, let alone physically discipline a student."

"Ha," chirped Tony. "You haven't sat in any of her classes."

"Shut up!" Carol snapped out.

Mr. and Mrs. Burns were surprised to hear Carol address Tony in that matter, which probably didn't help her case.

"... But Tony has been very abusive toward Miss Schor lately." Swanson continued. "I'm not defending what Miss Schor did. But I'm sure there was a very good reason that led up to this incident."

"Yeah!" Tony yelled out. "I accidentally broke one of her fingernails trying to defend myself from that simple JAP!"

"Your turn will come, young man!" announced Swanson.

"I don't care if Tony broke her arm! Who does she think she is, General Patton?" declared Mrs. Burns.

"Hey!" Tony yelled out.

"She is not to lay a hand on my son. That is my responsibility! If Tony was being abusive, I should have been notified!"

"Yeah!" Tony called out.

"And why weren't we notified?" asked Mr. Burns.

"Why not?" Tony asked.

"Well," replied Swanson, "it was to my understanding from you and the school psychologist, due to his Tourette's syndrome to let Tony do whatever he feels comfortable to express himself as long as he doesn't hurt himself or those around him."

"Right!" Said Tony.

"Well," said Mr. Burns, "we still feel that it is in Tony's best interest to let out his frustrations the best way he knows how."

"So, fuck all of ya!" Tony called out.

"No! I'm sorry!" Carol interrupted.

"What?" asked Tony.

"That's not how to treat disobedience, or an alleged mental disability."

"Alleged mental disability? Do you also have a degree in psychology, Miss Schor?" asked Mr. Burns.

"No!" Tony said.

"No, Mr. Burns! But I have your son for five and a half hours a day. That's more time than you probably spend with him all week."

"Carol!" Swanson shouted out.

"Hey!" yelled Tony.

TAKING THE SHORT BUS

"No, Jim! It's time to let the cat out of the bag! The topic here is not that I took disciplinary action against Tony. The real topic here is responsibility! Why do teachers have to discipline students to begin with? That's not what I'm paid for! I didn't spend close to ten thousand dollars of my hard-earned money, twenty years of schooling, and waiting on tables to be a truant officer. That job of learning proper etiquette in the classroom belongs to his parent's years before Tony reached preschool. By the time he was in first grade, mentally disabled or not, Tony should have been familiarized with proper etiquette and behavior skills for school. When a child has a foul mouth, passes gas loud enough for the entire class to hear, sets his pants on fire, or repeatedly drops his desktop down while I'm giving a lecture, I reflect on his upbringing.

Is there any medical documentation on Tony to prove Tourette's syndrome? If there is, it was never presented before me. I am tired of his sexist lewd remarks against me! I'm paid to teach your son the basic skills he needs to defend himself academically in this world. Your job as parents should be to teach him the behavior skills he must have to survive in his environment. Letting Tony do what he wants to do as long as he doesn't hurt anybody or himself is not responsibility, it's copping out, giving up! Why has your son been kicked out of every school from Abington, Glenside, to Cheltenham? What's wrong with this picture here? Don't you get it?"

The Burns were speechless, the room was silent. Tony was staring down at the floor. Swanson wanted to stand up and cheer. This is what he had wanted to relay to Burns for the past two years. At this point, Carol figured she was fired. She might as well get the last word in.

"I don't want to discipline your child. But it's not too late for you to take charge. Tony is old enough to be treated as an adult and should bear the consequences of his actions! Either he grows old with Tourette's syndrome, or he's cured, Tony must grow up now and be responsible! Yesterday, it was a slap across the face! When he's out of this school in the future, it could be his life!"

103

There was a second pause of silence. "Yeah." Mr. Burns acknowledged softly.

"Well," said Swanson as he cleared his throat. "Is there anything else anybody would like to add?"

Tony was about to say something, but Carol gave him a threatening look as a warning to keep his mouth shut. Tony remained silent.

"Thank you, Miss Schor. You and Tony are dismissed."

"I didn't get a chance to say my peace!" Announced Tony.

"You've said enough for the past couple years, young man!" Stated Swanson.

It was awkward for Carol to walk down the second-floor hallway alone with Tony. He was a pace in front of her and with every step they both took; Carol was getting more furious.

"You have nothing to say to me, do you?" She asked. Tony stopped to face her. "Nothing at all?" Carol continued. "Not an apology, or an acknowledgment? Nothing? Nothing!" Tony remained silent as they both proceeded to walk down the staircase to the first floor.

The whole day Carol's anxiety grew not knowing if she would be returning to Webster the following day. Eric was sympathetic. He didn't tease her about Warren or make any cute little passes.

It was at the end of the school day when Swanson and Carol had a short conference in his office.

"I talked to Mr. and Mrs. Burns out of sending a complaint against you to the Montgomery County, and Pennsylvania school authorities. Look Carol, I don't put you at full blame. This is not a normal school by any means. This is a school for special needs. But you knew that when you signed up for this job. Tony can push anybody of any caliber to the brink. All the kids here can be very tiresome and challenging. Before this happens again -and I trust that it won't- my suggestion would be to walk out of the classroom. Take a breath. People like Burns forget that teachers are only human. They forget that when that classroom bell rings for the last time of the day, teachers go home to their own families, go to ballgames, take their own kids to the movies, wash clothes, cook dinners, and pay bills. All I ask is that you be more careful. We're a small institution. We can't afford bad press. That's all."

Carol stood up from her chair, scraping her body by the desk, and proceeded to walk toward the office door threshold till Swanson called her back in to say, "Thanks." Swanson put his glasses back on his nose to read silently a letter from his desk. It then became apparent to Carol that the lecture to Tony's parents was a blessing in disguise. The 'thanks' from Swanson was a pat on her back of gratitude.

CHAPTER 5

ALL THE PRESIDENTS' BOYS

AFTER SCHOOL, ERIC drove to the Steak 'n Brew restaurant at the Cheltenham Mall. Since Aunt Frieda had informed Mrs. Blum about the employment offer Opie had made to Eric the night prior, Mrs. Blum refused to give Eric extra spending money unless he applied. Eric's second thought was, if he could get a steady paying job on his own, this could be his ticket to prove to the school that he was ready not only academically but mature and emotionally stable enough to graduate from Noah Webster. Perhaps, if scheduling permitted, he could also remain with Pete D'Angelo.

The interior at the Steak 'n Brew restaurant was of an old English pub with Victorian pictures and nick-knacks hanging off the dark brown oak wood walls and ceiling. There was a common salad bar in the center of the dining room. The male servers wore long white button-down shirts, white pants with white aprons. The women servers wore white dresses down towards the center of their calves with white aprons. A thin, attractive, young bleached-bottle-blonde hostess approached Eric at the foyer.

"How many?"

"I would just like to speak to the manager please." requested Eric.

"Okay. Just follow me."

Eric followed the hostess into the dining area. The restaurant was busy but not crowded.

At a table for four sitting alone, Marty -the restaurant manager- was eating prime rib, house fries and salad with a glass of merlot. The hostess left Marty and Eric alone at the table. Marty was an attractive, twice-divorced man in his early forties with thin light brown hair combed to the side that suggested it will be gone within the next fifteen to twenty-years. He was dressed in a black sport jacket, white shirt, red tie, and dark blue slacks. To his employees Marty was known as a gambler, alcoholic, and an infamous womanizer known to take up with a young waitress or two.

"What can I do for you?" asked Marty as he chewed.

"I heard there's an opening for a job."

"Who told you I had an opening?" Marty asked as more steak fell into his mouth.

Eric felt uncomfortable canvassing for a job in front of a man who was gorging himself. "Opie O'Neil." Marty almost gagged on his steak. "My sentiments exactly sir," Eric responded.

Marty wiped his mouth with a maroon cloth napkin, then took a swig of the red wine. "Yeah, well. Do you have any experience?"

"Well, I never worked at a restaurant before. But like any monkey, I'm sure I could learn."

"I don't hire monkeys." Marty seriously replied. "How old are you?"

"Eighteen."

"Do you want to wash dishes?"

"Sure."

"Learn to make salads?"

"Yes."

"Okay. Well, I may be looking for somebody. Leave me your phone number and I'll let you know when you can start. I'll send you a banana."

"Thank you," frowned Eric, then sneezed.

Eric assumed he had gotten the job. If he could stay with Pete D'Angelo, keep his grades up, and remain cool, the end of Noah Webster Preparatory could very well be in sight.

....

The following morning at Webster on the first-floor hallway, Eric was approached by senior Sam who was known by wearing a jeff cap and junior students Aaron, Tom, and Tony who were known as the school goof-offs. Eric sneezed.

"Bless you," Aaron said. "Eric, we're coming to you for some advice. Ever since the Carol Schor/Tony Burns slap incident..."

"Hey!" Tony squeaked.

"... The school called all our parents with ultimatums. If we don't take our studies seriously, and start passing our grades, the school will advise our parents to look elsewhere for our education. My parents can't financially afford to keep me at this school if I don't apply. I personally can't deal with a public school. Neither of us can."

"We asked the teachers to help us catch up before Christmas break." Said Sam.

"We're all going to funk this semester if we don't catch up." Said Tony.

"Well. I don't understand." Replied Eric. "The way you been behaving I never thought you guys cared if you flunked or passed."

"Well, I for one," announced Tony, "I'm on the limb. After that meeting with Swanson, my parents laid down the law. If I don't behave and pass this semester, I lose my Mustang!"

"You're in good with the teachers. You're, student body president." said Aaron. "Talk to them. Get them to be a little more lenient toward us with all this missed work till we catch up before Christmas break!"

"Me talking to the teachers won't help." Said Eric. "I can't change the way they teach or grade. It's not their fault nor mine that you guys clowned around these past few years." Eric stopped to think for a moment.

"But there may be another way around them. Look, Carol usually goes out for lunch. Let's all meet in her office on the second floor at lunch time where we can talk in private."

During the lunch hour on the second floor, Sam picked Carol's office door and got it unlocked. The interior of Carol Schor's office was half the size smaller than Principal Swanson's. It was probably a bedroom at one time. Besides Carol's office, the room was also used to store student records in a couple of tall metal filing cabinets.

Eric turned on the florescent overhead light from the light switch by the door.

Closing the office door behind them, Aaron, Tony, Tom, and Sam squeezed in on the floor or on top of Carol's desk. Eric sat in Carol's chair and placed on the floor beside him one of his creased brown paper lunch bags stained from peanut-butter oil that once harbored his double-decker peanut butter and jelly sandwich.

"What do you have for us?" asked Aaron.

"Gentleman!" announced Eric. "Whatever is said in this office from now on must stay in this office. If any of this slips-out there will be some very serious consequences. Is that understood?" The boys all agreed with anticipation.

"The plan that I have in mind will work, provided that it is carried out under strict military discipline. Did it ever occur to you why school is let out at one-thirty every Friday afternoon?" asked Eric. "It's because the teachers have their meetings in room twenty at that time." Eric slipped his hand into the paper bag and pulled out a small Radio Shack cassette tape recorder/player. "I found this recorder on the bookshelf in the English teacher, Mrs. Slain's classroom." Proclaimed Eric. "I don't think she'll miss it. With this recorder planted in room twenty during the teachers' meeting, we will know everything the teachers are saying about us and planning before any of the other students. We'll have next week's assignment, next month's, maybe even next year's! All on this cassette player. I'll hide it on the bookshelf in room twenty. For any reason I can't get this recorder out of the room in time, Sam, you must be the one to retrieve it."

"But what about the assignments we've already missed?" asked Tom.

"Good question," replied Eric. "You see these filing cabinets behind me? In those cabinets are all the records on all the students. So, this Friday as we bug the teachers' meeting in room twenty, Sam, you and Tom will break into this office, study our files from these cabinets, copy information, and report back to me what everybody missed since the beginning of the school year. I'll find a way to get the necessary materials needed to catch up."

Tony made a few disgruntled sounds as he hopped off the desktop. "I'm out!"

"What!" everybody asked.

"I'm out! I can't take this chance. I'm on probation. I have no more options. There are no other schools that will accept me! If I get caught breaking into school files, my parents will sell my car! I'll be dead till I'm eighteen!"

"Look, Tony," announced Eric, "you came to me for help. I didn't come to you. This is all I can offer. And you're right, you have no other option. The teachers will not listen to me, so I figured out a way to get around them. And I'm confident we won't get caught."

"How?" asked Tony.

"Can you keep a secret? And that's how we keep from getting caught. We keep our mouths shut!" Tony sat back on the desk. "Now Sam," continued Eric. "I'm going to have to depend on you. I need you to be responsible for the files. When you're finished copying them, put them back the way you found them. I think it will be better if everybody helps each other catch up on their work. I figure if we all pull together like a union, we can get away with murder.

"Why am I the only one that has to be responsible for the files and cassette player?" Sam asked."

"You're the only one who knows how to break into this office. As for the recorder, I trust you as my back-up."

....

Friday afternoon at approximately one-fifteen, all the students from Noah Webster had gone home for the weekend. The Radio Shack cassette/record player had been planted within the bookshelf in room twenty and already turned on before the teachers arrived for their meeting.

Down at the reception area on the first floor as the school secretary was doing her secretarial duties, Eric gave the signal for Tom and Sam to begin their covert cloak-and-dagger operation in Carol's office. The two boys climbed the staircase to the second floor. Aaron, Tony, and Eric stayed behind as lookouts. Suddenly, Carol appeared by the reception area from her classroom passing the three boys as she headed up toward her office on the second floor. Eric was startled.

"Oh no, no, no!" panicked Eric.

"Holy shit!" howled Tony. Eric nudged him to his side to calm down.

"What are you guys doing here?" Carol asked.

Before answering Eric sneezed, then coughed. "Um… we're staying to finish an art project down in the art room. I thought you had already headed up to the teachers' meeting."

"I was heading up, but I had to put something away in my classroom before I forget. Does the art teacher know that you're in his art room unsupervised?"

"Yeah. He knows that we take care of the equipment," Eric said with a sneeze.

Carol's office door had already been picked open, and Sam was into Carol's files as Tom held a flashlight over his head. Eric down at the reception tried to stall for more time.

"Uh… are you going to see *Warren* this weekend?"

'That is a strange question coming from Eric,' Carol thought. Eric never mentioned Warren unless he felt emotionally threatened.

"I don't know… maybe," Carol teased with a smile, as she climbed the steps toward the second floor. "Are you catching a cold?"

"I think so," replied Eric.

Meanwhile, Sam and Tom heard Carol approaching from the hallway as they were searching through files. Thinking as an ostrich, Sam buried his head in the filing drawer while Tom turned off the flashlight, bowed his head and closed his eyes waiting for the inevitable.

Carol slid her office key into the keyhole and her left hand around the doorknob. She stopped to think for a moment as she glanced at the closed door of room twenty toward the end of the hall before attempting to turn the knob. Changing her mind, Carol slid the key out from the tumbler, and proceeded to walk to the teachers' meeting.

In the dark office, Sam and Tom continued their work at a faster pace. Within a few minutes and with all the information needed, copied, handwritten from all of files, the two boys scurried out of the office closing the office door behind them.

In the reception area passing the school secretary who was too busy typing to notice the infiltrators, the five boys walked out through the French doors in the cafeteria onto the stone patio leading to the school's parking lot to go their separate ways for the weekend. Sam carried the information with him. Later at home he will shuffle through it.

At home, Eric ran straight to his bedroom and plopped down on his bed to rest. He suspected that it would probably be a long night with Steve, Pete, and Lou. The phone on the night table rang. Eric opened his eyes, jumped out of bed, and coughed before he picked up the receiver on the third ring. It was Renée.

"Why did you stay after school?" she asked. "Did you have a detention?"

"No, I had some artwork to catch up with."

"Will I see you this weekend?"

"Uh, yeah," Eric said accompanied with a cough. "Saturday. We'll have all afternoon together."

"Afternoon? What ever happened to Saturday night?"

"Well, I have to work with Pete Saturday night. But next weekend is all ours. I promise."

"Are you sure?"

"Have I ever lied to you before?"

"No. You never had the time."

"Well, besides that. Why should I start now?"

"Okay, I'll see you tomorrow afternoon. By-the-way, are you catching a cold?" Asked Renée.

"Yeah, I think I am."

When Eric hung up, he reached under his bed to retrieve an eight-ounce plastic bottle of ammonia. After unscrewing the top, he took a snort. "Yes! I can see the trails!" Then sneezed.

....

That night, Eric found himself sharing the back seat in Pete's caddy with Steve. Lou was sitting in the front as they cruised through the Frankfurt section of the city.

"Okay, listen up, gang!" Announced Pete as he drove. "Nolan's Nightclub opened last week. She's a little short on cash, so I'm going to help her out. What I have here is about three-hundred dollars' worth of invitations cards printed up to be handed out. The cards read that we'll be throwing a 'PD dance party' tomorrow night -Saturday-at the Liberty Ballroom in Frankford'. All the proceeds from this dance will be given to Nolan as a loan. That means we must hand out all these invitations by tonight."

"Who are we handing these cards out to?" asked Steve.

"The kids coming in and out of the dance halls and the movie theaters. I'm picking up Stanley who will be giving us a hand."

"Oh, no! Not Stanley the ogre!" Steve cried out. "He's retarded!"

"Retarded or not, he's an extra hand," Pete replied as Eric started to cough. "Eric, are you sick?"

"I don't know. I have been coughing a lot lately."

"Great! Just keep him away from me," Lou remarked.

The Caddy pulled up by a curb somewhere in Frankfurt. Stanley, a burly, husky looking seventeen-year-old dimwit who looked like he could hardly fit into his denim jacket was one of Pete's goons. Stanley squeezed into the back seat alongside Eric and Steve.

"Stanley! I hope you don't have any pens or combs in your back pocket," announced Pete. "This is a brand-new car, and I don't want any punctures in my upholstery."

"No. I don't have any pens or combs in my back pocket," Stanley established. "Just a penknife."

"Then take it out of your back pocket, moron!" Pete declared.

The Caddy floated off to The Tunnel, a dance hall in the Frankfurt section of the city. The Tunnel had a reputation of being a rough and tumble venue. Fights had broken out between gangs or a flirting girl or two. Teenagers were in line on the sidewalk to get into the hall.

As a local celebrity and not wanting to be recognized, Pete discreetly pulled over to the curb.

"Okay," said Pete, "people are beginning to enter The Tunnel. I don't want anybody to see me. So quickly Steve, Eric, and Stanley, you three get out and begin to solicit these cards." Pete twisted around to face the back seat to give each of the three boys an equal number of cards to hand out. "Lou, stay in the car with me."

The three boys rolled out of the Caddy to the sidewalk as Steve closed the car door behind them. The car pulled away with Lou smiling and waving from behind the window.

"The nerve of the guy!" Said Steve. "He stays in that warm car with Pete, while the three of us freeze to death out here in some God-for-saken neighborhood."

"Yeah!" agreed Eric, with a sneeze. "I'm still pissed about The Three Degrees song. Lou got all the credit for that one. And we're the ones who discovered it!"

For about fifteen minutes, the three boys handed out the invitations for the dance at the Liberty Ballroom. Peter's bronze Caddy cruised back to the curb without celebratory notoriety. The three boys climbed into the back seat. Pete peeled away.

"How many?" asked Pete.

"I have about five left," replied Steve.

"Seven," said Eric, accompanied by a sneeze.

"How 'bout you, Stanley"

"Oh, about twenty-five left."

"Twenty-five!" Pete yelled angrily as he twisted his torso to face the back of the car while driving. Eric could never figure out how Pete could drive that way. "I gave everybody thirty! You mean to tell me you only gave away five?"

"I didn't know who to give them out to," squealed Stanley. Eric began to snicker.

"You were supposed to give the cards out to the people who were going in and out of the dance hall!" Pete shouted.

"I could have done better than all of them," admitted Lou.

"Why didn't you?" asked Eric.

"That's not my job."

"Well then, what is your job?" Eric asked.

"Okay! No fighting," Pete interjected. "Let's just try to get rid of these cards. We'll hit the movie theaters. They should be letting out by now."

The Caddy pulled in front of the Castor movie theater in the Northeast Oxford circle section of the city.

"All right," announced Pete, everybody out and get rid of these cards." Pete tugged Lou's arm. "You better go with them."

The Caddy pulled away from the curb as the four boys began to distribute the invitations to patrons who were entering or leaving the theater. Two uniformed policemen leaning against a parked car in front of the theater watched the boys solicit with suspicion. Within fifteen minutes Pete drove up to the curb. Eric and Steve piled into the Caddy.

"Let's go, Stanley!" Lou called out as he held the car door open.

"Just a minute!" Stanley shrieked back. Stanley walked over toward the two patrol officers.

"Excuse me, I have to leave now. Would you two do me a big favor? Could you please hand out these dance invitations for me? Because Pete D'Angelo will get really pissed-off if I get back into that car with a handful of cards."

"Is that D'Angelo waiting for you in that car?" asked one of the police officers pointing toward the bronze Cadillac.

"Yes," replied Stanley, "and he's not really in a great mood tonight."

"Oh really? Well, I'd like to ask him some questions. Perhaps I can put him in a better mood," the second policeman said.

With alleged mobster dealings, and the dubious teen club, the cops were always willing to spend some quality time with the local celebrity -Peter D' Angelo-.

"Well, I wouldn't know about that," said Stanley. "But will you hand out these cards?" he asked as he surrendered the stack to the police.

"Sure," said the first policemen caustically as they both inspected the cards. Stanley raced toward the Caddy and squeezed into the back seat alongside Steve and Eric. Pete noticed the two policemen walking toward the car.

"Holy shit Stanley! Did you invite the fuzz here?" Yelled Pete as he stepped on the gas pedal and peeled off the curb before Lou had a chance to completely close the car door, almost dragging him outside.

"They just want to ask you some questions," said Stanley.

"I bet they do, you moron! How many did you guys give away?"

"All!" replied Steve, Lou, and Eric.

"What was their reaction toward the invitations?"

"Sounded enthused," said Steve.

"How 'bout you, Stanley?" Asked Pete. "How many did you give away?"

"I gave out fifteen; then I gave the rest to the policemen who wanted to talk to you."

Pete's face went totally white as Eric began to laugh and cough at the same time. Again, Pete twisted around to face the back of the car as he drove. "You what?"

"I gave the rest to the two policemen who were watching us."

"Why did you do that?" Pete asked angrily.

"Well, I saw how mad you were at me last time I didn't give enough out. So, when you pulled up, I had to get rid of them somehow. The cops said they would hand them out."

"Hand them out!" Screamed Pete. "They sure will, to the nearest trashcan! I spent three-hundred dollars on these cards! Stanley, you have got to be the world's biggest schmuck I have ever met! And Eric, stop laughing, this isn't funny!" Eric promptly stopped laughing but couldn't hold in a cough or keep from smiling behind his hand.

"Do you people realize what's at stake here?" Pete pointed out. "I have to raise a few thousand dollars between now and Sunday night! I'm serious! It's a matter of life or death!"

"The policemen seemed to know who you were," said Stanley.

"Yeah," replied Pete, "I'm sure they wanted my autograph!... Moron!"

....

The next morning, Eric was awakened by the phone in his bedroom. It was Sam from school.

"I just wanted to let you know what I found in the teachers' files." Sam reported. "You're doing okay, but you're missing a science report from Biff's science class that's been past due since October. Tony is missing follow-ups in science, math, and history. Tom has a make-up test in math. Aaron is missing a follow-up in English and math. I'm missing a few follow-ups from English. I found a report in Schor's desk about Tony. He's on his way out of school. Carol is trying to get him expelled. Now, will you get the recorder out from room twenty Monday morning?"

"Yes. First thing Monday." Replied Eric. "On Monday night, I'll give you guys a call and tell you what the teachers have in store for us."

"Fine, Eric. I have to go. See you Monday."

"Take care, Sam," Eric said with a cough. "Thanks."

"No. Thank you, Eric."

....

That night, Eric drove the old Chevy to a reception hall called The Liberty Ballroom on Torresdale Avenue in Frankfurt. The two bouncers, Charles Gammer and Bruce Fisher from the South Philly club were bouncing the door collecting cover money.

"… So, this is how we do it," Bruce explained to Charlie in mid-sentence. "The codeine comes in one-gallon brown-tinted glass jugs. I arranged with the drugstore in Roxborough to pick up two gallons. We transport them to Atlantic city. Our contact will meet us in front of the White House Sandwich sub-shop. Boy I can taste those foot-long hamburger hoagies now."

"Yeah," agreed Charlie, "but the codeine is accounted for by the FDA. How is the drugstore going to cover the count?"

Charles and Bruce abruptly ended their conversation when Eric approached.

"We'll talk more about this later Charlie," said Bruce. "Hey! Let's go to the Bent Elbow bar up in Bells Corner after the dance." Bruce suggested as he strolled away leaving Charlie collecting and counting cover charges from teenagers.

"Listen Charlie… Steve told me that you were in Nam." Said Eric.

"Yeah."

It was a kind of 'yeah' that didn't invite continuous discussion. But Eric pushed on. "I had a brother in Vietnam."

"Uh huh," said Charlie as he collected cover money from the young people walking in. "It's a two-dollar cover charge son," Charlie said to the boy who was thumbing through his wallet.

"My brother was killed there," announced Eric.

"Uh-huh." It was a cold 'Uh-huh' as Charlie didn't care.

"Maybe you knew him?"

"I doubt it… That's eight dollars for the four of you… Thank you," Charlie announced to the two boys and girls that approached and surrendered their money.

"Elliot Blum?" Asked Eric. Charlie said nothing but continued to collect money. "What did you do in Nam?"

"I flew cargo planes."

"Dangerous?"

"Look, this is really not the right place or time!" Charlie barked out. "I had friends who were killed over there. Your brother was killed over there. But that's war! Now, what do you want from me, a pity party? A shoulder to cry-on? Sorry son, I got my own nightmares to deal with!"

"I really don't know what I want. Sorry, Charlie."

"Then let me go on with my job here!" Charlie barked back.

"Sure, Charlie. I'm sorry." Eric walked off with a cough.

In the lobby, Pete appeared out from the crowd of young people and walked toward Lou and Steve who were talking to a couple of girls.

"Steve, I want you to work the turntables tonight. Lou, you stick around with me." As Steve walked off, Pete and Lou glanced over toward the other side of the lobby to find Eric approaching.

"I know just the right job for him," Lou smirked.

"What job is that?" asked Pete.

"'Coppertone detail'."

Pete smiled as Eric approached. He put his huge arm around Eric's shoulders, and both proceeded to walk side-by-side from the lobby toward a long hallway.

"Now Eric, I want you to come with me. I have a special assignment for you."

"You can count on me, Pete. I won't let you down."

"I know, Eric." Eric glanced back to find Lou chuckle which made him feel apprehensive.

Eric and Pete walked into the men's bathroom. Perhaps the rumors about Pete being gay were true. Eric was willing to do anything for Pete on an employment level. Homosexual favors were not on Eric's menu.

"The owners of this place are very skeptical about having all these kids here tonight," announced Pete. "So, to avoid vandalism, I want you to stay in here, and make sure that nobody comes in to rip out the copper pipes from the sinks or walls."

Pete walked out of the men's room leaving Eric relieved that Pete did not want a sexual favor, but disappointed on the assignment. Two boys walked in to take care of their personal business.

"Bathroom attendant," Eric said to himself.

He couldn't understand why he should stay in the bathroom all night when Pete had goons like Charles Gammer or Bruce Fisher to take care of this type of work. At that moment, Bruce Fisher bounced into the bathroom.

"Coppertone detail'! Yeah!" Bruce jested as he walked toward the urinal. "Yeah. I've been there too."

"I don't know why this is called 'Coppertone detail'," said Eric.

"You're here to make sure nobody rips out the pipes, right?"

"Yeah?"

"The pipes are made from copper. Hence the code name, 'Coppertone'."

"Well, this is not what I had in mind when I told Pete I would do anything for him."

"You have stars in your eyes my little friend. We all have to start somewhere," said Bruce as he continued to urinate.

"And how about you?"

"Me?"

"You! Pete!" Asked Eric.

"Oh, I'm just one of Pete's runners. You?"

"I'm still in high school, not too sure what I want to do with my life."

"This is a shitty business. Stay in school." Bruce proclaimed as he pulled up his zipper and walked over toward the sinks to wash his hands.

"What do you expect to get from Pete's as a runner?" Eric asked.

"He has connections. So, I'm biding my time. Collecting nontaxable dollars."

"Connections? Biding your time? For what?"

Bruce smiled as he dried his hands with a paper towel over the sink. He briskly glanced around before answering.

"With some of Pete's connections, I'm waiting to be discovered."

"Discovered as what?"

"As a writer."

"What do you write?"

"Books, TV, movies."

"Have you ever had anything published?" asked Eric.

"Oh, well, not at this point," admitted Bruce. "Pete won't even let me write for his TV show. I had asked him if I could write, but he kind of shrugs me off. He's just too involved with this -Lou- character to take notice of the talent he has around him. But he pays me well to be one of his goons."

"Well, obviously this is not how I want to make it," said Eric. "Not for me. I'm tired of playing second fiddle to Lou, and him taking all the credit for the work I do!"

Eric bent over and began to cough and hack repeatedly enough to scare Bruce.

"You okay, bro? You want me to call an ambulance?"

Eric waved Bruce's worries off as he coughed out last of the phlegm. He followed Bruce out of the bathroom, down the long hallway, and made a beeline past Charles Gammer still collecting cover money by the front door.

Just before walking across Torresdale Avenue, Eric heard his name being called. Eric stopped and turned to see it was Charlie Gammer.

"Eric! Look. I'm sorry to sound so cold. I'm sorry that you lost your brother."

"Why is it every time I ask a veteran what went on in Vietnam, they tell me I don't want to know? How do you expect us to respect you if we don't know?"

"It's because every time somebody asks us about Vietnam, it awakens the nightmares we been trying to forget. Look, I had a co-pilot. He was a war buddy. Just as he opened his mouth to say something, a piece of shrapnel broke through the windscreen into his mouth and took out the left side of his head. I still live with that nightmare every single day of my life. And so, until you can smell, taste, feel and live the agony of war, no matter how many times I try to explain to you, you'll never understand, because you weren't there. And so, it's just as easy for us veterans to say, 'You, don't want to know'. Look, let me tell you something about the military. They tear you down to build you up. And when all is said and done, they don't teach us how to come home. They just pat us on the ass and say, 'thanks for your service'. Where're you going?"

"I don't Think I was cut out for this business." Eric replied.

Charlie broke into a slight grin, turned, and walked back to the Liberty Ballroom. Eric walked across Torresdale Avenue coughing all the way to his car.

He pulled out of the parking spot and drove north along Torresdale Avenue. Eric spotted a phone booth outside a closed gas station and pulled over to call Renée.

"I was going to go out with my girlfriends tonight. After all, you stood me up this afternoon. Where were you? We were supposed to get together." Claimed Renée.

"Oh, man… I forgot, Renée. I'm sorry. I'll make it up to you. Why don't you break your date with your girlfriends? I'll be at your place within thirty minutes."

"What's this? No Pete D'Angelo?" she asked derisively.

"No, not tonight, or tomorrow night."

"What happened?"

"It's too embarrassing. I'll explain when I pick you up." Eric said with a cough.

Renée and Eric caught the nine o'clock showing of Blazing Saddles at the Southampton Shopping Center Mall in Southampton Township. During the scene where actor Harvey Korman shoots actor Slim Pickens in the foot for using the cliché, "Head them off at the pass?", Eric started to cough. He felt queasy and warm, hard to breath accompanied by the shakes.

"Renée, feel my head," he said.

At first, Renée thought it was a ploy for Eric to get her closer to make out. She played along by putting her hand over his forehead.

"Boy, you're burning up! What's the problem?"

"I feel as sick as a dog. I'm congested. Having a hard time breathing."

"Do you want to go home?"

"No, I think I can make it through the movie."

It wasn't easy for Eric to drive home in the condition he was in after his date with Renée coughing most of the way home. That night in his bedroom, Mrs. Blum took Eric's temperature. He was running a fever and she told him he was not going to school on Monday.

"The cassette!" Eric thought to himself. "But I have to go to school Monday!" He insisted to his mother.

"Not if you're still running a fever! And I don't like that cough!"

It was a good thing he told Sam where the recorder was hidden in room twenty if for any reason, he could not retrieve it.

. . . .

The next morning before the light of dawn, Mrs. Blum went back into Eric's bedroom to take his temperature. He was soaked in sweat. She noticed that his eyes were three-quarters closed and he was not responding to her presence.

"We have to take him to the hospital! His temperature is at 103!" She called Mr. Blum who was still in bed in the master bedroom.

Eric's parents would never have the strength to pull him out of bed, carry him down a flight of steps to the first floor, then drag him into the car. Mrs. Blum called for an ambulance and requested they not use the siren for not to alarm the neighbors. Mr. Blum drove the old Chevy from the back of the house to the front and waited for the ambulance to arrive. In his bedroom, one of the two paramedics wrapped an oxygen mask around Eric's semiconscious head and proceeded to record his vital signs. It was a challenge for the paramedics to carry Eric on a stretcher squeezing down the narrow second-floor staircase. As the ambulance drove off to the hospital, Mr. Blum carefully followed the ambulance under the watchful eye of Mrs. Blum to the emergency entrance of the Albert Einstein Northern Hospital in the Logan section of the city just a couple blocks from Cousin Opie's house.

At the emergency entrance to the hospital, two waiting orderlies helped the paramedics gently wheel Eric out from the back of the ambulance to an examination room, then transferred him onto a hospital gurney. A couple of nurses appeared and began to work on Eric. Another nurse with a clipboard blocked the Blum's from entering the examination room with their son.

"Do you have any medical insurance?"

"Yes. We're completely covered," replied Mrs. Blum as she and her husband watched the double doors of the examination room swing open then close with each medical technician that walked through.

"Is he on any medication, or controlled drugs?" asked the nurse.

"No," said the Blum's. Mr. Blum put his arm around his wife's shoulders.

It was about eight A.M when Eric was admitted to room 252 where he continued to lay semi-conscious. Eric shared a room with -Jack- a man in his sixties admitted for cardiac arrest who was sleeping in the next bed close to the window. Jack was attached like a puppet with tubes and wires. Oxygen was hissing from the hoses attached from the outlets on the wall behind his bed.

Eric's parents sat on the chairs by Eric's bed and kept a vigil as a doctor walked in from the hallway.

"Mr. and Mrs. Blum? I'm Doctor Hermann." The three walked out into the hallway so as not to wake up Eric's roommate. "Your son is suffering from viral pneumonia. Given his young age, and the fact that he's a strong individual, we expect to break his temperature sometime tonight. Even though he's slightly dehydrated, there will be no IV given at this point depending on how much fluids he'll drink when he awakes. I have the results of his chest x-rays and found previous scars on his lungs. How long ago did your son have pneumonia?"

"In 1966," answered Mr. Blum.

"The x-rays are showing a high level of fluid in his lungs." Announced Dr. Hermann, "We'll treat him with respiratory therapy and antibiotics. Good thing you got him here in time. If you had waited another day or two, his lungs would have completely filled with fluid. And if we got it in time, after draining I would have to see if there was any permanent damage." Mrs. Blum put her hand over her mouth at the thought. "He's very lucky you got him here when you did. Some people wait 'til it's too late." Dr. Hermann continued. "I'll come around later this morning to check on him. If you have any questions and wish to get in touch with me, here's my card."

Dr. Hermann handed Mrs. Blum his business card from the pocket of his white lab coat, turned, and walked down the hallway.

Dr. Hermann was approximately and inch over six feet tall, medium build, and in his early forties. Although he was cordial and polite, his bedside matter was strictly business. After so many years of practice at a major city hospital such as Philadelphia's Einstein Northern, seeing dozens of patients at a time daily, one's demeanor can easily become sterile.

"Boy, if he was awake now, I'd kill him for not buttoning up or wearing underwear before he went out into the cold," Mrs. Blum said to her husband. "And I know he doesn't wear any underwear. I do his laundry!"

Mr. Blum shook his head in agreement.

....

The next morning just before dawn, Eric was lying on his back when he fully opened his eyes for the first time since he was admitted into the hospital. He could hear the hissing sound of oxygen from his roommate's side of the room. The room was so dark, that Eric could barely make out the two men leaning over his hospital bed rail. One man was tall and thin, the other short and robust. Both dressed in traditional Black Victorian undertaker's garb complete with top hats.

"You thought you could get away from us, didn't you?" asked the tall thin man as he leaned in closer toward Eric. "But don't worry. We're going to finish you now."

The short man smiled as he put his right hand on the bed rail. Eric grabbed it. The two men laughed as they dissolved. Eric began to float. He looked down to find his body lying in a bed. As he floated higher, Eric felt all the feelings that a human being encounters in a lifetime. Hate, anger, love, pity, pride, guilt, honor, sorrow, and joy. Then he felt peacefulness and serenity. There was a loud reverberation that was annoying without being deafening. He wanted to cover his ears, but he couldn't move his arms that were stiff by his side. Eric sped head-first through a grey tunnel with a bright pure blue light toward the end. He was curious what the tunnel was made of. But a soothing mental voice assured him that it wasn't important. After a few moments of meaningless time, the vibrating sound ceased. Visions and events of Eric's life from the time he was admitted to the hospital until being in his mother's womb were seen and heard in fast reverse. For every event, Eric physically regressed and dressed in whatever style or fad was popular at that moment in time. Once he regressed to a fetus, an explosion brought him back to adolescence in his contemporary street clothes. He opened his eyes and found himself standing in the middle of a very lush field of green grass at the edge of a jungle. The colors on the plants were vibrant. There were some colors he had never seen before. The sun was bright, clear, and warm. The air was fresh, sweet, and pure. Lying on the ground before him on his back looking up at Eric was a man impeccably well dressed in a black three-piece suit. Eric knew the man was dead.

"Excuse me," said the dead man in a thick cockney accent. "Would you mind if I decompose here?"

"Why would you want to do that?" asked Eric.

"Well, it's such a lovely day. I thought I give it a try."

"No. I don't mind." Eric shrugged bewildered.

As the man dissolved, Eric heard from behind a chopping noise he recalled in a letter his brother had described from Vietnam. Two US military H-1 Huey Bell helicopters flew above no more than one hundred feet. Three loud explosions snapped Eric's head back to ground level. About fifty yards behind, an American Vietnam soldier carrying an M-16 rifle ran out of the jungle yelling over the thundering sounds of the explosions. Mortar shells exploding followed the soldier's heels.

"Eric! Go back!" The soldier yelled out. Eric squinted his eyes for better focus and found the soldier to be his brother Elliot. "Eric, go Back! Go back!"

Without a moment's notice, Eric found himself in front of Barson's neighborhood restaurant eating a double scoop of Breyers mint chocolate chip ice cream on a vanilla cake cone alongside his brother. Eric gazed down at the ice cream as he seized a lick. When he glanced up, he was sitting next to Elliot who was drinking a can of Ballantine beer while smoking a cigarette on the third level of the Connie Mack baseball stadium. The Phillies' pitcher, Jim Bunning was up at bat against the Los Angeles Dodger's Don Drysdale.

"Don't tell mom or dad that I'm smoking or drinking, okay?" said Elliot.

Mortar fire brought Eric back to the field. He was determined not to let his brother go a second time and proceeded to run toward him. "Elliot!"

"No, Eric! Go back. Go back home!"

Eric turned to run away as the shelling was getting louder and closer with every step. The ground vibrated. The dust from the impact just about surrounded his brother as he advanced. Eric looked back to find his brother was no longer behind. But at the edge of the field retreating into the jungle was Alice Cappadonna with a reassuring smile and a nod that told Eric he would be safe.

Eric continued to run until he noticed that the shelling had stopped. He found himself walking along a peaceful country dirt road toward a lake. As he approached the lake, a well-dressed man in a dark suit was surrounded by hundreds of pails of water. One by one the man was emptying the pails into the lake. Eric stopped to watch and asked him what he was doing.

"Dumping these buckets of tears," replied the man.

"Tears?" Asked Eric.

"Yes, tears." Said the man holding on to a full pail. "This bucket represents the number of tears that a human being will cry in a lifetime."

"Why are you dumping them?" Asked Eric.

The man resumed dumping. "Oh, well, these are the tears from people who have no need to cry anymore." The man handed Eric a bucket. "Would you like to dump this bucket into the lake?"

Eric investigated the bucket. "But this bucket is not full."

"Oh, yes. Well, that bucket is yours."

"Mine?"

"Well, let me ask you. Is your bucket half full or half empty?"

"That's one of those old philosophical questions. It's half empty."

"Old philosophical? Perhaps," grinned the man. "But it's a pity you decided that your bucket was half empty. If you had chosen half full, I would have suggested for you to go and don't come back till you fill it to the top."

"Go back? I have a choice?"

"You do. At least you have more of a choice than these people. Here in these buckets, the young and the old. They lived their full lives."

"I want to live my full life!"

"Good! Now you know that your bucket is not half empty. So, go! And don't come back until your bucket is filled."

From his dark hospital room, Eric sat up in bed screamed out, "Get out of here! Get out of here! Get out of here!"

A robust black nurse ran into the room and pushed Eric back down on his bed. "Mr. Blum! Mr. Blum! You're okay. Relax! Lay back and relax."

"Did you get them?"

"Get who, Mr. Blum?"

"The gravediggers! They were right here! Two of them!"

"Mr. Blum, nobody ran out of this room."

"I swear! I grabbed one of them!"

"You had a dream. Your temperature must be breaking. Open your mouth."

The nurse pulled out a small electronic device from her lab coat pocket and popped a plastic stick attached to a wire connected to the handheld device into Eric's mouth.

"What's this?" mumbled Eric.

"An electric thermometer."

"How do you know you didn't shove the rectal end of that stick into my mouth?"

"I tasted it. Now lay back and be quiet."

Eric laid back. "Where am I?"

"Einstein Northern Hospital. You have pneumonia."

"Oh, great! What time is it?"

The electronic thermometer beeped. The nurse slid it out of Eric's mouth. "Want some water?"

"No. I can hardly swallow. What's my temperature?"

"I'm not permitted to tell you," Eric smirked. "It's' 100. It's coming down. Now try to get some sleep. It's almost four-thirty in the morning. Close to dawn."

Although it was a cloudy winter's day, at seven-forty-five, the morning light from the window by Eric's roommate drenched the bright white walls of the room. Eric was awake in bed lying on his side looking over his roommate who was still asleep with plastic tubes shoved in his nose and wired electrodes to his chest along with an IV drip. Air could be heard hissing from the release valve on the wall behind and above his roommates' head. A blonde nurse walked into Eric's room with a tray of needles and test tubes.

"Good morning," announced the nurse.

"Good morning," replied Eric. "What's all that?"

"I'm going to take some blood from you."

"No!" Eric refused, "I can't stand the sight of blood. Especially mine."

"I'm just going to fill these three test tubes."

"Those three test tubes are as long as Karl Malden's nose," Eric cried out.

"Now, come on!" Grinned the nurse.

Eric held his arm back from the nurse. "I already know I have pneumonia, so you don't have to stick me with those needles to run any tests."

"You know, you're right," said the nurse as she grabbed Eric's arm, tying a rubber tourniquet around it. Eric watched in defeat as the nurse stuck the needle into his arm. Blood dripped into the test tube at the other end. Eric passed out.

Eric had no idea how long he was unconscious, but when he opened his eyes, the nurse was gone, and Dr. Hermann was standing in front of his bed jotting down notes on his clipboard.

"Good morning. Did you just wake up?" Hermann asked.

"I don't know," replied Eric still in a dazed. "I had two dreams. One was about a couple of gravediggers, and the other was about a beautiful vampire. Don't tell me. You're here to do the autopsy."

"No," Dr. Hermann laughed. "I'm Doctor Hermann. You have viral pneumonia. You still have a fever. If it goes down, and therapy goes well, I could have you out of here by the end of the week providing you drink a lot of fluids."

"Therapy?"

"Respiratory therapy. Antibiotics. You have phlegm in your lungs that must come out. The therapy will be issued twice a day. I'll come around and see you tomorrow. Now drink your fluids. That will help get your temperature back to normal."

"Why do you sound like my mother?"

As the doctor walked out of the room, a female dietitian came in with two trays of breakfast. She dropped Eric's tray on his night table, then dropped his sleeping roommate's tray on his.

"And how do we feel today?" she asked.

"Well, you may feel great," said Eric. "If I felt great, would I still be here?"

"You eat this, and you'll feel much better," she replied with a smile.

"Then could I go home?"

"No, I don't think so." Smiled the dietitian.

The dietitian walked out of the room as Eric's roommate woke up navigating the tubes and wires to inspect his breakfast on his night table.

"What are you in for?" He asked without introduction.

"Pneumonia." Replied Eric "How 'bout you?"

The man mechanically reached over and took a cigarette box hidden from under his pillow. He opened the box, pulled out a cigarette, held it up to his nose and took a hard sniff. "Heart attack, I'll be home in two days. Cigarette?"

Eric was amazed that with all the plastic tubing leading to an oxygen outlet on the wall, plus the IV draining into his roommate's arm, incarcerated by cardiac arrest, here was this man dying to have a cigarette.

"No, thank you. I don't smoke." Replied Eric.

"Where are you from?" asked Jack as he returned the cigarette back into its box.

"Mt. Airy. You?"

"Fishtown."

A young respiratory technician rolled a small portable machine with an oxygen mask into the room and placed it beside Eric's bed.

"What's this?" Asked Eric.

"This is your respirator. It's to clean out your lungs," said the technician. "All you have to do is put this oxygen mask over your face, and this tube in your mouth and inhale till you hear a click from the machine. Then exhale."

"Will it hurt?"

"Nah," said the technician. "When I'm not on duty, I get high off it." He admitted with a snort of a laugh. "Do this for about fifteen minutes. I'll be back to pick it up." The technician walked out leaving Eric under mask and sucking on a plastic tube.

There were two twenty-inch Zenith televisions sets on either side of the room mounted on the wall by the ceiling. Eric's parents didn't want to pay for the television on his side. They gave him a radio.

"If you don't buy your clothes from Krass Brothers…" Announced the obnoxious radio commercial. Eric slid the radio dial. "Silo is having a sale! A what? A sale! A what? A sale!" Another commercial for a local electronic /appliance store. Eric slid the radio dial to a disco song as his roommate turned his television on with a remote and perpetually changed the channels until Let's Make a Deal hosted by Monty Hall caught his attention.

"God damn them! Look at all those niggers jumping up and down for all those free prizes! They get their housing and their cars practically for free. What else do they want?" laughed his roommate. "What's your name, by the way?"

"Eric," Eric replied as he sucked on the plastic tube (click).

"Hi Eric. I'm Jack!"

"Ass," Eric continued under his breath (click).

"Mind if I change the channel?" asked Jack as he punched the buttons on the remote to the network news. A segment about the Middle East caught Jack's limited attention. "Middle East oil embargo! With all of them damn kikes out there! That's why gasoline is so expensive! We give arms to Israel, and the Arabs won't deal with us! I think we should bomb the hell out of Israel to save us all!"

"Oh great," Eric thought to himself. "I'm stuck here with Archie Bunker!" (Click)

Jack eventually rolled over and fell asleep with the television broadcasting the soap opera, Another World. Eric's mother walked into the room and gave Eric a kiss on his forehead, then took the chair in front of his bed. Eric took the mask off his face and the tube out of his mouth to say "hello".

"I see that you're looking better. You had us scared. You almost didn't make it." Announced Mrs. Blum.

Eric slid the tube back into his mouth and took a breath. (Click) "Thanks, mom. I knew you'd come here to bring me joy and encouragement." (Click).

"Did you see your doctor this morning?"

(Click) "Yeah. He gave me a week in this place." (Click)

"Don't count on it."

(Click, click) "Oh, and you know better?" (Click).

"I know when it's cold outside you should bundle up, Mister Disco! Walking around in sub-freezing temperatures all night, (Click) wearing just a sport jacket and a thin shirt unbuttoned down to his navel. (Click, click) And I know you haven't been wearing any under-wear. (Click, click, click) I do your laundry! Is this a new fad with your disco buddies?"

(Click, click, click, click) The tube came storming out of Eric's mouth. "Look, mom! I'm not going to argue with you here. You want to argue? Go home!" Eric glanced over to see if he had awakened his roommate as he slid the tube back into his mouth (Click).

Mrs. Blum sat back in the chair to get more comfortable. "Did you meet your roommate?"

"Yeah. Some roommate (Click). He's the only one who can judge a man by the size of his nostrils" (Click).

Mrs. Blum looked over at the food tray on Eric's night table. "Did you eat anything this morning? It looks like you didn't eat anything."

(Click) "No. I don't have an appetite. (Click) Besides, I still can't swallow." (Click)

"Well, you better start drinking your fluids to get that temperature down." Eric rolled his eyes. (Click, click) "The school misses you. I think Carol Schor is coming up on Friday night to visit. She called to see how you were doing. She's very thoughtful. I always liked her."

"Me too," replied Eric in a sly voice (Click).

"Steve called last night. I told him you were sick in the hospital. He told me you walked out on Pete D'Angelo. Why? I thought you liked that job."

(Click) Eric pulled the tube out of his mouth. "I did, mom. But it wasn't what I expected." He replaced the tube and sucked in (Click).

"Well, that's just as well. That's not the type of business you should be into anyway. Renée from school has also been calling. She wants your room phone number. (Click) I gave it to her, but I told her not to call you yet. I wanted to see what condition you were in before you received any phone calls or visitors."

(Click) "Thanks. So, Carol Schor is coming up to visit me Friday?" (Click, click) Eric asked with a grin.

"Yes, she is. And don't do anything crazy to her!" Mrs. Blum warned as she got up from her chair. "I'm going out to look for your doctor. I'll be back tomorrow."

"Okay (Click)... Oh, mom (Click)?"

"Yeah?"

"(Click) Don't drive the doctors' nuts. I'm still under their care." (Click)

Mrs. Blum took offense and sat back down on the chair. "Eric, I want to tell you something, and I'm very serious about this."

(Click) "What is it, mom?" asked Eric, rolling his eyes, anticipating a lecture.

"Now, look, Eric... you're all we have..."

Eric snapped the tube out of his mouth. "Now you look mom! I've had it with this Elliot lecture!"

"Listen, Eric!"

"You listen, mom! I'm tired of being in Elliot's shadow!" said Eric as he popped the tube back into his mouth. (Click) I'm not Elliot! I'm Eric! The war is practically over! I'm safe! There's no more draft! I'm not going anywhere! (Click).

"Oh, but you're wrong, Eric," Mrs. Blum replied in a soft voice. "You are very wrong. This war will never be over for me or your father. Not until your brother comes home." Eric put his head in his hands as tears rolled down his mother's face. (Click) "We almost lost you, honey. The doctors were prepared to operate on your lungs. I don't know what your father or I would have done if we lost you too."

(Click) Eric glanced over to see if Jack was up from his nap to witness the drama. The actress in Another World on the television was crying as though she was sympathizing with Mrs. Blum.

"Okay, mommy, (click) stop crying. I'll be careful. I promise (click)."

"You have to promise me, honey."

"I just did, mommy. I promise. So please stop crying (Click)."

"Okay," Mrs. Blum took out a Kleenex from her brown handbag and wiped her eyes, then blew her nose. "I'm going to see your doctor."

Mrs. Blum got up from her chair for the second time with handbag in hand and walked over toward the doorway.

"Now, be good and do what the doctor tells you, and drink your fluids. I love you, and I don't want to lose you."

(Click) "I love you, too mommy. I'll see you tomorrow."

A nurse with a tray of needles and test tubes walked into the room before Mrs. Blum walked out.

"Oh, no!" Wailed Eric. "I just gave at the office!"

"Oh, come on now!" said the nurse with a smile as she put the tray down beside the food on the night table. "This is for another test. What are we, men, or mice?" asked the nurse.

"Why don't you put a piece of cheese in front of me and find out!" Eric replied in the voice of Groucho Marx.

"Eric! Don't give the nurse a hard time!" his mother ordered. The nurse tied a rubber tourniquet around Eric's right arm, then stuck the long needle in. Blood began to trickle into a test tube. Eric took a quick peek, then passed out.

•••••••••••••••••••••

A couple of days later, the phone rang on his side of the room. It was Renée.

"I'm calling from the school pay phone in the lobby," she said. "Your mother asked me not to call you yet, but I just couldn't wait. Are you okay? When are you coming home?"

"I think Tuesday."

"I miss you. I want you," she said more discreetly.

"Yeah, I know," replied Eric. "I know."

"I have some of the kids from school with me."

At that moment, Eric heard the phone being snatched away from Renée's hand. "Give it back, asshole!" Renée called out.

"Blum! It's Mark Stern. I'm holding down the fort. I think I could make a better Student Body President than you."

"Well, just as long as you keep thinking that way."

"When are you getting out?"

"Wednesday."

"All right little buddy, here's Sam."

"Give me that fuck'en-phone-back!" Renée demanded in the background.

"Eric!" Said Sam.

"How's everything going, Sam?"

"Like a dream, Eric. And we're working on all our late assignments and going to be handing them in. I'm glad you told me where you placed the recorder before you were sent to the hospital."

"Play it again, Sam." Replied Eric in the voice of Humphry Bogart.

"Alright, Eric. Here's Tony."

"I want that God-damn-phone-now!" Renée scolded.

"Eric?"

"Tony?"

"I'm being investigated by the teachers."

"What for?"

"Unprescribed Drugs."

"Why?"

"Cause, I been behaving in class, and we're starting to hand in all our missed assignments. And the teachers can't figure out how we know which assignments we're missing."

"What are you going to do about it?"

"Nothing, I love it! It's another way of getting back at the whore/cunt, Carol Schor. Now she can't get me expelled."

"Well, you know what they say, Tony. No good deed goes unpunished."

"When are you coming home?"

"Friday."

"Alright. Here's your bitch."

"… Clothes-tearing, leather-wearing, grease dirty monkey, Tourette's ridden ASSHOLE!" Renée called out as she grabbed the handset from Tony. "I miss you, Eric. And the kids here want to sing something to you."

The students sang the first verse of Wish You a Merry Christmas accompanied by applause and cheers.

"Eric, I have to go now. I miss you. Come home soon." Said Renée.

"I will, Renée." Eric replied a little choked up. "And tell them… thanks. I really needed that."

"Okay, Eric. Goodbye. I love you."

"See you around, Renée."

It was difficult for Eric to reply to Renée that he loved her. Eric liked Renée, but he wasn't in love with her. And even though he had expressed his love toward Alice, it was Carol Schor that Eric was truly in love with. More than a student/teacher crush. And as he got older his feelings toward Carol became passionate. Every year it became more difficult and frustrating to hide his devotedness. Every so often Eric would slip out an innuendo toward her, but Carol always took it as an innocent flirtation. She accepted Eric in only two ways, as one of her students, and an entrusted friend outside of school.

After hanging up the phone, Eric climbed out of bed, and walked over toward sleeping Jack's side of the room to look out the window in thought.

One of the nurses by the front desk in the hallway raised the volume on her radio just as John Lennon and Yoko Ono were singing Happy Xmas. Eric glanced down onto the floor beside Jack's bed and noticed a page from the day-old Evening Bulletin. reading: Kissinger confirms All American Troops out of Vietnam by the spring. A tear followed by a full cry. For the first time in a long time realizing how much he missed his brother. With snow beginning to trickle down and being cooped up in a hospital, it was a depressing moment. The phone on his side of the room rang out the mood. Eric rushed over his side to pick up the receiver.

"Eric! It's Opie. I'll be right over."

"Opie!" Eric said as he wiped the tears from his face with the sleeve from his hospital gown. "You have the room number?"

"Yeah. I spoke to your mother, and she gave it to me… Boy did she give it to me! You know Eric, you should always bundle up before you venture out into the cold! And what's this crap about you not wearing any underpants?"

"Shut up, Opie!"

"Your mom told me not to call you yet. But you know me. I figured I'd give you a hoot. I'll be over shortly."

Just as Eric replaced the handset onto its cradle, Opie's head popped through the doorway of room 252. "I haven't even hung up yet! Where were you calling from?"

"The waiting-room." Opie grabbed the chair in front of Eric's bed. "Is that your roommate?" he asked pointing toward sleeping Jack.

"Oh, please," said Eric.

"When are you getting out of here?"

"Saturday."

"Well, how 'bout school?"

"Friday is the last day before Christmas vacation. I'll go back on the sixth of January."

"Well, because of the Philadelphia school strike earlier this year—which I was not involved in and one of the many things I cannot be blamed for—I have a short vacation. I go back on the second. You want to go to school with me?"

"Me at Central High?"

Opie looked down at his watch. "Well, I only stopped by for a couple of seconds. I'm already late. It's a good thing the school's across the street from the hospital. But who cares, right?" Eric smiled as Opie got up from the chair. "I guess I'll see you on parole."

"Oh, and by the way," mentioned Eric, "I never heard from your restaurant manager, Marty, about the job."

"You still interested?"

"Never was to begin with."

"Well, don't worry about it. They hired somebody else with more experience. Besides, Marty was probably too drunk to remember you." Opie walked out of the room.

"Hey, Op!"

Opie pulled his head back in. "Yeah?"

"Merry Christmas, little buddy."

Opie grinned. "Happy Hanukah, little cuz."

The moment Opie left the room, Jack carefully twisted his body to face Eric. "Are you a Jew?"

"Yeah… ?"

"Was that your cousin?"

"Yeah… ?"

"He looks scruffy."

Eric stuck out his tongue as Jack rolled back over.

....

The next morning when Eric woke up, he found Dr. Hermann in front of his bed jotting down notes on his clipboard. "Good morning," he said.

"Good morning, Doctor."

"You still have a fever. If you don't start drinking your fluids, we'll have to put you on IV You want that?"

"No, Doc."

"Well, that's what's going to happen. I'll check on you tomorrow."

"When can I go home?"

"Drink your fluids!"

Dr. Hermann closed his clipboard and walked out of the room as the nurse with the tray of needles and test tubes walked in.

"I'm not gonna look! I'm not gonna look!" Eric declared as he hid his eyes with his right hand. The nurse tied the rubber tourniquet around his left arm, and stuck the needle in. Eric peeked, then passed out.

....

Eric was awake but his eyes were closed when his mother entered the room and sat on the chair in front of the bed.

"Hi. Did you see your doctor today?" asked Mrs. Blum."

"Yeah."

"I can't stay long. I have things to do at home. I'm here to see how you're doing and to pick up your dirty laundry. Carol Schor is coming up to see you tonight." For the first time since his mother's arrival, Eric's eyes opened wide. "I'm telling you, Eric! Don't do anything crazy to her!" Eric closed his eyes. "Alright, I'm going to look for your doctor. I'll see you tomorrow." Mrs. Blum reached to the floor for the paper bag of dirty laundry. When she left the room, Jack rolled over to face Eric.

"Out of all the people who come to visit you, not one of them seem to want to stay long. Isn't there anybody who can tolerate you for an extended period?" Jack rolled back over as Eric gave him the finger.

....

That night, Eric was peeking from behind the door jamb of his room waiting for Carol Schor to stroll down the hallway. A housekeeping cart was sitting unattended in the hallway by his door. Along with the plastic trash bags, brooms, mops, and disinfectants, was a plastic gallon jug of ammonia. As a baseball pitcher looking for a runner to steal a base,

Eric stole a quick glance around before he unscrewed the cap and took a whiff. "Wow! There you are God! I feel much better now!"

Carol was approaching from down the hallway wearing a heavy coat looking like Nanook of the North carrying schoolwork in a plastic bag. Eric screwed the cap back on the jug as fast as he could, hopped back into his room and jumped back into bed, laid under the covers, slipped his oxygen mask over his face, turned on the respirator, and closed his eyes as Jack watched on. Carol walked into the room and got emotional by the pathetic sight that Eric was portraying.

She took off her heavy coat, threw it over the plastic bag at the foot of Eric's bed, grabbed the chair, and sat next to him.

"Oh, Eric. Are you okay? Are you awake? (Click) I had no idea. Eric, is there anything I can get for you? I have to use your bathroom. I'll be right back." (Click)

Without waiting for a response, Carol got out of the chair and headed for the bathroom. She had a date with Warren that night and wanted to fix her hair and makeup and make sure her nails dried just right.

While she was in the bathroom, Eric sat up in bed and splashed water on his face from the plastic water jug from his night table. It made him appear as though he was perspiring.

Jack observed lying on his side in bed with his hand holding up his head. Carol walked out of the bathroom and sat down next to Eric on his bed. (Click) "Are you sure I can't get you anything?"

"Wor (Click)…" Eric mumbled.

"What?" she asked as she moved in closer.

"Wor (Click)…"

"You want water?"

"Yeaaah (Click)."

From the night table Carol poured water from a plastic jug into a plastic glass. Then gently removed the oxygen mask from his face to his forehead to feed him. He downed the glass, then asked for more. Carol repeated the operation a few times.

"More…"

"There isn't anymore," she said.

"No more… ?"

"No more, Eric."

Eric slowly sat up, taking the oxygen mask from his forehead and in a cherry voice. "Thank God. I hate water. You know, the doctor told me…"

"Why, you little bastard!"

Carol jumped and grabbed him by his throat, which wasn't an easy feat since she was trying to avoid breaking her highly polished red fingernails at the same time.

"You scared me to death! That's not funny!" Carol sat back down on the chair. "You're okay! Why aren't you back at school?"

"I'll be back on the sixth," Eric said as he laughed.

"I brought some homework for you to catch up on."

"Oh. Is that the only reason you came to visit me?"

"No! I wanted to see how you're doing."

"Because you miss me."

"I do, Eric as one of my students. Nothing more."

"Here I am on my death bed…"

"You're not going to die, Eric!"

"… Will you be honest with me for the first time in four years?"

"I've always been honest with you. Since when I haven't been honest?"

"Do you have any feelings for me?" Asked Eric.

Carol glanced over to find Eric's roommate leaning on his right arm waiting for a response.

"Oh, come on, Eric!" Said Carol.

"Carol, do you?"

"Look, I'm going to leave. Catch up with your homework."

Carol grabbed her coat and got up from the bed but stopped shortly at the door. "I care about you very much, Eric."

"More than the others at school?" Asked Eric.

She tossed the coat onto the bed and sat back down on the chair. She looked at listening Jack and asked him, "Yes?" Jack just stared back.

For Jack, this was better than any of the soap operas he had been forced to watch since been admitted. Carol jumped out of the chair and pulled the curtain between the two beds, then sat back down on the chair in front of Eric's bed.

"Do you love me, Eric?"

"No, Carol. I'm madly in love with you."

"And how about Alice? Didn't you love her?"

"I'm not a real fan of monogamy. Humans have the capacity to love two people at the same time. I loved Alice. But Alice is dead. And now there's you."

"Who's Alice?" Asked Jack from behind the curtain.

"Jack!" Eric called out.

Carol pointed her thumb toward Jack to ask who in hell is he? "And Renée?"

"Ha. Renée. Oh, yes. She's just a toy. Something to keep me amused."

Carol paused quickly to get her thoughts in order. "Eric, I think you're old enough to be spoken to as an adult. And I think it's time that we have this little talk. Teachers are not paid or contracted or permitted to express personal emotions toward their students. But I must admit, we attend a unique school. Small and close enough where we can't help but get emotionally involved or attached to our students. Through the years I've got to know your parents. I lived through your pain, your anxieties. And Eric, you don't know this, but there were times when I cried with you. That's far beyond a teacher's responsibility at any school. Okay you're not just one of my students. We do have a special relationship. Outside of school I grew to love you as a friend. But there shouldn't be and can't be anything more between us. I don't feel that way toward you. I'm not attracted to you in that way. I'm an adult in an adult relationship. I have a boyfriend that I'm in love with."

"So, I'm not capable of having an adult relationship?" asked Eric.

"That's not what I'm saying, Eric. I have responsibilities. And with these responsibilities there are consequences. Your innuendos toward me mistakenly taken by somebody else at school could cost me my job, my reputation, and my career. Do you understand Eric?"

Eric seemed to understand what she was driving at. He made no comment.

"Good. Cause it must stop! Now that we have that cleared up, there's another reason why I'm here tonight. I want to tell you there are some strange things happening at school. Today, my office door had chewing gum over the latch, and Sam's hat was found on top of my desk next to Tony's open files. Files that were in a filing cabinet."

Eric started to panic. "What? Maybe you left the files out by accident."

"I have no interest in Tony's files. Besides, I have the keys to my own office. I don't have to gum over the latch to get in. The weird part is that Tony, Sam, Aaron, and Tom have been quickly catching up on all their work without asking any of the other teachers for assistance. And they all have been behaving different lately."

"If you ask me, I think Eric had something to do with it." Jack announced from behind the curtain.

"Shut up, Jack!" Eric snapped back.

"You know, Tony handed me an assignment a day after I handed it out." Announced Carol.

"Well, you should be happy about that," said Eric.

"Oh, I was. But the assignment was designed to take three weeks to complete."

"Have you spoken to the boys?"

"No, not yet. But I did mention it to Principal Swanson. He suggested that we wait till after vacation to investigate this matter."

'Visiting hours are now over,' a female voice announced over the hospital hallway intercom. 'Visiting hours are between 8:30 a.m. to 8:30 p.m. Visitors please leave by the nearest exit. Thank you.'

"Well, I guess that's my cue," Carol said as she got up from the chair and grabbed her coat from the bed. "Hey! come back. We miss you."

"Yeah, well, I'll miss breakfast in bed." Eric and Carol stared at each other intently for a moment.

"We really miss you," she said seriously. "See ya around." Carol headed out into the hallway, but then stopped short. "Oh, um, I was thinking about a class camping trip in April. You into it?"

"Yeah! Carol?" Eric called after her. She pulled her body back into the doorway for the second time. "Where are you spending Hanukah?"

After that lecture about their relationship, he shouldn't ask such a question.

"You know where."

Eric stared at her for a moment. "Happy Hanukah."

"Happy Hanukah," she replied.

After Carol left the room, Eric snatched his phone from the night table beside his bed to call Sam.

"Sam! Do you know where your hat is?"

"No. I think I left it at school today."

"Carol Schor was just here. She found your hat."

"Where did I leave it?"

"Where you left it. On top of Schor's desk in her office, next to Tony's files. She also found her office door latch gummed opened."

"Holy shit, Eric! I had to rush out of the office. I heard somebody coming."

"Yeah. It was Carol Schor. She also noticed the overnight change in you guys. Sam, the evidence of foul play is all pointing in your corner. You better call the others and tell them to enjoy their vacations. It's going to get pretty hot when it's over."

"You're not going to leave all this in our hands, are you? I mean, you are going to help us out of this, right? This was your master plan!"

"Of course, I won't leave you guys in the cold. As long as I'm not fingered, I'll have time to think of a way out."

"Okay, Eric. I'm sorry. Thanks."

"Don't thank me. I'm just the messenger with bad news."

As Eric hung up the phone, Jack was heard from behind the curtain, picking up the TV remote and repeatedly punching in different channels. "Was that your teacher who was just here?"

"Yeah?" replied Eric, waiting for an off-color comment.

"I bet she teaches sex education."

Eric rolled out of bed and pulled open the curtain between the beds. "You know Jack, I would love to donate that TV remote to you as a going home present."

"What would I do with it? My TV at home doesn't have the remote hook-up."

"That's not the problem," replied Eric. "I think the problem will be people laughing at you."

"And why is that?"

"Because you're going to look awfully funny walking around in life with that remote protruding permanently out of your ass." Eric pulled the curtain closed and plopped back down onto his bed leaving Jack speechless. "Leave it to good ol' Opie for the last word!"

....

The next morning Eric woke up to find the curtain between the two beds open and two nurses making up Jack's empty bed. Air hoses were silent, coiled and tied up against the wall. No wire leads. Jack was nowhere to be seen.

"Where's Jackass?" Eric inquired.

"Jack passed away last night," replied one of the nurses as she finished making the bed.

"I'm sorry." Eric had a slight chill thinking he must have caused Jack to have his fatal heart attack after threatening to place the TV remote in his ass.

"Did you get to know him?" asked the second nurse.

"No, not really." Eric found a smiley face printed on a sugar packet with his breakfast on the night table. He hopped out of bed and used the tape from the rolled-up paper napkin to stick the smiley sugar packet onto the hallway door. "That's what we need around here. More smiles," said Eric jumping back into bed as Dr. Hermann walked into the room. The two nurses walked out.

"Good morning," Dr. Hermann announced.

"Doctor." Replied Eric. "Can I go home?"

"Well, let's see. I have to check you over." Dr. Hermann sat on the edge of the bed and checked Eric's heart with the cold stethoscope. "Where's your roommate?"

"He already checked out." Eric flinched every time the freezing cold stethoscope touched naked skin from his chest to his back.

"Your heart sounds good. Your lungs are cleared. Your temperature is normal. Drinking your fluids, I see. Well, I guess you could check out tomorrow just like your roommate."

....

Mid-morning in his bedroom lying on his bed catching up with homework with the television on, Eric was spelled bound by a TV commercial for a board game called Ball Busters by MECO. It seemed to be an inappropriate commercial for network television. The phone rang.

"Eric! It's Opie. I'll pick you up around twelve-thirty. We're going to the All-Boys Central High School. Do you think your mother will let you go?"

"I don't know, Opie. I just got out of the hospital a few days ago. I think she's going to want me to stay in the house until early next century. But I'll try to convince her to let me go."

"All right Eric. But remember, when you go out, bundle up and wear underpants. You might catch another cold."

"Shut up, Opie!"

....

Philadelphia's Central High School located in the Logan section of the city was known country wide for its high academic standards. It was considered by the populous of academia as the Ivy League of public high schools. It was the only high school in the United States that was granted by an Act of Assembly in 1849 to hand out a Bachelor of Arts Degree to graduates who meet the requirements. Central also confers high school diplomas upon graduates who do not meet the requirement for a college degree.

Central's first president -principal- in 1839 was Alexander Dallas Bache, professor of natural philosophy and chemistry at the University of Pennsylvania. And a great grandson of Benjamin Franklin.

Cousin Opie was accepted at Central on the account that he was academically brilliant. But putting Opie into a public school did not curb his behavior. The public schools were not as strict on discipline as in the parochial schools.

On the third floor of the building, Opie and Eric were about to enter the science class.

"What did you think about my history class?" Opie asked.

"I think I like mine better. At least my teacher likes her students."

"Well, do you want to stay for science?"

"If it's anything like your history class, not really."

Most of the students in the science class at Central High waiting by their lab tables were brainy, nerdy-looking boys wearing thick horn-rimmed or wired granny glasses. Wallet-size calculators by Texas Instruments were strapped against their hips like six shooters. When it came to looks, Eric with his long curly hair, bell bottom dungarees and a printed shirt stood out like a Beeker in a Tupperware party. Opie could sort of pseudo fit in with his glasses and dull clothes. Both boys sat in the back of the classroom.

"This teacher is always late," Opie said to Eric. "You'll see. He'll rush in and conduct this class like a chicken without a head. But not today. We're leaving early!"

Opie got the class's attention. "Listen up, everybody! Somebody turned on the Bunsen burners! We'll fake being unconscious. The teacher has a sense of humor. He'll go for it!"

"The teacher's coming!" a student yelled out from the classroom hallway door. Another student turned on the hissing unlit Bunsen burners, and every student including Eric either laid on the floor or faced down on top of their tables. A few giggles accompanied the gag. Just as Opie had predicted, a bewildered and tardy teacher bounced into the room, heard the Bunsen burners hissing, and saw the entire class of students 'unconscious.'

"Oh, my God!" yelled the teacher, as he lifted a chair from behind his desk and tossed it through the third-floor window. Students trying not to laugh sat up with fake coughs. Buried amid the confusion of students and teacher, Opie and Eric ran out of the classroom.

"That's one way to end a class!" Said Opie as he ran down the hallway among panicking students and the sound of the fire alarm.

"Damn, Opie," announced Eric, behind in close pursuit.

....

Late that afternoon a few blocks from Central High School, above the O'Neal's Funeral Parlor, Eric ended up lying on the top covers of Opie's bed in Opie's third-floor attic bedroom which was the full length of the house. Large enough for a queen size bed, ping-pong table that was mostly hidden under clothes, books, sports paraphernalia, and magazines. Eric was watching the local news with anchorman Larry

Kane from a sixteen-inch color Admiral television set sitting on top of a dresser.

Opie was head-first on his knees in a clothes closet throwing out clothes, magazines, and other junk in a desperate search. After a slight struggle, a yank, and a pull, out popped a bong. With bong in hand, Opie joined Eric on the bed. The twelve-inch dark-blue translucent acrylic tube was filled about a quarter of the way with water. A metal bowl sat screwed-in halfway up the tube filled with marijuana. The top of the tube was wide open. Opie wasn't too concerned about being caught by his parents for smoking dope in the house. They were too busy working down in the basement at the funeral parlor. Plus, the redolence from the embalming fluids killed any odor that might sneak down from the third floor.

"Here, Eric. Light it." Opie sat next to Eric on the bed and passed the bong with a BIC lighter.

At first, Eric was apprehensive. "You do realize that I was just released from the hospital from ammonia and respiratory therapy?"

"Good! This will not only clear your lungs, but it will also make you think more clearly," said Opie.

Eric had never smoked marijuana before but felt peer pressure from his cousin and recollecting what Alice told him the last night he saw her. 'Don't knock it 'til you try it'. Eric lit the bong and took a heavy toke. He began to cough and choke violently as Opie laughed on.

"What in hell do you have in here?" Coughed Eric.

"Good Cambodian Red." Opie said still laughing. "Straight out of Vietnam."

"You mean to say that you watched me take a big toke of this shit and never thought about warning me?"

"Well, by hanging around with Alice, I thought you knew what you were doing."

"You, son of a bitch!" Eric choked.

Within twenty minutes, Eric and Opie were deathly stoned. Eric was relaxed, docile, and sleepy. He liked it.

The boys lounged in bed and continued to watch the early local Action News on television. Under the mind-altering drug, Eric dissected what was being reported on television. He read between the lines and understood clearly what he thought was a new reality in the world.

As Larry Kane introduced the local weatherman Jim O'Brien, Opie announced a confession.

"I stole this bong from a head shop. The one in Cheltenham Mall across from Gimbles."

"Who cares?" replied Eric.

"Have you ever stolen anything, Eric?"

"Well, when I was in fifth grade..."

"Fifth grade!" Opie laughed out.

"Yeah!" Eric snapped back. "Fifth grade! Now listen! When I was in fifth grade, a couple of friends and I were stealing candy from Cedarbrook drug store on Vernon Road. The old lady who owned the store caught us. So, as I was running out of the store with the stolen goods in a wool hat, the lady yelled out after me, 'I'll never forget your face! I'll never forget your face!' That following year she becomes my sixth-grade teacher."

By now, Opie was passing a lit joint to Eric. "Did she remember your face?"

Eric took a toke from the joint, then passed it back to Opie. "She flunked me," Eric admitted with a straight face. The two boys suddenly broke out in laughter.

"Well, what do you know? It took me six years and a joint to laugh at that," said Eric.

"Is that why you're in a retard school? Stealing candy, flunking your grades?" Asked Opie.

"No. I go to that retard school for other reasons."

"What other reasons?"

"Well... no! You'll laugh at me."

"I won't laugh at you. What other reasons?" Opie insisted.

"Well, I'm only telling you this cause I'm high and you're my cousin. After tonight, I'll deny everything. Even the fact that you're my cousin." From within the mental haze of marijuana, Eric swallowed his pride. "This was kept from you. You weren't supposed to know this. My parents wanted to keep this a low profile from the family. But I had a learning disability. I suffered from dyslexia. The Philadelphia schools didn't have the time to help me. That's why I was sent to a private school. I didn't know how to read till I was in eighth grade. Plus, I had an emotional breakdown when Elliot was killed. I've seen more shrinks in the last four years than you can imagine. When my brother was killed, my parents turned off their life lights. Remember shortly after Elliot's funeral, my mother was sent to the hospital?"

"Yeah. She had a heart attack," said Opie as he took a toke and passed the joint.

"No. That's what you were told." Said Eric as he inhaled the joint and passed it back. "My mother had a nervous breakdown. My father and the family doctor had her committed to the mental ward at Jefferson. Now, my parents are trying pull the shroud of mourning over me. But I'm not letting them, Op! It's hard. At times they tear me apart by comparing me with Elliot. I'm competing with a dead man, Op." Eric tried unsuccessfully to hold back the tears.

"Well. I always knew you were retarded," said Opie. "The whole family knew that."

"Do you remember my brother?" asked Eric.

"Yeah. But he was too old for me to keep my interest."

"My mind went totally blank after he was killed in Nam, Opie. I couldn't read, think, or even reason."

Opie holding the bong in his right hand and the joint warning of its extinction in his left. Opie knew it was time to change the subject. It was getting too depressing to waste on a good joint.

153

"I guess it's a good thing that you're in a private school. I mean, the Philly school system is constantly on strike."

"Strike?" announced Eric. "You'd be lucky if any of the school board members ever show up for work. My mother wrote hundreds of letters to school superintendent Richardson Dilworth, explaining how awful the Philadelphia schools are being managed. She never received a satisfying reply. My mother had always said that Dilworth should had given up his life jacket from the Andrea Dora to a more deserving person!"

"Opie!" yelled Aunt Frieda from the bottom step of the third-floor staircase. "You're late for work!"

"Holy shit! It's my mother!" Opie said in a panic as he jumped out of bed to ditch the joint and stashed the bong back into the clothes closet. Eric jumped out of the bed to open a window.

....

On the first morning back to Noah Webster Preparatory from mid-semester break, Carol and Principal Swanson had a conference in his small office.

"So, what do you suggest?" asked Carol.

"We'll have a hearing to get this whole thing out in the open. But first we must have a case, which means that we have to piece this puzzle together." Swanson suggested.

"Besides finding Sam's hat on my desk. I've already pieced this puzzle together with some more intriguing evidence." Said Carol, "There are greasy fingerprints on Tony's file folder."

"Fingerprints?"

"Yeah. Kind of like… motor oil."

"Motor oil," Swanson repeated, with contemplation. "Tony!"

"No," said Carol. "He doesn't have a car here to work on. Besides, as smart as he is, this operation is too smart for Tony to execute.

"Do you think Eric had anything to do with this?" Inquired Swanson.

"No!" Carol replied with confidence. "He was in the hospital when all this was taking place. Why do you think him?"

"He's a bit behind on his work. He's smart enough to pull such a coup. Maybe he wanted to help his friends. Could have run this whole operation from bedside."

"I don't know, Jim. I think he was in bad shape when the bulk of this was going on. I don't believe that Eric Blum, who wants to get out of this school so badly, would stoop so low, and take a chance in blowing his freedom to have somebody break into my office, and for whom? Tony and his stooges? Well, let me get out of here and grab a bite to eat. I'll be back within an hour. Don't start the hearing without me."

Out to the stone patio through the French doors of the cafeteria, Carol headed for the parking lot. Eric, Tony, Sam, Arron, and Tom were grouped together.

"If you don't want to answer any of the questions," Eric advised his goons about the up-coming hearing. "Just reply. 'I don't remember, I can't recall'."

With car keys in hand, Carol passed by the boys and climbed down the stone steps onto the parking lot. She walked over to an empty spot where she thought she had parked her VW. But there was no VW to be had. Carol glanced around the lot swearing she had parked the car in that very spot when she drove in that morning. In fact, she was sure about it. Carol walked back toward the patio.

"... So just deny. Deny everything" Eric continued to advise the boys.

"Where is my car?" Carol demanded from the parking lot. The boys looked down upon her from the stone patio as though she was speaking in Chinese.

"Where-is-my-car!"

Tony lifted his head ever so slightly in the direction of the street. Carol followed his glance to find the VW off property obstructing traffic.

"I am going to kill all of you!" Carol said softly to the goons as she raced down toward the street.

"Did you guys pick up Carol's car and move to the street?" Eric asked the goons.

Tony, with a bland expression till it gradually turned into a wide grin, said, "Yeah".

....

About two-thirty that afternoon in Principal Swanson's tiny office, Swanson sat behind his desk overlooking an outline he had prepared for interrogation. Tony, Sam, and Carol had the three chairs in front of Swanson's desk. Tom and Aaron were sitting on the floor. The evidence of foul play piled up on Swanson's desk. Sam's hat and the radio Shack recorder, a manila folder with Tony's name and greasy fingerprints.

"I believe within the last month somebody has been breaking into Miss. Schor's office and been reading confidential files on some of our students." Announced Swanson. "Students who are very far behind in their academic work. We have every suspicion to believe that the spy or perpetrator in this case is sitting in this office among us. I think you all know who that is."

"What makes you think we know, fucker!" asked Tony.

"Well, at the same time the files were being pulled out from their drawers, your attitude and academic conduct improved, Tony."

"That doesn't prove anything, stupid cow" defended Tony.

"Maybe not," continued Swanson. "But as a formality, I must ask you a few straightforward questions. Have you been breaking into Miss Schor's office perhaps looking for overdue follow-ups, future tests, and assignments?"

"Jackass. No, sir."

"Are you on any other federally controlled drugs besides the one that is prescribed for Tourette's syndrome?"

The rest of the students in the office giggled.

"No. Only Pimozide prescribed by the school psychiatrist, who's an asshole," Tony replied seriously.

"Will you please tell us, why this overnight change in your behavior?"

"I knew that I was behind in my work, and that I was on the verge of being kicked out of Webster. That's no secret."

"You've been kicked out of many schools. Why would you care if you were kicked out of this one?" asked Swanson.

"I like it here...fuck'en' zoo."

Sam and Carol clicked their tongues against their teeth in disbelief of Tony's answer. Aaron and Tom laughed.

"Besides," continued Tony, "there ain't anymore schools that will take me."

"Who told you that you were going to be kicked out of this school?" asked Swanson.

"I don't remember," said Tony.

"Was it, Miss. Schor?"

"Cunt! No."

"Jim!" Carol yelled out slapping the palm of her hand on Swanson's desk from Tony's lewd remark.

"Maybe another student?" asked Swanson.

"I can't recall."

"You don't remember?" asked Swanson.

"Yes, sir," replied Tony.

"Well, Mr. Burns, the only way for you to have known that you were going to be kicked out of this school, or if you were missing any particular follow-up is if you sat in one of our Friday afternoon teachers' meetings. Were you ever at any one of our Friday afternoon teachers' meetings, Mr. Burns?"

"No, sir."

"No, sir, you were not! But this recorder was found on the bookshelf in room 20 and recorded one of our teacher's meetings!" Swanson reached over to his desk to pick up Sam's hat. "Do you know who owns this hat?"

"Yes. Sam Harris."

"Do you know where it was found?"

"On his head? No, sir, I can't recall."

"It was found beside your files on top of Carol Schor's desk whose office door latch was bubble gummed over. Why do you think Sam Harris would want to break into a teacher's office to see your files?"

"What makes you think that I broke into Carol Schor's office?" Sam blurted out.

"That hat was not in my office before lunch. After lunch," Carol yelled aiming her tirade toward Sam, "my office was broken into and your hat and Tony's files with the greasy fingerprints were lying out on top of my desk. Now tell me you weren't in there!"

"Would you like to tell us, Mr. Harris?" Swanson asked calmly. "Did you break into Carol Schor's office before Christmas vacation and left your hat on top of the desk?"

"I didn't break in. But I could have had a meeting with Carol in her office at any time during the day before Christmas vacation and left my hat on top of her desk. Maybe she didn't notice it at the time."

"Ms. Schor, did Sam Harris have a meeting with you in your office the day before Christmas vacation?"

"No, he did not, Mr. Swanson!" Carol replied.

Principal Swanson picked up the manila folder from his desk. "Mr. Harris, it's funny that these files were discovered out of their drawer on the same day I overheard you telling some of the other students that you were going to work on your car during lunchtime. Are these your prints? I think they are. And I will have them checked."

Sam began to panic. Eric was not there to protect or back him up. And Sam was not going down on this ship alone.

"Okay, okay," Sam said as he got more comfortable in his chair. "Yes, we been recording the teacher's meetings and those are my prints on those damn files. I wanted to be seen working in my car during lunchtime. I needed an alibi in case something went wrong. Look, it was after the meeting you had with Tony's parents. We stopped Eric Blum in the hallway."

"Who's 'we'?" asked Swanson.

"Tom, Aaron, me, and Tony. Our parents told us that you had contacted them with an ultimatum. So, we asked the teachers to help us get caught up. They didn't give us all the missing follow-ups. We were so far behind we would never have the chance to catch up. Since Eric was president of student council, we asked him to talk with the teachers to be more lenient with us. He told us he had a better idea and to meet in Carol Schor's office at lunch time when she goes out for lunch where we wouldn't be detected."

"No! No! I can't believe it!" Carol yelled toward Swanson. "Eric wouldn't! There's no way he would break into my office! That is not like him. I will bet on that. But just in-case, I want that little fucker here and now!"

"Tom," Swanson said calmly, "would you please find, and get the little fucker here and now?"

Tom scurried out of the small office. Within a few moments, Tom with Eric's head popped through the office doorway with an Ernie Kovacs smile.

"Come in and have a seat, Eric." Invited Swanson, even though there were no seats to be had. Eric walked up to Tony Burns and scuttled him off the chair.

"Get up, get up, get up!" Eric ordered.

Tony slid off the chair, stepping on Carol's toes as he landed on the floor next to Tom. Eric took Tony's seat next to Carol. She was staring at Eric just inches away from his left ear. Carol couldn't believe after all these years of trust and confidentiality that Eric would order a break-in at her office. She felt violated.

"So, you were behind all this?" asked Swanson.

"No! He was not behind this'. Said Carol. "He would not do this to me. Were you behind all this, Eric?"

"I don't know what you're talking about. I've been sick these past weeks," Eric said.

"Sick!" Carol yelled out. "Sick! Boy let me tell you something. If you had anything to do with this, you're going to be dead in a minute!" The other students chuckled.

"Carol let's calm down," said Swanson. "Mr. Blum, even though you've been elected student body president for the past four years, if we find that you were involved in this incident, we can have you impeached."

Eric glanced down at the floor, finding leaning up against Swanson's desk a David Frye comedy album Jacket entitled -Richard Nixon a Fantasy -. "I won't leave without honor," Eric protested.

"You'll be lucky if you leave this office with your fuck'en head!" Carol yelled. "Did you give the orders to break into my office?"

"Carol, stop!" demanded Swanson as he continued to interrogate Eric. "We could also have you suspended."

"I know nothing of such crimes. I am as shocked as you are!" Eric maintained.

"Mr. Blum, your friend Sam Harris just blew the whistle on you."

"He's no friend of mine."

"This little shit gave the orders to break into my office! What in hell were you looking for, boy!" Carol yelled.

"Carol!" intervened Swanson. "We've had you, Mr. Blum. Give up. We're going to call your parents. I'm sure your mother would love to hear what you have been up to."

Mr. Swanson picked up the handset from his desk and began dialing the rotary phone. Eric couldn't let his parents know about his shenanigans in school. They had already been through enough disappointments in their lives. Eric was their hope, their last frontier.

"Don't call my mother." Every number Swanson dialed took about three seconds to rotate back to its starting point. "Why do you have to do that?" Swanson continued to dial. "Why do you have to be that way? Please don't call her. You know she's a little nut. Perhaps we could plea bargain."

"I'm going to bargain your ass to the front of your head! Call her!" Carol yelled out.

Eric turned and looked straight at Carol. "Man. You look so hot when you're angry," he discreetly said.

"I'm going to fuck'en' kill you," Carol replied softly. "Call her!" She yelled out toward Swanson.

"Okay, Eric," said Mr. Swanson as he hung up the phone before he dialed the last two numbers. "You cooperate, and then we'll see who gets called. Did you order your friends to break into Carol's office to collect information? And did you also have the teachers' meetings bugged?"

Eric swiveled comfortably in his chair. "Yes, I did it!" admitted Eric, sounding a bit like Humphrey Bogart from the movie, The Cane Mutiny. "I had to do it. I'd do it again if I had to!" Eric took two metal pinballs out from his pants pocket. They made a clinging sound as he fondled them. "They approached me in the first-floor hallway. At first, I thought they wanted me to steal the key to the milk locker in the lunchroom. I knew it was the strawberry flavored milk they were after."

"Mr. Blum!" interrupted Swanson. "Eric, are you aware that you breached a constitutional amendment when you violated somebody's privacy?"

"The Constitution, Mr. Swanson? Under the Constitution, a man is innocent until proven guilty. If this is the case, then why is he locked up until the day of his trial. And sometimes for years?"

"That's not the point here, Eric! The point is that you did something illegal. You in-violated the Fourth Amendment—something that the President of the United States was almost impeached for. You invaded an individual's privacy."

"Yeah, mine, you little son-of-a-bitch!" Carol yelled out.

"Nobody got hurt," defended Eric. "Nobody was going to get hurt. You know as well as I that these boys would never have passed last semester. They wanted to find out what they missed. They wanted to catch up. They just needed a little boost. I showed them under the Freedom of Information Act how to receive that boost. There wasn't any cheating. They tutored themselves."

"Your stunt is not classified under the Freedom of Information Act. That act only applies to the Government." Carol responded.

"As long as my name is on those files, I have a right!' Eric yelled back.

"That was my private office!" Carol yelled louder. "Not under the jurisdiction of the Freedom of Information Act!"

"Eric," Swanson calmly intervened. "You conspired to break into a teacher's office and had confiscated confidential information. It was a given that this would never happen here. Let me explain our philosophy. What we have here is a small school, Eric. We don't even have a dress code. We turn a deaf ear when students address their instructors by their first names. We follow liberal Quaker standards. But what we will not stand for, what there is no room for, is dishonesty. I'm quite surprised at you, Eric Blum, President of Student Council. You want to graduate from here this year? All you had to do was to keep a low profile and do what was required for graduation… but not after this stunt. Except for some of the members of the U.S. Senate, this behavior is unacceptable in society and especially from any of our graduates. Do you think you're mature enough to leave this place? I think not. And I'm not singling you out, Eric. But you have been here longer than any student in this room. You're the one who is next in line to graduate."

"Yeah, how many times I've heard that in the course of two years?" Eric replied under his breath.

"I'll have re-evaluate your behavior and decide about your attitude. I will surely talk to Dr. Goldman about this event. And how you behave for the rest of the school term will determine whether you spend another year here to qualify for a diploma. The rest of you I will decide your punishments. You're all dismissed."

Outside in the hallway as Eric and the goons walked out of Swanson's office.

Renée was listening in by the door

"I had no idea that you had anything to do with this. I love you, Eric. And I'm with you all the way." Renée gave him a kiss on the cheek and a hug of confidence.

"Thanks, Renée. But I don't feel that you should get involved. Now I'm worried about Swanson calling my parents. If he does, I'll never be able to go home."

"You could stay with me. We have lots of room in our house."

"Thanks," grinned Eric. "But I don't think that's going fly with your parents."

Carol walked out of Swanson's office and spotted Eric and Renée walking arm-in-arm toward the staircase leading down to the first floor.

"Eric!" Carol shouted out, "Wait!" Eric and Renée stopped at the top of the staircase. "I admit that I wasn't fair when I saw that the boys were trying to catch up with their work. That was my fault. But you know after all this time the boys were never serious about their studies and I didn't want to waste my time. That was their fault. Sometimes teachers forget that we're teachers. That's just being human and that's nobody's fault. Swanson and I decided to let you and your cohorts have lunch detention from now till Easter. But I have some bad news about the future. I think you may lose any chance of graduating this year unless you can pull something short of a miracle to prove to the staff that you can handle yourself emotionally, academically, and mature enough to be a responsible young adult."

"My parents won't be called?" asked Eric.

"Swanson believes the threat of keeping you here another year and calling your parents is enough punishment to keep you in check."

"I'm sorry about your office, Carol. Can we still be friends?"

"I don't know Eric. I wasn't hired here to be your friend. I'm your teacher. It's just that I could have had very important and personal things in my office, which I did! And it's just the feeling of violation that ticked me off. And by you, Eric! Of all people. To be a friend with somebody who did this to me is something I'll have to work at."

"I'm sorry, Carol. It won't happen again. So, my parents won't be called?"

Carol surrendered a smirk to both Eric and Renée as she turned and continued to walk down the stairs to the first floor.

"Renée! I can't believe how easy I got off!" Eric said as he hugged her.

"So, what are you going to do now that you're not getting out this year?"

"Oh, I'm getting out." replied Eric with a look of thought.

"What do you have in mind, Eric?"

"I heard there's a job opening down at the Philadelphia Spectrum."

"What job?"

"My mother heard from a friend that they were hiring for change-over crew. I could go down there after school and apply. I heard that it's hard work, and the hours could be long. I'll be working side-by-side with other normal people. I could do it. I know I can. Man, if I keep my grades up and stay cool. If I could get this job on my own, the school would have no other reason not to let me go at the end of the school year. Besides, I could then afford to take you to nice places—not just to a movie or to a mall."

CHAPTER 6

THE PHILADELPHIA SPECTRUM
THE ENTERTAINMENT CAPITAL OF THE WORLD

THAT AFTERNOON AFTER school, Eric drove to the Philadelphia Spectrum sports arena across from Veteran Stadium on Patterson Avenue in South Philly. The parking lot was empty except for the few cars that belonged to the Spectrum employees. Eric parked as close as possible to the arena, walked through the employee entrance, and was stopped by a uniformed security guard.

"I'm looking for employment with the change-over crew."

"It may be too late. I think everybody went home for the night." Replied the guard. "Just walk down this hall and turn right at the end. Walk straight through the tunnel till you get to the arena. Ask for Ted. He's the change-over crew manager, if he's still here. You'll need a pass. I'll write one up for you."

With the pass in hand, Eric walked down the red industrial carpeted hallway passing the front offices. The walls of the hallway were made of cinder block painted white adorned with framed pictures of basketball, hockey, soccer, and rock n' roll icons that had endured the arena since it's opening in 1967. Eric opened one of the double glass doors dividing the hallway from the maintenance tunnel which wrapped around the arena under the bleachers. Toward the end of the tunnel, he made a right into the arena. The transformation from a maintenance tunnel to an open air 18,169 red chair cathedral was overwhelming at first. The arena had a combined odor of steel and odorous popcorn. From I-beams over above the arena floor, banners and flags draped down acknowledging the 76ers basketball, Flyers hockey teams.

The Spectrum was one of the first sports arenas to have a scoreboard coincided with a message board. It was approximately a twelve-foot square that hung extended by cables over the center of the arena floor that could be electronically lowered for maintenance.

The message board was the first dot matrix screens in pro hockey or basketball capable of photos, animation, and instant replays as well as messages.

The day crew were finishing laying a professional basketball court for the 76ers when Eric spotted two boys around his age about to roll out a red carpet on the floor in front of the north bleachers. He told them he was looking for Ted.

"Sorry." Replied one of the boys, "He's in his office. Go back to the entrance of the tunnel and make a sharp left. His office door is always open."

"Thanks… I think," replied Eric bewildered about the apology. Eric walked back to the maintenance tunnel, then turned left. The workers were correct. The office door was wide open. Hanging on the walls in this twelve-by-fifteen-foot cinder block office painted mint green were framed building certifications and posters of past events. A couple of metal filing cabinets stood at attention in one corner. The office was lit by double tube florescent bulbs twelve feet above.

The change-over crew boss -Ted- was a stocky middle-aged man with short grey slicked back hair reading a memo from behind his metal industrial desk. Eric knocked on the open steel door.

"Yes!" said Ted in a booming condescending authoritative voice as he continued to read without looking up.

Eric felt like the cowardly lion in the Wizard of OZ who wanted to run away after hearing the yelling wizard.

"Hi, um, my name is Eric Blum."

"Who?" asked Ted.

"Eric Blum?"

"What can I do for you?"

"I'm applying for the job with the change-over crew?"

"How old are you?"

"Eighteen."

"Can you work nights?"

"Well, I still go to high school during the day. But I'm free on the weekends."

At that moment Eric realized, what about Renée? Would she tolerate another weekend job? But this was a real job, with real money. And this real job with real money would be a more convincing job for Webster to lead him back into the real world.

Ted finally dropped the memo on his desk, reached into the side desk drawer, pulled out an application, and handed it to Eric.

"Here. Read this. Fill it out, -both sides- and bring it back to me. If it's not completely filled out both sides, don't bother coming back." Eric thanked him and turned to leave. "Can you start Friday? Be here by eleven P.M. pm with the application filled both sides!"

"So, am I hired?" Eric asked.

"Get out of here or you'll be fired."

....

The next morning Eric pulled into Webster's parking lot. The news that reverbed through the car radio caught his attention.

'An early morning three-alarm fire gutted the center city nightclub known as Nolan's, which had its allegedly outlandish grand opening about a month ago. Fire commissioner Joseph Rizzo remarked that the blaze looked suspicious, and arson is suspected. The owner of the club, Tommy Lorenzo, a.k.a. Mary Nolan, has been missing for the past week. His whereabouts are unknown. It was rumored that the club was financially backed by a Philadelphia organized crime syndicate...'

In the school's first-floor hallway Eric spotted Renée walking toward him.

"I got the job down at the Spectrum yesterday. I did it on my own. I didn't need the school's help. I start Friday night!"

"Another weekend job?" whined Renée.

"Look, Renée," Eric snapped back, "you know for me to get out of this school with a clean slate I have to prove that I am capable of getting a normal job on my own. That I can fit back into the world. This is my exit. I'm out of here!"

"But on the weekends?" Renée continued to whine.

"I have to prove to the school that I can do it. Mostly, I have to prove it to myself, Renée. I don't belong here anymore. I have to get out of here! And weekends are all I can find right now."

"Well, I guess we'll work it out. What will you be doing at the Spectrum?"

"Building stages for concerts, probably or making ice for the Broad Street Bullies. I saw a crew erecting a basketball court for the 76ers!"

Carol was walking through the hallway when she found Eric and Renée together.

"Eric! I was just looking for you." Announced Carol as she walked on by. "Goldman is here. He's waiting in his office on the second floor."

Renée and Eric stared at each other for a moment. "Only on the weekends?" Renée whined again.

....

In a dark office on the second floor, Goldman sat behind his desk sucking on his pipe. The manila folder was open with papers and a legal-size lined tablet laid out. Eric sat in the leather armchair in front of him.

"I heard about the stunt you pulled with your classmates before the Christmas break," announced Goldman.

"I felt I had just cause to do what I did," replied Eric.

"You probably lost the opportunity of getting your diploma at the end of the school year." A billow of smoke poured out of Goldman's pipe in anticipation of a reply.

"Well, we're in the middle of the school year. Maybe I still have time to make up for my misgivings," replied Eric.

"Perhaps. Assuming this will be your last year, have you given any thought about where you want to go next year? I mean as in college?"

"I would like to start off at Harvard-Yale." Eric replied with a straight face.

"Well, let's work on the community college level first." Suggested Goldman. "Do you think you can afford it?"

"I don't know. I don't think so. Not at this moment."

"Well then, how do you expect to get into college?"

"I need a grant or a loan."

"And if you can't get the grant or the loan, what then?"

"I don't know. Work, I guess."

Goldman peered down through his bifocals at the manila folder on his desk. "Are you aware of the options offered to you if you leave here at the end of this year?"

"What do you mean by 'options?'" Asked Eric.

"If you plan to get into college, you might be placed back into the Philadelphia public school system in twelfth grade."

"Twelfth grade?" Eric called out.

"Since you've been attending a school for special needs, you might not have the acceptable credits for college. And even if you do, you might not be accepted into college without taking the SAT."

"I don't understand."

"Let me explain. At most colleges, outside of a community college, you must take the Scholastic Aptitude Test, SAT. It's a placement exam. Many colleges determine who they will accept by the results of this test. Now, this school was designed to get students back on an academic track. We are not qualified or equipped to give the SAT."

"Well first, if the Philly school system would have helped me from the start instead of pushing me through, I would never be in this mess! Now where do you suggest I go after this year if not college?"

"If not college," said Goldman. "I suggest going back to a Philly school to catch up."

"A Philly school? If you send me back, I'll be where I started four years ago!"

"Not exactly. First, we'd place you into twelfth grade," explained Goldman.

"Doc, you're putting me back another year! I already flunked sixth!"

"Blum, you are not being put back!"

"Then what do you call it?"

Goldman tried to remain professionally calm. "How could you be put back into a grade that you were never in?"

"I'm in twelfth grade now!"

"Since when does this school have grades?" Goldman barked back. Eric stopped to think for a moment. "We're trying to place you where you'd be comfortable."

"Yeah, well, I can't go back into twelfth grade."

"You're not going back into a grade you were never in!"

"I can't go back to a Philly school!"

"Why?"

"Cause, I can't."

Eric didn't want to openly admit it to himself—let alone to Goldman—but the issue was his pride. Fourteen years in a twelve-year academic system would be downright embarrassing. He would be a couple of years older than his classmates. How could anybody concentrate on catching up on their studies with that sentence over their heads. One more year of high school would devastate Eric's spirit.

"Look," said Goldman, "if we can't get you into a college next year, that could be the other alternative."

"If I have to go back to twelfth grade, I'll quit!"

"Blum, if I'm alive, I'll make sure you get into a college, even if you have to repeat twelfth grade seven times over! I'll kick your ass to make sure you get there. And I'll do it! Your parents have invested too much time and money in you. Thousands and thousands of dollars they never had to get you where you are today."

"To get me where I am today? Where am I? I'm going back into twelfth grade next year."

Goldman slammed his palm on the desk. "You're not…" He caught himself raising his voice but composed. "Let me remind you of something." For the second time Goldman looked through his bifocals at the open files on top of his desk. "Within the last four years, you went from reading on a fourth-grade level to twelfth. We here at Noah Webster are ninety percent sure that you could now function normally in a college or in a mainstream public school."

"Then why can't I get a clean break from here?"

"We have to make sure. And making sure is another alternative that I have to offer on the table."

"Which is?"

"If we can't get you into a college, and if you're really not comfortable in the public-school system, there's always one more year at Webster."

"You're just like the others here! 'Next year! Next year!'" Eric yelled out. "And I thought you were different! Well, you fooled me!" Eric shot up from his chair taking a step toward the door. "I have no more years left in me at this retard school! I'm not coming back here next year and that's for sure! You know, you can't keep me here. I'm eighteen. I'm legal! I could walk straight out of this place at the end of this school year!"

Eric could hear the crackling of the leather chair as Goldman sat back to get himself more comfortable as smoke bellowed out from his pipe.

"That's right. "Goldman replied calmly. "We can't legally keep you here, or even force you to go to college for that matter. I don't think after all the money spent by your parents to get you back on an academic track, especially your mother will be very pleased about your decision not to continue your education. And I was only making a few recommendations. Now come back and sit your ass down!" Goldman ordered. Eric waited for a beat or two then walked back and plopped down on the chair. "We just want to make sure you're okay. Look! Why don't you take that restaurant job?"

"What's that have to do with school?

"It has to do with you being emotionally stable, maturity, capable of fitting back into society."

"I don't need the restaurant. Don't you think working as an usher or for a disk-jockey was proof enough? Look! I just got a job down at the Philadelphia Spectrum with the change-over crew."

"How did you manage that?"

"I heard through my mother that they were hiring. So, yesterday after school, I applied. They hired me. I start this Friday night."

"Are you sure you can handle it?"

"You just told me that you were ninety percent sure that I'm all right. If I can't prove it to you, and to the rest of the school that I can do it on my own, I'll be in twelfth grade for the next four years!"

Goldman took a puff from his pipe and folded his hands in front of him. "I think you can handle it, Eric," he said as he grinned. "I think you're going to fit right back into the world."

"Well, that's funny. You're the first person in this school who has ever said that to me and seemed to mean it. And apparently, you're the only one who holds the key to my exit out of this retarded place. I just know I don't belong here anymore, Doc. I have to move on."

There was a moment of silence. Smoking his pipe, Goldman waited patiently for Eric to compose.

"I remember listening to my friends talk about their teachers and what they did together at the public school." Eric continued. "The football, and the baseball games they participated in. The girls they met. I learned very early not to share my school experiences. I mean, what could I possibly tell them? I went to see my shrink today. I can't read. I need psychiatric care and testing. I knew my friends wouldn't understand. I had to keep my mouth shut these past four years. Not an easy task for a teenager. When I would listen to my friends talk about their school, I felt out of place; I felt dumb."

"But that's all behind you now." Goldman interjected with smoke bellowing out from both sides of his mouth.

"Oh yeah! You think so? My old friends have moved on in life. I'm still here."

"Did any of your old friends ever find out what kind of school Webster is?"

"Well, one day in the summer of 1970, before I attended Noah Webster Preparatory, the kitchen window was open as my mother was explaining to my father about the school. It just so happened that two of my so-called friends were walking by and overheard the conversation. Well, before long, the word was out that I was going to a retarded school. It wasn't until that fall the confirmation of my death warrant circulated throughout the neighborhood."

"Death warrant?" asked Goldman.

"Yeah. That Lil' yellow school bus in the morning that pick up the retards to their special school, then drops them off at home in the late afternoon." Eric's eyes begin to water. "I was picked up, then dropped off to my special school in a little yellow Dodge van with yellow and red warning lights on the roof while the neighborhood kids walked to and from their public schools snickering." conveyed Eric. "Even some of the neighborhood parents believed that I was taking the short yellow bus because I was retarded. Some parents on the block were suspicious and did not want their children to associate with me. Other parents were compassionate, and would speak slower when addressing me thinking that I would be able to Un-der-stand-them-bet-ter. You still think this is all behind me? Behind is being able to forgive and forget. I don't think this will ever be behind me Doc, for I will never forget."

Goldman waited patiently while Eric fruitlessly tried to hold back the tears. "You want a tissue?"

"No." said Eric as he wiped his hose with his sleeve. "I couldn't wait till I got my driver's license so I could travel outside of Mt. Airy and start fresh. No questions, no past! Just the present and future!"

"Parents can usually be big children themselves," remarked Goldman, after taking the pipe out of his mouth.

"Is that your only professional opinion?" Eric asked smugly.

"No. That's my professional fact. Parents, just like their children, can be mean without thinking. Do you think you're retarded, Eric?"

"I suppose. According to most of my old neighbors. I know I ain't normal."

"In which way *ain't* you normal?" Asked Goldman.

"I'm not generally comfortable around people. I just feel different," said Eric as tears rolled down both cheeks. "I get this feeling that people stare at me as though I'm some sort of freak."

"Do you think you make people feel that way?"

"I don't know. Maybe it's this persona or this aura I project. I don't know. I never been comfortable in my skin."

"Are you sure you don't you want a tissue?"

"No," Eric said as he wiped the tears from his cheeks and his nose with his shirt. "I just feel at times that people think I'm one of those retarded special kids in that Lil' yellow school bus."

"Do you really believe this is a school for the retarded, Eric?"

"Compared to the public schools? Yeah!"

"Well, can you pick out one retarded person here?"

"How 'bout three? Mick Maze, sadist. He's going to turn out to be a mass murderer. Tony Burns! Speech impediment, foul mouth. Farts loud in the middle of class. Has outbursts of verbal abuse toward his teachers."

"Tony has Tourette's syndrome." Declared Goldman.

"Tony is bullshitting! I know it! The other students in this school know it! Tony knows that we all know it!"

"Is that your professional opinion?" asked Goldman.

"That's my professional fact! He sells his prescription drugs for Tourette's to the neighborhood kids."

"Well, if you think he's bullshitting, why do you think he's retarded?"

"He just is!"

"Why do you think he's doing it?"

"For attention! He doesn't get it at home. And I know that's a fact! I spent time with him at his house. You want me to pick out another retard? How about Joey Pearlman? Fragile little mouse. Swaying back and forth in his chair all day. Scared of the world. chasing after helicopters. Our own Don Quixote! That ain't normal, Doc."

Goldman retreated, laying his pipe down on the desk. "Joey's autistic."

"Artistic?"

"No, autistic." Eric shrugged. Goldman continued. "Autism is a syndrome that was discovered in the 1940s. There isn't a single convincing theory of its cause, but some researchers feel that it might be biological rather than psychological. Some of the symptoms of autism are treating other people as inanimate objects. Another is something we call echolalia, which is when a person repeats a word or words that they have heard without any apparent reason or understanding of the meaning. Like a parakeet. Not speaking is another symptom of autism. Extremely passive behavior, or nervousness. Swaying in a chair or being unable to sit still for extended periods of time. Pacing."

"Wow! That describes every New Yorker I've ever met." Said Eric.

"I'm a New Yorker," Proclaimed Goldman. "And I don't have autism. But Joey Pearlman displays some of these behaviors. And he has inlets of competence where the average teenager lacks. Did you know that Joey understands and can explain mathematically a portion of Albert Einstein's theory of relativity and is presently working on a thesis paper? Do you know calculus?"

"No. I'm retarded.

"No. You're not retarded! Like you said, you're different. I don't know calculus myself. I have a hard time helping my kids with their third and fifth grade math homework. Am I retarded? No! We're all different. No matter what color school bus you rode here on, you're not retarded or dumb. You wouldn't be here if you were. That, I guarantee professionally. Your parents invested too much in you to be labeled retarded. And this school doesn't just deal with special needs. We have students here that can't cope in public schools. Like your friend Sam Harris and Mark Stern. There's nothing wrong with them. And there are others. But, like I said before, if we can't get you into college next year, and the public school doesn't work out, there's that last alternative of coming back to Webster." Goldman put the pipe back into his mouth.

"No way, man!" Retreated Eric. "Besides, my parents can no longer afford it here. My parents..." Eric repeated as the tears once again began to roll down his cheeks, "...are so beat, man." Eric began to hyperventilate as he cried.

Goldman picked up his pen to write but stopped short thinking it would be better just to sit back and observe Eric having his moment.

"Want a tissue?"

"No." Eric wiped his tears with his shirt collar. "I had a dream when I was in the hospital."

"Dream?"

"Yeah. I don't remember much. What I do remember was seeing my brother. No! It was more than just a dream. Do you believe in astro projection?"

"Its astral projection, and no."

"Whatever, same difference. Did you ever do any research on it?"

"Some. When I was attending graduate school. I haven't found any documented proof of its existence. What was your brother doing in the dream?" Goldman picked up his pen and resumed writing.

"He was telling me to go back to mom and dad."

"Go back?"

"Yeah."

"Have you been thinking about your brother lately, Eric?"

"More or less since we started our sessions. I was young when he died."

"How old were you?"

"Thirteen. We were five years apart."

"Do you know how he was killed?"

"Well, it was in Vietnam. But I don't know the details. I think it was by mortar fire. My mother is known to write excellent inquiring letters. She always gets a response from whomever she writes too. But out of the hundreds of detailed inquiry letters about my brother's death, my mother never received a satisfying reply from the military. They're not widely known for sharing information. Anyway, my parents constantly compare me to Elliot. I think that's why up to this point I was so callous about the subject. It wasn't until recently that I started asking questions about the war.

My father served in the big one. World War II—and fought with pride. Back then, there seemed to be a reason to fight. But this war in Southeast Asia, my father wasn't so gung-ho about. He was getting concerned because Elliot was approaching draft age. Well anyway, in '68, during the Democratic run for the presidential nominations, my father, who is a die-hard Democrat, wasn't too impressed with McCarthy or Vice President Humphrey who was openly advocating for the war. Then it was the Republican National convention in Miami. Nixon made his candidate acceptance speech for the presidency. And man, what a speech. Have you ever heard it?"

"No," replied Goldman abruptly stopped writing, not expecting a question, "not that I remember."

"Man, it was good." Continued Eric. "I watched it on television with my father. Nixon had perfect insight into what this country was going through internally and externally. He made mention of the fact that our country was being torn apart by a war that had gone on long enough. He talked about our college campuses turning into battlefronts of protest. Nixon said he had a secret plan to end the war in Vietnam. My father was impressed. So, on the first Tuesday of November 1968, for the first time in his unprofessional political career, my father forgave checkers' owner, and voted Republican. I would have voted for him if I were of age.

Well, Nixon won the presidency without my help, but the war raged on. My Brother was drafted and then killed in action just three weeks in country, and until this day the war continues to rage on. After his resignation my father heard Nixon in an interview stating that he never had a secret plan to end the war in Vietnam. He just needed the votes to be president. My father felt that political knife in his back twist up to his heart. The way my father figured, he voted for Nixon to have his eldest son killed."

"How did you find out that your brother was killed?"

Tears rolled down Eric's cheeks as he began to cry, fighting to get every word out."

It was a Sunday. We were having breakfast. My parents were eating whitefish. I hate whitefish. My parents would pick at it with those dead eyes looking up at you. The doorbell rang followed by a hammering knock. We jumped out of our skins. My father went to the door to see who it was. My mother and I stayed behind in the kitchen as My father let them in. There was some conversation then silence. My mother and I walked into the living room and there were two soldiers holding up my father. My father who was on bended knees clenching papers. My mother dropped to the floor and screamed. She knew.... She knew.

After my brother's funeral, my mother had a nervous breakdown, then was committed to the psychiatric ward at Jefferson Hospital. My father had a slight heart attack. And me? Witnessed it all! A Thirteen-year-old with no place to go, no place to hide. Soaked it all in until I couldn't take it anymore. Then I had my breakdown. Do you know who the real victims of this war are Doc? Not the dead soldiers. They are our heros. We are the victims of the Vietnam war. The living. Waiting forever for our brothers and sons to come home that never will."

Goldman not knowing what else to say, but to watch Eric have his moment as Eric continued to cry hysterically. Goldman took the pipe out of his mouth, his glasses off his nose and tossed them both down onto the desk as if the mask of psychology had been disrobed. And for the first time in his professional career, Dr. Goldman became unprofessional and human.

"Do you want a tissue?"

Eric wiped his nose and eyes with both arms. "No. I'll have a cigarette."

"I didn't think you smoked."

"I don't. But I feel like one now."

Goldman stared at Eric for a moment, then grinned as he reached into his breast pocket of his sport jacket to pull out a soft pack of Newport's. He tossed the pack and a Zippo lighter toward Eric on the desk.

"I didn't think you smoked cigarettes too," said Eric behind the tears.

"I smoke a pipe to relax. Cigarettes are a habit. Don't mention to the school I gave this to you."

Eric reached for both the pack of cigarettes and the lighter. "Your secret's good with me, as long as I don't get a subpoena."

CHAPTER 7

CIRCUS BOY

IT WAS ABOUT ten-forty-five P.M. Friday night when Eric parked his car at the Spectrum's parking lot between the Spectrum and Veteran Stadium. The lot was mostly empty since the basketball fans had already vacated. Eric approached the employee entrance and was stopped by a different uniformed guard. Eric explained to the guard that this was his first night on the job. The guard let him pass.

At the entrance to Ted's office, Eric knocked on the open steel door. Ted was reading another memo from behind his industrial desk. "Eric Blum?" asked Ted, dropping the memo, and looking up at him.

"Yes."

"Did you bring your application?"

"Yes, sir." Eric pulled the folded application from his back pocket and dropped it on Ted's desk. "Both sides filled out, sir."

Ted picked up the application and skimmed through it front to back, then dropped it back down onto his desk. From one of his desk drawers, Ted snatched a red T-shirt with 'Spectrum' printed in white on the front.

"Here's your shirt. Five dollars will cover it." Eric handed Ted a five-dollar bill from his wallet. Ted handed Eric the shirt. "Take good care of it. That's your identification to get into the building. If you decide to leave us, give us back the shirt and we'll refund your money. I'll start you off at two dollars and fifty cents an hour. We have a stage union here. Local 104." Ted frowned. "The union will take five percent for dues. If you do what you're told, keep your mouth shut, we'll get along just fine." Ted took a contract out from his desk drawer. "Please sign this agreement with the union so I can send you out to work." Ted sounded a bit disgruntled.

Eric signed without reading, then stared at Ted as Ted went back to read his memo. Ted slowly looked up to find Eric still standing before him.

"That's it! You can get to work now!"

"Thank you, sir!" Said Eric with a broad smile as he darted out from the office.

In the arena as the basketball court was being disassembled by the house change-over crew, all other technicians were coiling, folding, or wrapping up their equipment. Eric slipped the Spectrum T-shirt over his shirt as he walked around the arena floor. Since he didn't know where to start or what to do wanting to lend a hand to anyone who he thought might need his unprofessional service. Bright floodlights caught Eric's eyes as he found himself looking up at the second level press super-box. Al Meltzer, the local NBC sports commentator, was finishing a live report on television about the evening's game. Eric glanced at the small monitor beside Al Meltzer and could barely make out the local TV news anchorwoman, Jessica Savage who was sitting next to her co-anchor, Mort Crim back at the local NBC studio.

"Thank you, Big Al," acknowledged Jessica Savage from the monitor.

"Coming up next, weekend weather with Bill Custer..." Continue Mort Crim.

Eric looked down onto the arena floor and saw a young black man unscrewing screws from the basketball court floor with a hard wire electric drill. The extension cord reached across the arena.

"Can I help you?" Eric asked.

"Oh, sure," the man replied. Eric picked up the screws the man left behind. "You're new here, aren't you?"

"Yeah, I just started tonight. My name is Eric Blum."

The man put down the drill to shake Eric's hand. "I'm Mike." Eric caught himself off balance and dropped a couple of the screws as he shook Mike's hand.

"How long will the change-over take place?" asked Eric as he clumsily picked up the fallen screws that were still tumbling out of his palms like a waterfall.

"Well, we're changing over from basketball to hockey. At least six hours."

After the basketball court was disassembled into four by eight feet boards and stacked onto several dollies, a forklift came to pick up the stacks to be stored in the maintenance tunnel. Eric followed Mike to the west end to join the rest of the change-over crew which consisted of about thirty-five young, and a couple of middle-aged men.

"Where's the ice?" Asked Eric.

"Under these insulation boards that we're standing on." Said Mike.

At that moment all the workers on the west end of the arena laughed and pointed toward the east end at Mario the ice crew chief walking across the arena floor carrying a five-pound rubber mallet which happened to be his trademark. Mario managed the changeover from basketball to hockey. He was a short five-foot-four pudgy Italian man in his mid-thirties with a high-pitched thick South Philly-accent, sporting a thick cheesy mustache. All that was missing was a sombrero, and Mario would be the spitting image of Frito Bandito.

"Okay, let's get to work!" Mario screeched out.

The changeover crew mocked him as they usually did by repeating Mario's words with his accent. "I'll punch your timecards out!" Mario threatened as he continued to wave his mallet overhead. The more furious Mario became, the louder the crew laughed. "You want to see me punch you guys out? I'll punch your timecards out! I don't need this shit tonight. I want to get outta of here!"

A forklift pulled up carrying one of the empty insulation floor dollies and dropped it off by the crew. Then drove back into the maintenance tunnel to pick up another empty dolly. An older worker took an ice chopper and wedged it between one of the four-by-eight-foot sections of Styrofoam insulated plywood boards, then pried it. Two more workers picked up the board and carried it off to the awaiting dolly.

After about eighteen to twenty boards were piled, the forklift picked up the dolly with the insolation boards and took it back to a holding area in the maintenance tunnel by the disassembled and stacked basketball court.

One of the workers slipped and fell on the uncovered ice as he picked up the end of the board. As the crew laughed, a couple of co-workers lifted the board off his legs. The man shuffled up from the ice and continued to work unharmed and embarrassed.

Even though it got cooler as more ice was being unveiled, workers were sweating from work, and some took off their Spectrum shirts.

"Put your shirts back on!" Mario yelled out, "who told you to take off your shirt! Who? Who was it?"

Grunting, workers regretfully replaced their shirts. To Eric it reminded him of a scene from the movie Mr. Roberts.

The digital clocks on the second level at the north and south end read twelve-thirty A.M. Eric followed Mike toward the south stands where the two boys sat on a couple of red seats for their fifteen-minute break. Mike offered Eric a cigarette. Eric accepted it.

After the break, the Spectrum change-over crew had a difficult time sliding the slightly oversized hockey dashers into their slots forcing them in by using the steel tempered safety glass post as hammers.

Not all professional hockey rinks are the same size-give an inch or two. The Spectrum hockey rink dashers were meant for the New York

Madison Square Garden being built at the same time in 1967. But the Spectrum's construction was completed first and did not have their dashers. The Spectrum took Madison Square Garden's. The dents on the top reeling of the dashers were not from the embattling hockey pucks, but from the changeover crew hammering them into place.

At four-forty A.M. when the ice was uncovered. The Zamboni came out from the maintenance tunnel to sweep a new clean surface. Some of the workers stayed to play ice soccer using a folded Dixie cup as a ball.

"Where do you live?" asked Eric.

"Olney," replied Mike.

"Mt. Airy. Need a lift?"

"Sure."

The Chevy traveled west on the Philadelphia Expressway when Eric initiated a conversation.

"That Spectrum is an amazing place, and that Mario is strange."

"Do you know what he does during the day?" asked Mike.

"No, what?"

"He's a tailor."

"A tailor?" Eric responded with a laugh.

"He's supposed to be one of the best in South Philly."

"Well, why is he working at the Spectrum?"

"Nobody asks Mario why or what he does. Nobody!"

"You know," said Eric. "Every time Ted mentioned the union, he looked uncomfortable."

"Oh, yeah. The Bellies give him a hard time."

"Bellies? What are Bellies?"

"Bellies is another name for a union member."

"Why Bellies?"

"Have you ever noticed that most union workers have beer guts? Do you know how you can spot a hard-core union worker on a job site?"

"No, how?" asked Eric.

"Well, he's the one guy smoking a cigarette while hammering a piece of wood with his right hand, as he holds a belly bagel and a cup of coffee in his left, coughing his brains out without the cigarette leaving his lips or spilling a drop of coffee."

"Belly bagel?"

"Donuts. A couple of years ago, we had this union steward named Bill. A real nice guy. Bill took care of everybody. Kept management at bay. One night we were building a wrestling ring for Gorilla Monsoon. Even though he was still standing, Bill looked as though he had fallen asleep, which isn't unusual since Bill was also a member of the Teamsters. And you know why the horse is the symbol for the Teamsters, don't you?"

"No. Why?" asked Eric.

"Because the horse is an animal that can also sleep standing up. Anyway, it wasn't until Bill's son-Josh-picked up the belly bagel, is when we learned of Bill's death-by heart attack."

"Bill died Standing?"

"I told you; the Teamster's symbol is a horse."

"Bill's son works with us?" Asked Eric.

"Well, he did. Not anymore. We voted Josh in, and he tried to fill his father's shoes. Did a good job. He would just stand around and watch everybody work. Josh wouldn't play ball with management. So, behind closed doors due to the pressure of management, in a secret meeting by the order of the hall without ratification, they replaced Josh with these two jerks we have now."

"Jerks?"

"A steward and his assistant. Management lays down rules without our consent and the union has us sign contracts without letting us ratify or vote on them. We have this suspicion that the union is in partnership and gets kickbacks from management. Somehow, it ends up with -us-, the workers, having to pay higher dues with no representation. A word of advice. You can ask anything you want about the Spectrum, but don't go around asking any questions about the union. It's something you'll have to witness for yourself."

....

The next morning, the phone in Eric's bedroom rang while Eric was still lying in bed physically exhausted trying to recover from work just a few hours before. He stretched over to reach for the receiver on his night table. It was Renée.

"What did you do last night?"

"Hi Renée. I can hardly move. We changed from basketball to hockey within six hours."

"What time do you have to be in tonight?"

"Eleven." Eric yawned at the telephone. "What do you want to do tonight?"

"What can we do? That doesn't give us much time," Renée said with disappointment. "We can go to Neshaminy Mall. Pick me up at 7:30."

That night at the Spectrum, the crew started out by mocking Mario for a few moments then went back to work covering the ice with the insulated four-by-eight-foot insulated boards. During a fifteen-minute break, Mike and Eric sat on the south side first level bleachers. Mike brought out a joint and presented it to Eric.

"You want?" asked Mike.

Eric stared at the joint for a moment and took a swift glance around the arena to see if anybody witnessed.

"It isn't Cambodian Red, is it?"

"No," said Mike. "I wish it was."

"Sure. I'll take a hit."

Mike and Eric walked under the bleachers to light up.

As the two boys shared the joint, a five-pound rubber mallet came poking through a row of red folding bleacher seats, followed by Mario's head.

"Ahhh!" said Mario, with a broad smile. "I see ya! I see ya smoking that joint!"

Mike laughed into Mario's face. "Want some?"

"Nope!" said Mario. "I don't do that shit!"

Mike and Eric laughed as Mario's mallet and head disappeared from between the seats.

"Do you think he'll squeal?" asked Eric.

"No. I don't think so. He doesn't care."

"Who's playing here tomorrow?" Eric asked as he inhaled the joint.

"Led Zeppelin".

....

The following night, Eric went to work three hours earlier to catch the British rock n' roll band, Led Zeppelin. He was not a Led Zeppelin fan, but he thought he would take advantage since every student at Webster wished they could be in his shoes at that moment.

Eric walked down the maintenance tunnel toward the arena. The backstage sounds, sights and the excitement of the show filled the atmosphere. A long line formed outside the backstage men's bathroom. Tony -one of the changeover crew- was in front of the line.

"Tony, what's going on?" asked Eric.

"Some girl is giving head in the men's room. You want to butt in?

"No, I don't think so," Eric replied amused.

Ted walked by and noticed the two boys. "Tony, Eric! Get back to the work area!"

"Aw, c'mon, Ted! I waited about a half hour in line for this moment! I'm next!" cried Tony.

Ted refused to give-in, and the boys headed back to their work area.

In the arena the house lights went out as cameras from the audience flashed from every direction. The stage was dimly lit in amber light flooded with haze from the foggers. The impatient audience began to chant for the show to begin. From behind the stage the band Led Zeppelin walked past Eric.

"Ladies and gentlemen!" said the British announcer from an out of sight location, "Welcome to the Philadelphia Spectrum, the entertainment capital of the world! Now let's give a warm Philadelphia welcome to the British rock n' roll band, Led Zeppelin!"

The audience cheered wildly as the band walked to their positions on stage. The bands' name was light up with light bulbs in huge letters up stage hanging from the trusses. The band started with their first song, Rock n' Roll.

Behind the stage, Eric watched the Road crew at work for a few minutes then walked out into the arena to catch the show. The music was so loud from the eight-to-ten feet stacked speakers on stage plus the multitude of speakers hanging from the trusses, Eric's ears were ringing. He grabbed an empty seat next to a pretty girl on the first level down stage right. The girl was sitting up in her chair as still as a statue staring at the stage. Her eyes were deep and dark as though in a trance. Eric was infatuated with her.

"Pretty loud concert, hey?" Eric yelled toward her.

The girl continued to stare at the stage without a hint of movement, emotion or even realizing Eric's existence. "Are you okay? Are you alright?" Eric touched her shoulder. The girl slid off her chair as she threw up onto the steel bleacher where she laid in her own puke between two rows of seats. The people in the next row down were drenched in the girl's vomit. Eric covered his own mouth to keep from gagging at the sight. He jumped out of his seat and ran backstage where it was safe and appeared somewhat sane. Mike had just arrived at work and passed Eric in the tunnel.

"Are you okay, Eric?"

"Yeah," he said, walking toward Ted's office.

"Are you sure?"

"I said I'm okay!" Eric yelled back. Mike watched him walk off not wanting to pursue the matter any further.

Eric ended up sitting on the floor across from Ted's office smoking a cigarette, trying to keep himself together as the Roadies, techs, and groupies walked by.

After the concert, as the Roadies packed their gear into several semi-tractor trailers, some of the changeover crew began working on disassembling the wooden stage. The stage itself was covered with debris of girls' undergarments and other small deplorable objects. Three security guards were prying out a body from inside one of the stacked speakers on stage. Two Spectrum ushers were dowsing out a seat fire up on the third level.

On the floor, Mike and Eric leaped over bodies, spilled sticky beverages, spent needles, and picking up small joints-aka roaches-, hopping around droplets of blood, vomit, and other unidentifiable liquids to get to the west end of the arena to meet up with the crew to lay the 76ers basketball court.

••••••••••••••••••••••

That Monday morning, at Webster standing behind her desk Carol prepared her lesson plan before class started. In the back of the room, Eric was hunched over with his head on his desktop. He was exhausted from working just a few hours before. Mark Stern was reading another one of his Playboy magazines as the rest of the class looked on to inspect Miss January 1975 -Lynnda Kimbal-. Renée walked into the classroom and asked if she could sit in.

"Whose class are you supposed to be in?" Carol asked.

"Science. But Biff isn't here today."

"Yeah, sure." Carol said as she waved her in.

Renée took the empty seat between Joey Pearlman and Eric. Joey gave Renée a seductive smile as he continued to sway at his desk. Renée showed him an unassuming frown sliding her chair closer toward Eric.

"How was your night?" Renée asked sardonically.

Eric raised his head. "It was okay. Why are you asking me?"

"It seems that we don't have any time for each other."

"Well, Renée, you also know why I'm doing this. I have to prove to the school that I can do it."

"Look, if you want to prove to the school that you're normal, get a normal job." she said.

Students, including Carol, jumped with the sound of Eric's single pounding of his fist onto his desktop. "Well, damn it, Renée! I don't know how to please you!" Eric continued more softly. "I don't need this from you!"

"Well, I like to go out with my boyfriend on the weekends after a long week at school."

"Well then, find another boyfriend!" Eric laid his head back on top of his desk.

Renée paused for a moment stunned that Eric suggested a break-up.

"There's a party over at one of my girlfriend's house this Friday night." Renée announced.

"Okay. But you know I have to leave early for work."

That Friday night, Eric found himself in the basement of a house somewhere in the great northeast section of the city. As the disco beat of 1974–75 rung throughout from a record player, Eric stood at one end of the den conversing with some of the boys. Between points of non-interest, he glanced over to watch Renée who was sitting on the sofa with an ex-boyfriend laughing and having a wonderful time.

A couple of hours later backstage at the Spectrum, the crowd could still be heard chanting from the arena as Eric walked through the tunnel heading toward the stage. He was pushed aside by hoard of groupies and handlers rushing by with a British rock n' roller who just finished his act and was heading toward his dressing room. He had long wavy blonde hair and was thin as a rail. A reporter asked the rock star as they walked on when the world would hear his next album.

"I'm working on my next album now," said the rock star. "It's going to be a live solo album. I plan to release it early next year."

"Pete Frampton! Solo album, live!" Eric mumbled to himself as he walked toward the stage. "Nah, this cat will never make it."

....

Mid-morning at Webster, Eric caught up with Renée on the first-floor hallway. "Where were you last night?" he asked. "I called your house, and your mother told me that you were out all evening."

"I was with a friend," Renée replied, standoffish and cold.

"Your old boyfriend from the party?" Eric didn't have to ask. He knew the answer.

Renée was silent at first as she bit her lower lip. "Yeah. He drove me home from the party Friday night."

Eric paused to think. "So, now what?"

"I don't know, Eric. I mean, he has much more time for me than you do. And I think I remember you telling me to find another boyfriend."

"Well, I have a purpose." Renée joined in on Eric's next line. "I want to get out of here."

"Well, I do, Renée! Don't you?"

"I'm not going to kill myself in the process!"

"What do you mean? Who's killing who? What are you talking about?"

"You, Eric! I'm talking about you! Look at you! You're tired…you come home late from work. You fall asleep in class. Eric, why do you want to get out of here so quickly? Is it that bad here?" She points toward the hall-way window by Joey Pearlman who is swaying looking out. "It's crazy out there, Eric. That's where it's nuts! Unlike you, I'm not in such a hurry to jump back in!"

"If I can get out of work this weekend, will I see you?" Eric asked calmly.

Renée paused for a moment. "I don't know. Will you?"

She broke away from his clenches and walked down the hallway. A helicopter flew over, and Joey Pearlman was getting excited.

"Joey! Cut it out!" said Eric as he walked past.

Eric couldn't get out of work Friday or Saturday night, which brought his relationship with Renée to the breaking point.

....

At the Spectrum, Eric was watching the roadies behind the stage as the British rock n' roll group Mott the Hoople performed. In an instant, the sound went down. The audience began to chant for the show to continue. The sound tech was trying to figure out the problem with the equipment. Lead singer Ian Hunter stomped off the stage. From behind the stage Eric watched as Ian confronted the sound tech.

"What in bloody hell is going on?" Hunter yelled out.

"I don't know yet!" replied the tech.

"Well, you better bloody well know, or you're fuck'en fired! Do you hear me? You're fuck'en fired!"

Within a couple of minutes, the sound came back. Guitars, feed-back, and a few drum rolls were heard through the ten-foot-high stacked speakers on stage. The audience ceased chanting and continued with a high pitch of whistles and screams, holding up lit matches and lighters.

"All right! We're back! We had some technical difficulties," Hunter announced from behind the stand-up microphone down center stage.

The band played the introduction to "All the Young Dudes" and the concert continued without a hitch.

Within the week at the Spectrum, Eric sat beside Mike on stage right with their legs dangling over the second level watching Linda Ronstadt on stage. Eric noticed that the audience for Linda Ronstadt was different than the audiences of Mott the Hoople or Led Zeppelin. These people were older and more mature. They listened intently to the lyrics and less than a handful of people were smoking pot. Along with the rest of the audience, Eric was entranced by the slow, smooth, hypnotic tune 'Long, Long Time'. Before the concert ended, Eric and Mike rushed down behind the stage to meet the star. She was polite, and sweet and she thanked the stagehands and handlers who assisted and escorted her off the stage.

It was about one in the morning when the stage was struck down and tucked away in the tunnel. On the way home even though it was out of the way, Eric decided to take a ride by Renée house. But this would just be a drive-by.

It was unusual weather for this time of year. It had been raining and sleet was accompanied by lighting. The Roads were slick. In the northeast section of the city, Eric drove pass the Sears department store on Roosevelt Boulevard by Robbins Avenue close to the spot where Alice Cappadonna had been killed. The clock on the Sears tower was reading one-thirty A.M.

By the time Eric arrived at Renée's house the rain had subsided. He parked on the street. An unfamiliar car was parked in the driveway behind Renée's parents' car. Eric slid out of his car, and quietly climbed the damp cement steps that lead to Renée's front door. A dim light was shining through the translucent curtain hanging over the living room window. Eric peeked through the sheer white valance hanging against the front door window and could scarcely make out the image of Renée in the arms of her old boyfriend on the living room couch.

Eric slowly and solemnly sat down on the top cold damp cement step. He pulled out a hard pack of cigarettes and Zippo lighter from his coat pocket to light up. Taking a long draw, replacing the hard pack and the lighter in his coat pocket as he reflected about what went wrong with their relationship, or how he should have handled things differently. Eric didn't think he had strong feelings toward Renée. It was more a realization of not wanting to be alone. Lightning filled the sky. A couple of raindrops began to fall. Eric stood up, walked back to the Chevy, and turned on the ignition, then drove off Renée's dark, cold and wet deserted street.

On his way home through the suburban town of Willow Grove, eight miles northwest outside of Philadelphia, Eric was driving south on

Route 611 at least ten miles an hour faster than the recommended speed limit for road conditions. The roads were slick. The air was misty. He could hardly make out the white painted divided lines on the wet asphalt. But by riding and driving on this highway so many times within the last few years, he knew every curve by heart. Eric's mind was sidetracked by the sight of Renée in the arms of another. The Road took a sharp bend toward the left that Eric caught with the corner of his eye. His heart skipped a beat when he tried to miss the center concrete median strip as he applied the brake pedal. He was lucky there was nobody following behind. The Chevy fishtailed toward a patch of black ice, up onto the sidewalk and sideswiped a traffic signal timing box. The silver colored seven-foot-tall by four-foot-wide metal box jolted from its foundation damaging the right front fender of the old Chevy. Eric tried to control the car, but the car seemed to have another destination at hand. Fruitlessly stepping harder on the brake pedal, the car crashed square through the closed wooden main gate of the Willow Grove Naval Air Station and stopped dead just a few yards past the guardhouse. Eric opened his eyes to the sounds of running footsteps and guns being cocked. A military marine policeman knocked on the driver's side window with the butt end of his revolver. Eric slowly and carefully rolled down his window.

"Are you okay?" the marine asked.

"Yes, sir. I think I am," Eric answered with his heart racing.

"Would you please turn off the engine and slowly get out of the vehicle, sir."

"Yes," replied Eric, without taking his eyes off the two military policemen in front of the car with their drawn weapons. Eric took the key out of the ignition and cautiously opened his car door.

"Will you please step away from the vehicle and show identification for you and the vehicle, sir?"

With his right hand up in the air for submission, Eric carefully took his wallet out from his back pocket with his left. There were two more

MPs with cocked guns positioned in the back of the car and another armed MP on the right passenger side.

"I have to get back into my glove compartment to retrieve the car registration," Eric said, presenting his license and holding both hands up hoping to alleviate the tension with the MPs.

"Okay," acknowledged the MP. "But do it cautiously and wisely. These boys will not give you a second chance."

Without blinking, Eric glanced at all five-armed MPs that surrounded the car as he slowly and mechanically slid back into the passenger's side to open the glove compartment. Sliding slowly and mechanically out, he presented all the information to the lead MP.

"I had a draft card," Eric volunteered. "But somebody else burned it. I swear, it's the truth!"

The MP acknowledged that this was a civilian accident. Within minutes two Upper Moreland Township police cruisers with their lights flashing showed up.

An Upper Moreland police chief wearing a heavy jacket and a Smokey the Bear hat walked toward Eric by the Chevy. Three policemen behind the chief searched through the Chevy for contraband. Eric surrendered his identification to the officer.

"Have you been drinking?" asked the Upper Moreland police chief as he looked over Eric's license and registration with a long thin black flashlight. The beam bounced from the chief's hand holding Eric's identification to Eric's chest.

"No, sir," Eric said. "I just didn't see the road or the divided lines because of the ice."

"Do you travel this road often?"

"Yeah. Well, I'm familiar with the road but…"

"… Okay. We're going to have to fill out an accident report," the police chief said abruptly. Eric followed the chief back toward his patrol car. The chief pulled out a briefcase from the front seat and laid it on the hood of his cruiser. From inside the briefcase, he took out a couple of forms and began to write. "Do you have any insurance?"

"Yes. I'm under my parents' plan. State Farm."

"Was there anybody else in the vehicle with you at the time of the accident?"

"No."

"Where were you coming from?" The police chief's personality was as bland as melba toast.

"I was coming from work, sir."

"Where do you work?"

"The Philadelphia Spectrum."

The police chief stopped writing. "Looking at your address, that's in the opposite direction."

"Well, I went to visit a girlfriend on my way home."

"Where does she live?"

"Greater Northeast Philly."

"That still doesn't explain what you are doing out here."

"Well, I take the back roads to get home, which borders the suburbs."

Noticing Eric was still jolted from the accident, the chief figured a more human approach would calm him down. "So, you work at the Spectrum?"

"Yes, sir."

It didn't work. Eric was too worried about what his mother was going to say about all this.

"What do you do there?"

"I'm on the changeover crew. I make ice, build stages…"

"Have you ever met Bernie Parent or Dave Schultz?" asked the police chief.

"Yes. Several times."

A police officer walked behind the chief and handed him a slip of paper. "He seems to check out okay," said the police officer. "No prior violations. The head MP would like to speak to you."

"Okay," said the chief. Then he turned toward Eric. "I'll be right back. I'm going to talk to the MP. Don't move!"

"Can I have a cigarette?"

"Yeah. Need a light?"

"No."

As he slid the cigarette pack and the zippo lighter out from his jacket pocket, Eric watched the Upper Moreland police chief walk toward the MP in front of the Chevy. The MP showed the chief measurements related to the car and where it left debris and skid marks. Both the chief and the MP looked toward Eric and shook their heads. Eric was curious as to what was being said. It didn't look good. As he continued to shake his head the chief walked back to Eric.

"Okay, Mr. Blum. Apparently by the skid marks, and the debris you left behind, you were traveling way over the legal speed limit. But since this was your first reported accident and you have no prior violations, and because of the road conditions, I'm going to give you a break. I'm not going to give you a ticket for reckless driving."

"Thank you." Eric was relieved to hear that.

"But I'm going to give you a ticket for speeding. Montgomery county and the federal government will get in touch with your insurance company about the damage. It could have been a lot worse. Hopefully in the future you'll drive more cautiously, especially in poor weather conditions. Do you think you can drive your vehicle home?"

"I don't know. I don't trust it. Can I pick it up in the morning?"

"Yeah. We'll have it towed to the nearest gas station in Abington. There will be a fifteen-dollar-a-day storage fee."

"I need a lift back to Philly. What bus could I get from here?"

"The buses to Philly stopped running at twelve-fifteen. How 'bout your parents?"

"Well, no. Believe it or not. I'm the only one in the family who drives, and here's the car."

"I could give you a lift to the county line. It's just five miles south of here."

"Yeah. That's better than nothing."

Eric took the ride to the border of Willow Grove and Abington Township. Regretfully, the officer couldn't cross township lines. The police chief stopped Eric before Eric had a chance to completely step out of the patrol car and asked,

"Are you sure there isn't anybody you can call? It's about another five-mile walk to Philadelphia."

"No. I'm afraid there isn't. Thanks." Before Eric closed the car door, the police chief called him back.

"Oh, Mr. Blum!"

Eric knew he was in trouble now. The police always do that. He had seen it a thousand times on that detective television show Columbo starring Peter Faulk. The police let you off the hook, then they call you back for that one-more-question that lands you in jail.

"After all that happened to you tonight," continued the police chief, "you should consider yourself very fortunate."

"Fortunate, sir?"

"Well, according to that MP, if your vehicle would have slid another six inches into that naval base, those jar heads had orders to open fire."

"Oh great! That's all I need. If my mother found out I was shot, she kill me!"

The rain began to trickle down as the police car spun back in the direction of Willow Grove. Eric was alone at the boarder of Abington Township southbound on Route 611. He spotted a phone booth by what appeared to be a desolate intersection and called Carol, but her phone kept ringing. She was spending the night at Warren's apartment. Many times, Carol had given Eric Warren's phone number, but Eric was too jealous to keep it or even memorize it. With no way out of this situation, it was time to face reality.

"Hello, mom?"

"Where was the accident, Eric?"

How did she know? Eric had always thought his mother had ESP. "Mom, it wasn't a big accident."

"Yes, it was, Eric. It was a big accident! What are you trying to do, kill yourself?" his mother yelled. "If that car is totaled, I'm going to kill you!"

"Mom, let me talk to dad, please."

"It's your son!" Mrs. Blum said as she handed Mr. Blum the phone. "Talk to him about these suicidal tendencies."

"Are you okay, Eric?"

"Thanks, dad. I didn't think anybody really cared about me. I'm all right."

"What happened?"

"I'll explain when I get home."

"Can you drive the car?"

"I don't know, dad. I really don't trust it. The right fender is rubbing against the tire."

"How are you getting home?"

"I don't want him running home!" Mrs. Blum called out from in the background.

Eric could never figure out how his mother knew what he was planning. "I was thinking about running home."

"Your mother doesn't want you to."

"You think I should call Opie?" Eric asked.

"Well, I think Opie's in enough trouble." Replied Mr. Blum.

"What did he do now?"

"He's being punished for breaking a window at Central High School."

Eric suppressed his laughter. "Dad, I have no other alternative. I'll be home within two hours."

"Have him call Carol Schor!" Mrs. Blum yelled out.

"I did, dad. She's not home."

"All right, Eric. Be careful."

"Thanks dad, for caring."

It took Eric more than two hours to reach the front door of his house. His parents lounged on the worn green sofa in the gloomy, dimly lit living room as they did when they waited for him to come home late from Alice's house last October.

"What is the matter with you? Are you trying to kill yourself?" asked Mrs. Blum.

"No, mom," Eric replied sitting in one of the unmatched living room chairs gazing down at the floor across from his parents.

"Well, there's got to be something wrong."

"No mom, there's nothing wrong. I just had a car accident."

"Was anybody with you?" Mr. Blum asked in his quiet tone.

"No. I was coming home from Renée's house through Willow Grove. I couldn't see the median strip because the road was wet. So, I plowed through a traffic light signal timing box, and skidded through the main gate of the Willow Grove Naval Air Station."

"What were you doing at Renée's house at this hour at night? Weren't you at work?" asked Mrs. Blum.

"I went after work to see if she was still awake."

"Well, was she?" asked Mrs. Blum.

"No." Replied Eric.

"What was the damage to the car?" asked Mr. Blum.

"Like I told you, I just bent in the right front fender. I really couldn't see if there was any other damage. I had the police tow it to a gas station in Abington. There's a fifteen-dollar-a-day storage fee. I also got a ticket for speeding. I'll pay for it myself."

"Are you going to also help pay for the higher premium on the insurance?" Mrs. Blum inquired. "You better talk to Dr. Goldman about these suicidal tendencies."

Eric just rolled his eyes. Any Jewish boy will tell you, there is no use in reasoning with an unreasonable Jewish mother,

The next morning, Eric took the public bus to Abington Township to retrieve the car from the gas station. He paid the overnight storage fee, then inspected the damage. It wasn't as bad as he thought. The car was about ten years old and almost completely made of metal. It took the impact well. The front hood was slightly dented and scratched. Eric borrowed a crowbar from the mechanic to pull the right front fender out against the tire.

. . . .

That night at the Spectrum, Eric was called into Ted's office before he had a chance to walk out onto the arena. An agreement from the stage union sat on top of Ted's desk. Ted sat behind it with a grim look on his face.

"Sign this, or you won't be able to work here anymore."

Eric picked up the pen and proceeded to read the agreement that was previously signed by other workers.

"What's this? Why is the union agreeing with this, to take away our hourly minimum and just work on straight time?" Eric continued reading on, then looked up at Ted. "They're raising our dues to eight percent hourly. They want us to add in fifteen percent yearly quarter for our insurance premiums. What happened to the insurance cap? Where is that money?"

"Please sign," Ted ordered in an agitated tone.

"I'm not familiar with union business, but doesn't the body have a vote on this ratification before we sign? I don't remember voting for this agreement. Where's the representation?"

"Eric, I don't want to tell you again! Either you sign, or you're out of here!" Eric reluctantly signed.

In the arena new ice was being applied. Five members of the changeover crew including Eric watched from the bleachers as a water truck sprayed steamed water onto the bare cement floor.

Incorporated into the cement floor were copper pipes with chilled water. After one layer of spray at $1/32^{nd}$ of an inch, the water was left to freeze to eventually fill the rink. The second layer at $1/32^{nd}$ was painted in paintec white. A third layer of water at $1/16^{th}$ sealed the bottom layers. Then the Flyers logos were applied with stencil.

The final eight layers of $1/32^{nd}$ evenly sprayed end to end made the hockey rink over one-inch-thick of ice. Ted walked into the arena and over to Eric on the bleachers.

"Eric! I need a couple of favors! First, I need you to be on the ice crew during the next hockey game."

"Ice crew?" Enquired Eric.

"Yeah! That's when you and two other workers come out between quarters with the Zamboni to clean off the ice. All you have to do is straighten out the goals. You'll be out of here by ten. It's an honor to be on the ice crew! Also, the circus is coming to town. I need somebody with me as a liaison to help the circus people around the arena. You interested?

"Yeah! can I invite a few people to the circus?"

"Sure! Just let me know how many, and I'll get you tickets." With these little perks, Ted assumed Eric wouldn't be a challenge for the Bellies.

Four nights later at the Spectrum, a Philadelphia Flyer and a Canadian Toronto Maple Leaf danced together into the dashers and shared their faces against the safety glass as they beat the living hell out of each other with glove and fist. The referee skated over to pull them apart.

"Come on Schulz! Break it up. Break it up Schulz!"

As the two players skated off, blood was left smeared on the safety glass.

On the east end of the arena, Eric and two other workers lined up at the opening of the maintenance tunnel behind the Zamboni. When the quarter time buzzer sounded, both teams skated to their appropriate side benches.

The Zamboni headed out onto the ice from the tunnel. Eric and the two workers stayed close behind trying to keep their balance as they slid across the rink in their sneakers. Eric was a bit of stage fright in front of a near sell-out crowd of 17,000 people. Overly cautious, Eric slid by a tooth and droplets of blood that had splattered on the ice from the players who had been ice dancing. Once the west side goals were straightened out, the ice crew slid back over toward the east end. Eric slipped and fell. His sneakers refused to dig into the solid glass-like ice. It was embarrassing at first when he resembled a newborn fawn trying to get onto its feet for the very first time. With the help from his two co-workers, Eric carefully got back up to his feet, but his two co-workers had fallen. Laughter and jeers from the fans would have made the Three Stooges proud. The fans gave them a standing ovation when the three boys got up and slid back to the maintenance tunnel. Thank Goodness there was a commercial and the event was not telecast.

The following week, the Ringling Brothers and Barnum & Bailey circus took center ring at the Spectrum. At the entrance of the maintenance tunnel, Eric stood proudly where he could be seen wearing his red Spectrum T-shirt in front of his parents, some friends from school, and Cousin Opie with his new girlfriend. Eric had got them all third row up from center ring.

As the conclave of the animals encircled the arena, Ted approached Eric with a shovel, a broom and a thirty-gallon plastic Hefty trash bag.

"So, what's up?" Eric asked with a frozen smile.

"Eric, I have a very important assignment for you. You're going to have to walk behind the last elephant as it travels around the ring. Try to shovel all the shit that falls as fast as possible before it hits the floor, and into the plastic bag. You can't let any of the shit drip through the insulated floorboards under the sawdust. The heat will melt the Flyers ice."

Eric stared at Ted for a moment. "So, what's up?" he asked again, still wearing that frozen grin.

"Last year, we had these brown holes that had to be filled-in and repainted." continued Ted. "We don't have time to do that this year with the Flyers' in play-offs."

"You're kidding of course," Eric asked with a laugh in his voice.

"I wish I was."

Eric grabbed Ted by the shoulders and turned him in toward the tunnel out of view to talk in private.

"Ted," Eric pleaded in a very serious tone. "I have friends and family out there in the stands. I can't be seen walking behind elephant's ass shoveling shit."

"I understand, Eric. But you're the only one from the Spectrum I have here. The circus employees won't do the job fast enough from keeping the shit from dripping onto the ice."

"Now look, Ted, you said you needed me to help chaperone the circus people around the arena. And I did that. And right now, I'm willing to walk into that tiger cage without a chair or a whip and repaint its stripes. I'll let the snake lady French kiss me. I'll have the clowns run me over in their little car. And I'll even get the fat lady to sit on my face. All this in the center ring! But no way will you get me to walk behind the elephant's ass, picking up shit in front of my friends and family!"

"Somebody's got to do it, Eric. And it ain't going be me, cause I'm the boss!" Ted encountered sternly.

"Ted, I beg you, please do not make me go out there and do this. I'm begging you!"

"I can't get anybody else right now!"

"I understand that, Ted. But please!" By this time Eric was hanging onto Ted's shirt collar bended knee with his head navel-level pleading. "Ted, I'm begging you!"

"So, it's notoriety you're afraid of. Well, I may have a partial solution to that problem."

"What is it?"

"We can put you in costume."

"What type of costume?" asked Eric as he got off his knees.

"Clown."

"Okay. If I must do this, clown will work. But you said that was a partial solution."

"Well, we don't have time to put you under make-up. So, you'll have to go out there wearing a clown suit bare faced."

"What good will that do me?" Eric cried.

Eric never felt so humiliated in his entire life walking out in public dressed as a clown with oversized floppy shoes, baggy black and yellow pooka-dot pants, and a ruffled shirt, topped off with a dunce cap without make-up or a red nose.

As the last elephant walked out from the tunnel with its beautifully dressed female rider, a thought occurred to Eric, "Karma! Who in hell did I fuck over to deserves such a fate?" Eric strolled close behind picking up the animal's droppings to avoid the 'China Syndrome' of poop. He tried to hide his head amid the collar of the puffy clown shirt, but it did not alleviate his insecurity.

Not even a quarter of the way around the ring, out of all the gleeful screams of cheering children with their guardians who were pointing and laughing at the clown with the shovel, Eric heard his cousin Opie shouting as he sat next to his new girlfriend, Karen.

"Hey! That's my cousin in that clown suit! Yo, Rigoletto!" Opie called out. "I hope you're wearing underwear underneath those oversized pajamas!" Opie laughed along with his girlfriend. "I bet its cold down there over that ice! We don't want you to get sick again, Circus Boy!"

Eric continued to walk behind the last elephant staring into its rectum contemplating how to plug it up.

"I can't even get him to clean his room! But he'll dress up as a clown and sweep shit from an elephant in front of twelve-thousand people! And this is what we've been spending seven-thousand-dollars a year for school?" Wailed Eric's mother standing over her husband with her voice that could be heard well above all others. Mr. Blum stared straight on with a stone deadpan expression of a corpse.

If Eric had known this would be expected of him, he would never have volunteered for this position, or invited his parents or anybody else to the circus.

"Welcome to the real world, Eric! It's not all disco music, fun and games," Carol shouted out toward him as he passed. "Sometimes it really shits!"

That was a dig she couldn't resist. Carol was sitting in the audience with Eric's nemesis -Warren- which made it even worse for him.

Eric was no more than three-quarters around the ring sweeping and shoveling more dung into the plastic bag when La tour del la ring Ut Elephant was almost over. He could literally see the light at the end of the maintenance tunnel when he heard another unwelcome ear-piercing voice from the darkness of shame.

"I always thought you were full of horse shit Eric. But this will do nicely!"

It was Renée sitting next to her old boyfriend. "Where in hell did, she come from? I didn't get her tickets!" Eric thought to himself as he looked up from the halls of humiliation to see that shit-eating grin of hers.

It was embarrassing for Eric to go back to school the following week. The morning was a living hell taking in all the ribbing and laughter from all his classmates. He thought about taking a day or two off, but for him to complete the school year, he couldn't miss any more days since the week he'd spent at the hospital counted as time off.

By the time science class rolled around in mid-afternoon, Eric was ready to call it a day. Renée was one of the last of seven students who entered the classroom. Biff, the science teacher stood behind his lab table preparing the day's lesson in front of his class.

"Eric? What is a niche?" asked Biff.

"A niche is, uh, like your home. Where you come from, I think... I don't know... something like that."

It was a simple question with a simple answer. But Eric had enough humiliation for one day.

"Yeah. It figures," Renée said under her breath settling at her desk.

"What figures?" Eric asked out loud. "I know what a niche is. I also know that you're an immature brat with a lot of growing up to do!" The students made some cat calls.

"Okay, Eric!" announced Biff. "That's enough."

"Well, at least my boyfriend has a normal job! He doesn't have to pick up elephant shit to prove anything to anybody!"

"Renée!" shouted Biff as the class joined in with laughter.

"I bet your boyfriend never worked a day in his life!" Eric replied.

"Eric!" Biff roared.

"I just want to say one more thing!"

"No, Eric!" Biff called back. "Enough is enough! This is my class! And it's science, not human relations!"

But Eric continued. "Renée, I got a job for you and your boyfriend."

"Eric! I'm warning you for the last time!" Announced Biff.

"Nabisco is hiring. They're looking for someone who could stamp the assholes in the animal crackers!"

The class roared in laughter.

"That's it, Eric! Out! Out of this room! Out!" Biff hollered.

The class applauded as Eric got out from his chair and walked out of the room smiling.

"That seems to fit you, Eric!" Renée encountered. "You're the one with the experience with animals and assholes!"

"Renée, you want to join him?" Biff yelled out.

"I don't even want to be in the same school with him!"

"Then, shut up!" Biff replied.

....

Friday night at the Spectrum down across the stage, a white drape hung from trusses as a huge movie screen depicting a graveyard. Rock star Alice Cooper walked out from the middle of the split screen and yelled out, "Welcome to my nightmare!"

From off stage, Eric watched the macabre concert in amazement as Cooper sang in front of 15,000 screaming fans with a snake wrapped around his neck. After the concert backstage, Cooper walked by Eric holding on to a can of beer. His thick black macabre mascara mixed with sweat dripped down from his face. "I can't believe the kids love this shit." Cooper said to his handler as he walked toward his dressing room.

A couple nights later, while the Spectrum crew disassembled the basketball court for another concert. Two Belly union stewards walked among the crew stating that the agreement the crew had signed was found invalid and encouraging the crew to strike when the contract expired at midnight. The two stewards (one tall and thin, the other short and stout) looked awfully familiar to Eric. He couldn't place their faces, but he knew he had seen them before.

By the time midnight rolled around, the basketball court was three quarters disassembled to make way for the stage. The changeover crew stopped working and sat on the first level of the arena as the two Bellies took the center floor to show support. Ted ran out of his office and onto the arena floor to address the two Bellies.

"What are you doing? Get them back to work! You can't do this now!"

"We're sorry Ted," said the thin Belly. "There's a problem with the contract that was previously signed."

"It's a clerical error that can be cleared up!" Claimed Ted. "I got a show on their way down from Boston. They'll be here within four hours!"

"Well, until the contract can be cleared up, there's nothing we can do."

"You can stop this strike!" claimed Ted.

The Bellies shrugged. Ted took the center floor to address the crew.

"Men! As you know tonight the rock group Santana is on their way down from Boston. Santana's people told me that they could have their three trucks here within five hours. I told them that we can have this basketball court dismantled, and a stage up and ready in three! You new guys may not know this, but the Philadelphia Spectrum changeover crew has a reputation of being the fastest and the best in the country. Time after time we've built stages, made ice, and changed back to basketball in record-breaking time. The Santana people know this. When I guaranteed them that we could meet their trucks with a ready-built stage, and a fully seated arena, they didn't bat an eye."

"The contract agreement that you all signed had a flaw in its clause. A minor technicality that can be cleared up with the power of attorney which will have to wait for another eight hours. That's time we don't have. We've already lost time since you've been on strike! I'm not asking to go against your brethren's, I'm asking all of you to have faith and trust in me and believe in my word that this technicality will be cleared up, and you will have a legally binding contract. You have the power to over-ride your representatives and the right to vote this strike down."

Not satisfied with how the local met worker's conditions, and still sore over the circus boy incident, Eric had a loyalty toward Ted who had given him unforeseen opportunities. He decided to give Ted the benefit of the doubt. Eric who was sitting next to Mike got out of his seat from the fourth row and proceeded to march onto the arena floor.

"Eric!" Mike called out. "What are you doing?"

"I'm going back to work, gentlemen!"

Eric walked past Ted and the two Bellies on the arena floor and straight toward the waiting forklift which was holding a section of the wooden stage to be picked up and placed on spike.

"Eric, I'd sit down if I were you," warned the tall thin Belly.

"What are you going to do, kill me?" asked Eric. "Look, I don't know the details of the contract technicality. Plus, I don't care. What I do care about is having to sign papers without being given time to examine them or having our hourly minimum cut. If I'm paying dues, I want the opportunity to have a say in this local. I want a vote! If management weren't so greedy and unfair with conditions, there wouldn't be any reason to have a union. In fact, with condition as they stand, I can't find any reason for this one!"

"That's very nice, Eric," announced the short Belly as he clapped his hands. "That's nice to hear, indeed. But you see, nobody here is going to join you."

Eric continued to walk toward the unmanned forklift. He faked struggling to lift the section of stage from the forklift by himself. He knew he wouldn't be able to do it alone. One by one, six workers including Mike got out of their seats and walked down onto the arena floor to give Eric a hand. They lifted the section of stage off the forklift and placed it where it was spiked off. More workers gave up the strike. A few of the workers continued to disassemble the basketball court. The forklift operator jumped back on the lift and started the engine, put it into reverse and backed into the tunnel to retrieve another section of stage. A second forklift came out of the maintenance tunnel with an empty floor dolly to pick up the remaining basketball court.

Within the next couple of hours, three trucks carrying Santana's equipment with their tour bus from Boston were crossing the Delaware River from Trenton, New Jersey passing a sign that read -Trenton Makes the World Takes- and onto Route-1 in Morrisville Pennsylvania heading south toward Philadelphia passing a blue reflective road sign reading: 'Welcome to Pennsylvania. Milton J. Shapp Governor'.

At the Spectrum as the stage was getting bigger. Ted and the Bellies who stood and watched in despair from the center floor.

The changeover crew had never worked so hard or as fast. Santana's trucks were passing the second blue and reflective sign on the side of the road southbound Route-1 about thirty-eight miles north from the Spectrum reading: 'Welcome to Philadelphia, Frank L. Rizzo, Mayor.' Just about an hour later as the barriers and the last row of floor chairs were being put into place, the huge garage door in the back of the tunnel lifted to reveal the first of the three forty-five-foot semis. The changeover crew cheered. On stage, Eric wiped the sweat from his face with his Spectrum shirt sleeve.

"Very good, people!" the tall thin union man shouted out sardonically from the floor. "Well, you just might have screwed yourselves out of a four-hour mini to do this job! There goes our bargaining chip! Very good, indeed!"

Eric pulled a hard pack of cigarettes from his back pocket.

"Thanks, Eric!" Ted called up from the floor. "But that wasn't a wise thing to do." As Ted turned to walk back toward his office, Eric noticed the two Bellies who were still on the floor giving him a threatening look that could stop Roadie's trucks.

A week had passed since the -Belly- strike incident. Everything seemed to be getting back to normal. The Spectrum crew was working under a valid contract, and management seemed to be more sympathetic toward the workers' conditions.

The British rock n' roll band The Rolling Stones were scheduled at the Spectrum for two days on their national tour. Since the star-shaped stage was built and shipped from England, there wasn't much for the Spectrum changeover crew to do but to stand by and assist the Road crew.

As the house lights dimmed, a British announcer introduced the American soul group called The Commodores as a warm-up. Eric was backstage with the rest of the changeover crew and roadies waiting for Mick Jagger and the Stones to arrive. During The Commodores' twenty-five-minute set, the audience was beginning to get impatient and started chanting "Stones!"

After The Commodores finished their set, it took a few minutes for the stage crew to move their equipment and change the stage setting for the Stones while the audience continued chanting their enthusiasm.

Behind the stage out of view from the audience, the huge garage door in the back of the maintenance tunnel slowly opened. Three black limousines screeched in. The car doors on the first limo opened before it came to a complete stop. Just two feet from Eric, Mick Jagger and Keith

Richards walked by heading straight toward the stage with Bill Wyman, Mick Taylor, and Charlie Watts walking behind. Another musician-who was not an original member of the band followed suit. Eric walked next to the man trying to place him.

"Hey! Aren't you Billy Preston, the fifth Beatle?" asked Eric.

"Yes, I am!" Preston replied with a smile as he walked toward the stage behind the Stones.

"Holy shit!" yelled Eric.

Since Spectrum employees were not permitted onstage during performances, Eric walked from backstage to the audience fighting his way through the impatient crowd for a good view. He found himself pressed up against the partition/barriers he had helped build to prevent the crowd from storming the stage. A security guard -a couple generations older than Eric- was standing between the partition and the stage just about nose-to-nose with Eric.

"Hey! Did you know that's Billy Preston up there?" Eric asked the guard.

"Big shit!" Replied the guard.

If Theresa Brewer had been singing lead instead of Mick Jagger, the guard probably would have been more enthusiastic.

The Stones started the concert with Honky Tonk Women. Eric was pushed farther back from the stage by the crowd. Toward the center floor, as the song Give Me Shelter followed suit, Eric felt as though his back was pressed up against what felt like a hard wall. But there was no wall built toward the center of the arena. Eric turned and was face-to-face with an old, robust, Hell's Angel with a long gray beard and matching hair hanging over his weathered leather cut vest. He was probably one of the originals. The Angel looked straight down at Eric with no expression. Eric was fascinated.

"Hey! I like your colors. You know, I'm pretty much interested in American history, and I was wondering how I can get a vest like yours as a souvenir?"

The Angel, thinking this was some sort of joke, briefly glanced behind making sure that Eric was not addressing somebody else. He looked back down at Eric accompanied with a smile as he began to disrobe his weathered cut.

"Sure! You can have my vest as a souvenir. But now, out of Hell's Angel's tradition, if I take this vest, you're going to have to kill me!"

Eric had this instantaneous panoramic view of the documentary motion picture Give me Shelter, starring patron Meredith Hunter who enacted his only stellar performance.

Eric surrendered a chilling smile as he patten down and dusted off the vest preventing the angel from taking it completely off. "No thank you. I think I'll run home and make my own."

Eric bowed at the old Angel, then disappeared into the crowd as the angel laughed on. "What an asshole." said the Angel.

....

The Spectrum change-over crew had orders to build a seventy-five-foot by sixty- foot stage with two forty-five-foot towers made of scaffolding to support a video screen for the rock band Pink Floyd - Wish You Were Here- tour. At first Eric and Mike teamed up. Eric climbed to the top of one of the two towers with two other workers standing on planks putting in the last of the scaffolding pins. One scaffolding upright suddenly shifted to one side enough to throw Eric and the workers off balance. The three grabbed hold to the upright as the planks on which the three young men were standing on slid from beneath their feet. The two workers screamed for help. Eric yelled out "Mommy!" The tower the three were hanging on began to lean further out.

"Don't move!" a worker shouted out from the ground.

"Where in hell do you think I'm going to go, moron!" Eric called down as the tower leaned more over to one side from the unbalanced weight of the three workers. Other workers on the ground panicked as they tried to figure out a way to steady the scaffold and get the three young men safely down. Eric reasoned within himself as the other two continued to yell for their lives.

"Either I let go now and die from the fall, or I stay with the tower and get crushed from the impact. Eric had a decision to make on how to die. All right...I'll let go. On the count of three, I'll let go. People from the ground continued yelling different instructions for their safety, but Eric wasn't listening. One... two... three! Eric closed his eyes as the tower once again began to lean more and started to resemble the Leaning Tower of Pisa. Shit! Eric said to himself. I'm still here. My mind says yes let go. But my body says no.

It was only a matter of time when the over balanced weight from the three stranded men would overcome the support of the allegedly anchored scaffold.

Ted ran out from his office and called up to the three stranded men.

"We're going to hold down one side of the tower with the forklift. One by one, hand over hand, climb down the upright!"

Workers raced on the ground to hack away at the finish section of stage so the forklift could work its way to where the scaffold was supposedly anchored. Ted's idea worked, and when all three men touched down, relief and a round of applause was heard throughout the floor.

"I can't imagine what you were thinking while you were hanging up there," Mike said to Eric who was receiving pats on the back and handshakes from other workers.

"You know Mike, my whole life flashed before my eyes, and the only thing I could remember seeing were reruns of Gilligan's Island." Eric replied with half of a nervous grin and a chuckle.

"I think you better go home now, Eric." Ted requested as he gestured behind.

Eric looked over Ted's shoulder and saw the two Bellies sporting an indecipherable smile. It then dawned on him where he had seen them before. The tall thin man and his short robust friend appeared to resemble the gravediggers in his dream at the hospital when he had pneumonia back in December.

"We'll finish you now!"

CHAPTER 8

ONE'S SELF WORTH

IT WAS ON April 17, 1975, the day before the class camping trip. The government of Phnom Penh in Cambodia had fallen to the Communists. Through the eyes of the American government the political domino theory was becoming fact. President Ford was looking for a quick, honorable way out of Vietnam. Secretary of State Henry Kissinger who had seen the demise of South Vietnam for the past couple of years, suggested evacuating some of the civilians. Just two-weeks prior, an Air Force C-5 transport plane evacuating three hundred Vietnamese children with their guardians to the United States had crashed killing over two hundred people on board.

In a dimly lit office on the second floor at Noah Webster, as always, Dr. Goldman sat behind his desk smoking his pipe. A legal-size pad, pen, and a manila folder with a couple of papers laid open before him. Eric sat across from Dr. Goldman in the comfy leather armchair.

"So, you failed at the Spectrum." Goldman opened with.

"Oh no! Not at all! I didn't fail. I fought against a corrupt organization and won. Okay, so they tried to kill me. I figured I should quit before they do. But I stood my ground for what I thought was right. You see Doc, that's a sign of maturity on my own behalf. A sign of well-being and confidence. So, no matter what I decide for my future, if I want to go to college or not, you have to sign me out at the end of this school year. I must move on. I told you I don't belong here anymore. Can I smoke?"

Goldman nodded his head as he watched Eric take a pack of cigarettes and a zippo lighter out from his pants pocket and light up.

"Been smoking much?"

"Pack every other day," replied Eric as he exhaled.

"Who else smokes in your family?"

"Well, I know my father does. Not in front of my mother of course. He's not supposed to be either because of his heart. But sometimes when he comes home from work, I can smell it on his clothes. My brother was a chain smoker."

"Okay. So, what do you want to do now? asked Goldman.

"I guess I'll give that restaurant a try. Plus, it will keep my parents off my back about earning my own money since they refused to give me any. I do hate working with Cousin Opie again. I'm going on a class camping trip this weekend. When I get back, I'll go to that damn restaurant."

"What are you going to do if they're not hiring," asked Goldman.

"I don't know. Find another."

· ·

Friday April 18th, 1975, on a clear sunny late afternoon, Eric Blum, Joey Pearlman, Mark Stern and Carol Schor embarked to French Creek National Park in Pennsylvania from Noah Webster's Preparatory parking lot. The white 1966 window Dodge van the school had lent them was one of Webster's original school buses. It had been a few years since Carol had driven a stick on the column. Tricky at first, but once she regained the hang of it, it became second nature. Unfortunately, the van had a habit of sliding out of third gear on its own. The van was loaded with two

two-men tents, camping equipment, and a first-aid kit. The camping equipment belonged to Carol and Warren. Carol and Warren would go camping a couple times out of the year and this was the first time she was going camping without him.

Carol wasn't worried about her well-being with three sexually incorrigible adolescence. These were three good kids. Parents weren't too concerned either. The attendance at school was so small and tightknit that everybody-including teachers- were considered trusted family members. This was the first time Mark, Eric and Joey had ever gone camping. The other students from school who were invited to go camping were not interested in spending a weekend roughing it up in God's country -City Slickers-.

Carol and her three students traveled west on Route 76 via the Pennsylvania Turnpike outside Philadelphia on their way to the campsite. Cruising with the flow of the traffic, taking in the historic scenery of Valley Forge and passing Amish farmers with their horse drawn black buggies.

Run, Run, Run by rock band Jo Jo Gunne on rock radio station W.I.F.I-FM spilled out from the vans radio. Mark sat shotgun. Eric sat in the middle on top of the engine cover and without swaying, Joey was sitting on first bench seat smiling at everybody who was bopping and singing along.

"You see those cabins over there?" Carol asked as they sped past General George Washington's encampment at Valley Forge. "When do you think they were built?"

"I don't know," Mark responded. "Two hundred years ago?"

"No," Carol said. "About 1925. The originals are long gone. Has anybody ever heard of Dumas Malone? He just won the Pulitzer for his book entitled Thomas Jefferson and His Times. I suggest you read it!"

The four traveled down the turnpike for another five miles taking in the fresh air and the rural communities while the van intermittently popped out of third gear.

"You know, Swanson wanted me to take Tony Burns along," Carol announced waiting for feedback that never came. "But I flat out said no! I couldn't keep my eyes on him all weekend. I mean can you imagine if he would have gotten lost in the woods, and with his alleged Tourette's syndrome had to ask a park ranger for directions? That's all I need, to have uncontrollable Tony Burns out in the woods."

"Yeah. That would have been hysterical." Said Mark.

"I think you misunderstand him." Announced Eric.

Carol wasn't sure what she had just heard or where it came from. She looked through the rearview mirror and there was Eric's reflection staring straight back at her from his spot-on top of the engine cover.

"What?" she asked with a slight smile.

"As retarded as he may openly seem, I think he's highly intelligent," continued Eric. Mark Stern smiled as he looked out his window. Joey began to sway in his seat with a grin.

"What makes you say that?" Carol asked.

"I don't know. The way he could take apart a car engine and put it back together. He does have one of the highest IQ in the school.'"

"And how about the way he and Sam Harris go out every Tuesday night to that burlesque theater in Philly -The Troc - to see 'Sweet Betty, the Bottle Opener'?" Announced Carol. "Or staying up all hours of the night listening to Frank Zappa and watching Monty Python's Flying Circus when he could be studying or reading a book! He wouldn't have to worry about catching up on his schoolwork. How about the way he disrupts my class? He has no discipline."

"He hasn't disrupted your class since you slapped him across the face." Eric announced. "Besides he teases you because you're vulnerable. You're a woman."

Carol turned her head and gave Eric such a look. She wasn't sure if she should smack him or laugh.

"I spent some time with him last summer," Eric continued. "His parents are so out of touch. They're into their own social status. Away from the school and authority, Tony's different. He might have been different on this camping trip if he had had the opportunity. He just lacks attention."

"Who do you think you are?" asked Carol. "Doctor Goldman? You think you're a psychologist?"

"I should be! I've been analyzed enough these past four years to fill a textbook. We all have!" Eric sternly snapped back as he and Mark peered out the right-side window while Joey continued swaying in his seat with a contemplating stare.

What started out to be a pleasant vacation away from academia, was threatening to become a disaster.

"Look!" Carol said. "I don't want to talk about school anymore! School's out! Let's just have a good time, okay?"

"You started it." announced Eric.

Once again Carol glanced into the rearview mirror at Eric. "I'm sorry," she said. Eric nodded as he continued to stare out the right window at Mark, and the van once again popped out of gear. "I can't believe the school lent me this piece of crap!" Said Carol as she shifted back into third.

It was an hour and a half drive to French Creek National Park from the school in Cheltenham. The thick of the woods gradually surrounding the van as Carol pulled up to the ranger booth to pay the fee.

"It's just ya'll four?" asked the ranger in a thick southern accent.

"Yes sir." Carol replied. "We'll be here for two nights. Out by Sunday morning."

"That will be twenty-four dollars." The Ranger announced.

Carol paid the fee from her wallet, then slid the van into gear.

"Now, ya'll know about the coons, don't ya?" asked the ranger hanging his torso out the ranger booth window.

All four in the van glanced at each other not knowing how to react to what they perceived to be a racist remark.

"Well, we're from Philadelphia," Carol replied in an uninsurable manner. "So, we're quite used to them."

"All right. Just remember to tie up your garbage and hang it from a tree. Those coons don't like to climb. You're in lot number sixteen. Ya'll has a good weekend, ya'll hear?" The ranger smiled.

"Sure," Carol replied with slight trepidation. "Thank you."

As Carol slowly lifted the clutch and slid back into in gear, the van rolled past the booth. The four in the van were in total silence and despair. The thought of a federal or state representative speaking in those terms was appalling. Then it dawned. "Raccoons, right?" Carol asked the other three. "He's talking about raccoons. Right?"

"Yeah, yeah, that's it!" they all said with laughter and relief. "Raccoons!"

"But just in case", Eric asked Carol. "Are you wearing your mezuzah?

It was a month before camping season and all the other campsites around lot sixteen were empty. There were no bathrooms or showers. This was no KOA -Kampgrounds of America-. This was camping. They unloaded the van and Carol helped the boys set up the two tents.

"Before it gets dark, I suggest we go into town and gets provisions." Request Carol. "One of us will have to stay behind to watch the campsite and collect firewood."

At that moment, an old beat-up, dark blue Volkswagon Carmengia with a small sun catcher hanging from the rearview mirror, and a Grateful Dead and Fillmore East back bumper sticker pulled into the next lot. A twenty-year-old blonde hippie girl resembling Goldie Hawn in the movie Butterflies Are Free wearing tight torn blue jeans, a loose peasant blouse and Jesus Boots -sandals- rolled out of the car and walked over to lot sixteen. She was traveling with a small barking black mutt-of-a-dog.

"Hi," said the girl. "Are we allowed to have dogs here?"

"Yes, but I'm not too sure," Carol told her."

"The ranger wasn't at the gate when I pulled in. I'm supposed to meet some friends here and I still have to register. Incase we're not, could you watch my dog till I get back? It should only take a minute."

"We're on our way to the store. But Eric is staying. He could watch your dog," Carol volunteered.

"Thanks. I won't be long. I'll just tie my dog around this tree." Said the girl.

After the dog was tied, the girl drove back to the ranger station as Eric gawked.

"Well, I don't know, Eric!" Said Carol. "Just watch the dog! We'll be back!"

"Suppose I don't want to watch the dog! Suppose I want to go to the store with you?" whined Eric.

"Tough! You've been elected to stay! Now collect firewood. We'll be back soon."

Mark and Joey smiled as the three piled back into the van waving bye-bye to Eric all laughing their way to the town of Birdsboro.

Eric reluctantly collected firewood from around the campsite. He found a few rocks and made a fire pit, then put the wood inside the pit as the small dog intermittently barked tangling herself around the tree by her leash.

A truck was heard coming up from the road. It was a park ranger. Eric, not sure if pets were allowed scanned around for a place to hide the dog. He thought of the tents, but the dog was persistently barking. He tried to untie the leash from around the tree, but the dog knotted herself up. Earshot, only seconds before the park Ranger would have the camp in sight, Eric picked up the dog, and threw her into the plastic seventy-quart Coleman cooler partially filled with ice that was by the tree. Then closed it and sat on the lid. The dog could barely be heard barking.

"Have you seen a dog around here?" the Ranger shouted out from his truck.

"No," said Eric, sitting on top of the cooler with one end of the leash still attached to the tree and the other end leading into the cooler.

"Well, I heard some barking, and it came from around here. We don't allow dogs roaming lose."

"No, I'm sorry. I heard the dog, but I haven't seen it." Eric said offering a smile. The Ranger smiled back as he drove on. Eric took the dog out of the cooler. The dog was shivering with some ice deposits around her nose and paws. But at last, she stopped barking.

Within a few minutes, the young hippie girl drove back onto lot sixteen.

"Well, I'm registered. My friends are in lot twenty-one. Did my dog give you any trouble?"

"No. In fact, she kind of chilled out," said Eric.

"Thanks. I appreciate it." The girl untangled the leash around the tree, then walked off with her dog to look for her friends.

The van returned to the campsite as the hippie girl with her dog came back.

"I found my friends". The hippie announced to Carol as the boys unloaded the van with the provisions. "I'm in another lot." She presented Carol with a joint. "Wanna smoke?" Joey and Mark looked on as Eric's ears perked up.

"That wouldn't happen to be Cambodian Red, would it?" asked Eric.

"Well, in fact... said the hippie.

"Eric!" Carol interrupted. "No. We don't do that. Thanks anyway," Carol smiled at the girl deceitfully.

The girl shrugged. "Okay, that's cool. Peace." With her barking dog in the back seat of the old Carmengia, the young hippie moved on.

Mark wanted to go on a hike. Since dusk was approaching, Carol told him it was okay as long as they followed the yellow marked trees on the trail. With flashlights in hand, Groucho, Harpo, and Chico were off to explore the African safari while Carol settled the campsite.

During the hike, the boys discovered a lake. For some unknown reason, Mark pushed Eric into a mud hole. Eric jumped back up and tried to push Mark, but Mark was too big. Eric threw a stick at him, and Joey smiled as he watched Mark chase Eric. Eric was too fast and disappeared down the trail toward the encampment.

As Carol was preparing the hamburgers and hot dogs over the campfire pit, she observed Eric rushing into camp. Eric ran into the boys' tent and pulled out to expose a section of the plastic ground cloth from under Mark's sleeping bag. Mark and Joey returned to the campsite as Eric joined Carol at the fire. She asked Eric what had happened.

"Stern pushed me into a mud hole."

"Why did you do that?" She asked Mark.

"Because, it was there," he replied.

"Well, you all better get washed up. We're about ready to eat."

That evening after dinner, they all sat around the campfire for hours gazing into the flames, looking up at the stars. There's something about a campfire that turns people serene. The April night air was getting chilly, but the fire kept them securely warm and comfortably numb as the portable radio on the picnic table serenaded with Angie by The Rolling Stones.

"Having a good time, Joey?" Carol asked, hoping a different environment would open him up. But Joey just sat on a fallen log by the fire and continued to sway with a smile.

"My Cousin Opie would have had a great time here," Eric blurted out.

"My friend, let me tell you something," Carol declared. "If I had the choice, I would've rather had three Tony Burns here in replacement of one Cousin Opie."

"You don't like anybody I like," said Eric.

"That's not true!"

"You don't like my parents."

"Bullshit!"

"Alice?"

"Oh, she was a great influence on you, Eric!" Carol answered sarcastically.

"Renée?"

"Be real! I'm sure you can come up with somebody we can agree on who either isn't hooked on drugs or doesn't have the maturity of an eight-year-old."

"I'm getting tired," said Mark as he got off his section of fallen log and headed toward the tent. "I'm going to hit the hay."

"I think we all should hit it. We had a long day, and tomorrow is another," Carol announced. "It may rain tonight, so make sure your tent flap is down."

"How 'bout the fire?" Eric asked.

"It's okay. It will burn out on its own." Said Carol.

The three boys shared the two-man tent. Carol had the other for herself that was positioned far enough away from the boys. The portable radio was left playing Bob Dylan's Lay Lady Lay on the picnic table with his exasperate voice to discourage any nocturnal animal away from the campsite.

Not more than an hour had passed when Carol suspected everybody was asleep. Alice Cooper could clearly be heard singing Eighteen on the picnic table. Eric quietly slipped out of his tent and stood outside Carol's. She was still clothed, tucked in her sleeping bag as she filed her fingernails with an emery board.

"Carol," whispered Eric.

"What is it?" she firmly asked from in her tent.

"My tent is too crowded. And I'm cold."

"So, what do you want me to do, get you an electric blanket?"

"Well, aren't you cold?"

"I'm dealing with it," Carol replied.

"Do you need somebody to help you deal? I mean, I'm no *Warren*," Eric chuckled, "but thank God."

That was it. Eric was getting out of line. She struggled out of her sleeping bag on her hands and knees and battled to wrap a wool knitted poncho around her body. She flipped the tent flap up exposing half her torso.

"Let's get one thing straight!" She warned. "Do you know what would happen to me if there were any shadow of suspicion about us here?"

"No, what?" Eric challenged her explanation.

"First of all, even though you are of legal age, you're still under parental care! Your parents would have the school authorities after me! Even as a rumor they would prosecute me on the grounds of elicit sexual activities. The worst part, not caring guilty or not, the school would press the charges. I spent over ten thousand dollars of my hard-earned money, waiting on tables, cleaning houses, and fifteen years of schooling to get me where I am today! It's not much, but right now, it's all I've got! Even if I *was* interested in you in that way, -which I am not- you ain't worth the risk poisoning my career! Now, go back to your tent!" Carol flipped the tent flap down leaving Eric outside.

"Well, thanks a lot!" Eric proclaimed. "It's good to know one's self-worth!"

Eric stormed away from the tent. After a couple of thoughts and a deep sigh, Carol peeked out of her tent to find Eric sitting by the picnic table scanning through the portable radio dial till George Harrison was heard singing What is Life.

Carol crawled out of her tent. Once again struggled to wrap the poncho around her shoulders and walked over to the picnic table where Eric was smoking a cigarette.

"Eric? Eric! Since when you started smoking cigarettes?"

"Since you found me that God-damn shrink! What a trade-off. Insanity for cancer."

Carol glanced over toward the boys' tent to see if they were being watched. She knelt in front of him.

"Eric. I didn't mean it to come out the way it did. I like you very much. And I love you as my friend outside of school. I have told you that multiple times. I don't expect you to understand this now or if you ever will, but it's very hard for a woman to become successful in this professionally male-dominated world. I know that sounds feminist, but with you making all these innuendos toward me at school, it's risking my career and future."

"Is that all there is between us Carol? A risk?"

"No, Eric, I don't see you in the same light as you see me."

"You said 'risk'. And if there was no risk involved Carol?"

"Please, Eric. Don't do this to me. I'm begging you. I'm not interested in you that way. I told you I have a boyfriend. I'm in love with another man. And I want to do more with my life than just teach. And it's taking me too long. I fought too long and too hard. I'm still fighting with no end in sight."

"What do you want to do, Carol?"

"I haven't put my finger on it yet. To be honest, I really don't know, Eric. Like you. I don't know. But whatever I decide to do with my career, it won't be easy. Not for me because like you said, 'I'm a woman'. Please don't make it any harder than it is. Stop!"

Eric gently rubbed her cheek, then ran his right hand through her hair. She vigorously slapped his hand away from her face. Eric stood up and looked down at her with anger and a clenched fist. Carol eyes widen as she looked up at him and leaned back with anticipation of being kicked or punched. She glanced over toward the boys' tent to see if there were any witnesses. With his sneaker, Eric ditched his cigarette on the ground by Carol, then solemnly walked toward his tent leaving Carol behind with George Harrison.

The next morning at about seven-thirty, they were all awakened by a Saskatchewan scream from Mark Stern. Eric tumble sauced out of his tent and ran straight into Carol's. She pulled the sleeping bag up over her chest and against her chin.

"Get out of my tent!" She screamed at him. "Get out of my tent!"

"But Stern is going to kill me!" Cried Eric.

"Good! Now get out of my fuck'en tent, or I'm going to kill you!"

"But don't you want to know why? Do you want to see what I did?" Eric asked with a devious smile.

"No! The only thing I want to see is the back of your head! Get out of here!"

It had rained at dawn. The plastic ground cloth that Eric exposed the day before under Stern's sleeping bag was soaked. Stern woke up to a damp and cold environment, and he was furious.

"Can't I escape through your back door?" Eric pleaded.

"No! I don't have one! For the last time, get -the fuck- out!"

"Okay, Carol! Relax!"

Eric swallowed and then rushed out. "Now, look Stern..." ordered Eric in the center of campsite face to face with a furious and damp Mark. Joey peeked his head out from the tent smiling, then climbed out aggressively hoping, prancing, dancing around the campsite anticipating Eric's demise.

"Carol Schor told me to tell you that you deserved it for pushing me into the mud hole yesterday."

"The only thing Carol Schor told you is to get out of her fuck'en tent!" Yelled Stern as he approached closer toward Eric.

"Mark! cut it out!" Carol yelled out as she crawled out from her tent struggling with her poncho around her shoulders. "Just take your wet clothes and hang them up somewhere!"

"Where? It's drizzling!" Announced Mark.

It was a pity that it drizzled most of the day and Mark's clothes never got completely dry. But the weather didn't discourage them from driving into Peddler's Village and Daniel Boon's Homestead. Two reenactment villages of the late eighteenth and nineteen centuries.

At Peddler's Village, Eric acted a bit standoffish towards the others. It was in the blacksmith's shop Carol saw Eric standing alone watching the reenacting 19th century blacksmith smite his red-hot prong over an anvil. Carol approached him since they were away from the other students.

"Are we mad?" she asked discreetly.

"Mad about what?" asked Eric.

"Last night. "

"Nothing happened." Eric replied.

"Our little talk." Said Carol.

"No." Eric shrugged.

"So, you understand the grounds between us, right?"

"Right," replied Eric not swayed. "So, where are you spending Rosh Hashanah?"

"I'm spending it with Warren and his parents."

"You're spending it with '*Warren*' and his parents." Eric repeated with a push on Warren's name.

"Yeah! I'm spending it with '*Warren*'." Replied Carol with a push on Warren's name.

CHAPTER 9

COCHISE

AFTER SCHOOL, ERIC was by the grills at the Steak 'N Brew restaurant kitchen with restaurant manager Marty who was holding on to a cocktail. The two cooks were busy slapping steaks onto the grills while waiters and waitresses in white uniforms rushed around the stand-by station delivering and picking up orders.'

"So, when can you start?"

"Anytime," said Eric.

"How 'bout now?"

"Sure!"

"Okay. We'll start you off by making salads." Said Marty. "But first you'll have to do something with your hair. It's too long. I don't like it hanging down. It's not presentable to the customers; besides, it could end up in somebody's salad."

"I have a headband," proclaimed Eric as he took the white elastic band out from his pants pocket and placed it around his head.

"Let me get you a white shirt, then I want you to meet somebody," said Marty.

After receiving the long white shirt from the utility closet, Eric followed Marty into a walk-in cooler. Inside the cooler was another boy his age shredding lettuce.

"George! This... uh." Marty looked Eric over and noticed the olive complexion in contrast with his white shirt and headband. "You know," Marty said to Eric, "you look like an Indian. George, this is Cochise."

"How," said George as he raised his right hand with his fist clenching a handful of lettuce.

"Quite easily," Eric jumped in on cue. "I need this job."

"Cochise, George will show you how to prepare the salads. Go to it white man," Marty said to George as he walked out of the cooler.

"Are you really an American Indian?" George asked.

"First of all," said Eric, "Pardon me for being frank. I'm not crazy about this job. Why and how I applied is none of your business. So, let's just cut the small talk and chitchat and just show me how to make the damn salads."

Eric started on a strong foot. This restaurant business was not going to be fun and games for him.

"All right, all right." George replied. "Bum deal on Manhattan and they hate the whole world. We first start off by making the salads here in the cooler to keep them fresh..."

After fifteen minutes Eric got the hang of making salads on his own, and George went home for the night.

Inside the walk-in cooler the doorknob turned but did not release the lock. Eric wasn't shown how to open it. He kept the door slightly ajar so he wouldn't get locked in.

Cousin Opie working as a busboy, carrying a plastic bus tray with dirty dishes, glasses, and utensils walked by the cooler on his way to the dish room. Not knowing that Eric was inside, Opie kicked closed the cooler door with a free foot. Eric, in the mist of making a bowl of salad heard the door close behind. With a fistful of iceberg lettuce, he turned the knob that continued to turn with no avail.

"Cochise! Cochise! Where is that Indian? We need salads out here!" Marty called from the kitchen.

"I'm stuck in here!" Eric yelled out. "I'm locked in the God-damn cooler!"

The compressors and other kitchen machinery outside the cooler forbid Eric to be heard. Marty walked back into the dining area in search of the lost tribe. Out of temperament, Eric gave the doorknob one last punch. The door swung open just as Opie walked by carrying an empty bus tray.

"What's with you?" asked Opie, noticing Eric in a paler shade than olive.

"I locked myself in the cooler."

"You should try keeping it propped open just a bit," Opie offered. "Hey, Marty! I just found Cochise! Guess where?" Opie yelled out.

"Thanks a lot Opie! Asshole!"

"Okay, okay," Opie retracted. "I need a favor."

"I'm working with you, and I'm your first cousin. Don't you feel that's enough of a favor?"

"Yeah, yeah, blah, blah. Being a first cousin doesn't count. It's a birthright. I met this girl at a BBG function."

"At a what?"

"As part of my punishment for scaring my science teacher out of his mind, my parents forced me to join this Jewish social AZA -Aleph Zadik Aleph- chapter up in northeast Philly. Can you imagine, an O'Neal in a Jewish social organization?"

"My Jewish face is in a Catholic school yearbook, may I remind you," said Eric.

"Well, you know it's not in a name according to the Jewish law." Opie continued. "It's who you are maternally. Anyway, my parents think I'll find a better class of people that will help me curb my behavioral problem. Tell me Eric, do I have a behavioral problem?" Eric stared back at Opie deadpan. "Anyway, a few weeks ago, I met this girl named Karen at this lame social. She just broke up with her boyfriend and wants to go out with me. It just so happens I got this fake ID to get me into Penn State Ogontz campus to see that local rock band, Forest Green in concert next Saturday night! Karen's favorite band. This Karen wants me to fix her girlfriend up for a double date."

"This Karen wouldn't happen to be the one that accompanied you to the circus, would it?" Questioned Eric.

"The one and the same."

"The one who was pointing and laughing at me?"

"The one and the same."

"No!" Eric turned to walk back into the cooler.

"Oh, come on Eric! If not your best cousin, be my best friend."

Eric stopped dead in his tracks and turned to face his cousin. "What's the catch?"

"No catch Eric. I met Karen's girlfriend. She's really pretty, and she has nothing to do Saturday night. So, I figured since you have nothing to do Saturday night, it would be great to get two people who have nothing to do together to see Forest Green. I hear this girl is also crazy about them."

"And how are you going to get the rest of us in Penn State Ogontz campus to see Forest Green if you're the only one with a pass?"

"I'm supposed to meet another friend who goes to the school at the gate. He has a couple passes."

"Well, I don't know Opie. I remember the last time you tried to fix me up with a girl. I'm still waiting for the catch. How old is she?"

"She's, our age. They're both seniors at Northeast High. Just do me this one favor. Hey, I got your parents off your back by getting you this job."

"And that's why I don't owe you a thing."

"It's just for Saturday night, Eric. One night. This could be my ticket into Karen's good grace. You don't like her girlfriend; you'll never have to see her again. I'll even spring for a bottle of ammonia."

"Well, okay," Eric said begrudgingly.

"Great! I'll pick you up around seven-thirty. Oh, just one thing."

"Ah, the catch! You sound just like the policemen before they arrest you. Hit me! I'm ready. Right here in the kisser!"

"There's no catch, Eric. It's just, well, this girl has a slight handicap. She's hard of hearing. You'll have to speak up when you talk to her, but she reads lips."

"Oh, damn, Opie! What's her name?"

"Susie."

"All right. I'll do you this one outstanding favor."

"Great! Thanks a lot, little buddy. Hey! You think we should take the hearse?"

"No!!!"

"I'm only kidding, man."

"And I got one request," said Eric.

"Anything. You name it."

"I don't want to hear one word, one thought, one question, one remark about what I did at the circus."

"Relax. There won't be anything said. Hey Marty!" Opie called out as he headed toward the dining room. "Guess where Cochise was hiding! Was it cold in there, little buddy? Don't want you to catch pneumonia. You are wearing underwear, right?" Opie walked off laughing.

"Oh! You're such and asshole, Opie. Such and asshole." Eric called after him.

· ·

Somewhere in the Oxford circle section of the city in the middle of a block of identical stone front row homes was Karen's house. As Opie and Eric walked down the street, a few of the old lady neighborhood yentas peeked out from their windows or stood by their open front doors to see what stranger had invaded their territory. But that's just Philly.

Eric stood behind Opie on the front steps of Karen's house as Opie opened the aluminum screen storm door, then knocked on the solid thick white wooden door.

"Now, whatever you do," warned Opie, "don't mention anything about Susie's hearing impairment."

"Oy Vey!"

Karen opened the white front door and smiled. "Hi, Opie. Come on in!"

Eric followed Opie into the living room. There was a party atmosphere. Beer, soda, popcorn, pretzels, and potato chips were laid about in bowls on the coffee and end tables. Karen's parents were sitting in a beige and flowered pattern sofa covered by a clear plastic slipcover. Her older brother and his friend sat on the floor all watching the Flyers game in front of a twenty-four-inch console RCA color television set.

"Mom, dad? This is Opie," announced Karen. "And this is his cousin, Eric. You're from the circus, right?" Karen addressed Eric with a giggle. Eric scowled at Opie. "And this is my brother Paul, and his friend Scott."

While all were engrossed in a great hockey play on the TV, Eric saw Susie strolling in from the dining room. He was surprised to see how attractive the dirty blonde looked in a leather motorcycle jacket, blouse, and tight jeans. Susie eyed Eric. Eric wasn't sure if he was smiling or not but continued to stare at her until Karen shouted over her brother and his friend's excitement on the television.

"Susie, you know Opie, and this is his cousin, Eric." Eric thought he noticed Susie reading lips.

"Hi Eric." Susie's shouted out with a smile. "You're the circus boy, aren't you?" Eric smiled out of respect and then turned toward Opie with a less approving grin. Opie shrugged as an apology.

"Mom, dad? I'll be home by one," Karen yelled out over the television.

"Twelve o'clock!" Karen's mother shouted back.

"Mom, the concert is over about eleven thirty or twelve!"

"Just don't be any later than one!" Her mother replied.

Eric and Susie slid into the back seat of Opie's car, hopping over a few empty eight-ounce glass soda bottles that were on the floor. It was an awkward situation for Eric. He didn't know how to communicate with a person who was hearing impaired.

"Are you sure your friend will meet us at the theater entrance with passes?" asked Eric from the back seat.

"I'm positive. I called him just before I picked you up from your house," replied Opie as he pulled the car out of the parking space.

Eric noticed that Susie who was sitting next to him in the back seat had responded to the conversation. For somebody who was hearing impaired and not facing lips, she picked up sound very well.

"Where do you want to go after you graduate this year?" Eric called Susie.

"Temple University!" Susie called back. "And you?"

"I haven't made up my mind. I was thinking about Harvard!" Eric saw Opie's surprised expression from the reflection in the rearview mirror. "Or maybe just a community college as a warm-up."

Susie surrendered a peculiar smile. "Where do you go to school now?"

"Noah Webster Prep," Eric replied.

"Wester? Never heard of it!"

"No. It's Webster!" said Eric.

Anybody could have made that mistake hearing impaired or not. Eric noticed Opie and Karen in the front seat suppressing some laughter.

"Opie, I want you to know that I still talk to my old boyfriend. He called me last night." Karen mentioned.

"What did he want?" asked Opie.

"He just wanted to talk."

The conversation in the front seat was moderate over the music from the car radio. Eric couldn't help but notice Susie's reaction. Without seeing lips, she seemed to be following what was being said.

"So, what does that mean for us?" asked Opie.

"Nothing, Opie. But we're just good friends. I mean, I've known him all my life. His parents and my parents are like family."

"Well, maybe it's time to un-know him and divorce his family," suggested Opie.

"Well, it's hard to do when our families are close. I just thought I'd let you know. I don't want to keep any secrets from you. I'm sorry I brought it up. Let's just drop the whole topic."

"I don't like you calling him." Said Opie

"Well, he's like a brother. That's all there is, but okay! Let's drop it!"

"Fine."

The parking lot at the Penn State Ogontz college campus in Abington township was just about filled by the time Opie pulled into a parking spot. Eric, Susie, and Karen followed Opie as they walked to the front entrance of the campus theater where a campus security guard was checking IDs.

"You're sure he's going to be here, right Opie?" asked Eric with trepidation.

"I swear. He's probably here now!"

The four waited about fifteen minutes without any sight of contact. Music was heard coming out of the theater. Forest Green was on stage.

"Well, I guess he's not going to show up," said Opie. "I'm going to have to sneak you guys' in."

Eric expected it. But that didn't sit well with Susie or Karen. These two girls were brought up in a respectable middle-class environment. They never had to sneak into any place. Opie seized the moment when the attention of the campus security guard checking IDs was diverted.

"Let's go!" Opie grabbed Karen by the hand and ran off with her in tow entering the building passing the unobservant guard. Eric and Susie missed a beat. The guard went back to his post. Eric and Susie stopped dead in their tracks toe to toe with the guard. Eric looked up and could see by the theater staircase window that Opie and Karen had made it onto the second floor. Opie gesturing to Eric and Susie to try to sneak in.

Eric shrugged in defeat. Opie grabbed Karen's hand and for the second time a crowd of college students pushed them along.

"Karen!" Susie shouted out, "Karen!"

"Forget it. They're gone."

"Karen will not leave me here. She's my best friend."

"Karen is with my cousin Opie, nobody's best friend. Don't count on her coming back."

"I can't believe it!"

"Believe it!"

"So, now what?" asked Susie.

Eric faced Susie so she could read his lips. "I'm going home."

"How?" Susie asked, not realizing her own loud voice.

"Hitchhike."

"Hitchhike? You're gonna leave me here alone?"

"No. You could come along."

"I'm not gonna hitchhike! Where am I going to hitchhike to?" Yelled Susie.

"We'll hitch to your house. From there I can catch a bus home because I'm not gonna stay here!" Eric yelled back.

"Well, I'm gonna wait!" Susie defied.

"I'm not waiting for Opie! He always pulls this shit on me!" Eric shouted back as he turned to walk away.

"I can't believe you're leaving me here alone! What are you, an asshole?"

Eric stopped walking and turned to face her. "Susie, I don't want to leave you here alone. But you're not giving me much of a choice! You don't want to hitchhike, and I don't want to wait all night in this God-forsaken parking lot for Opie, and your 'best friend' Karen!"

Susie watched in disbelief as Eric turned and disappeared into the crowd of college students. After taking a few steps, Eric stopped walking and reconsidered his decision to leave Susie. He pulled out of his pants pocket a Zippo lighter and a hard pack of cigarettes. As he lit up, a young boy with two girls who looked underaged for college stood by looking complexed.

"You have tickets?" asked Eric.

"No." said the boy. "We were hoping to sneak in."

Eric heard his name being faintly called from behind.

"Eric! Eric!" Susie emerged from the crowd. "Wait up! Okay, fine, I'll hitchhike. But I gotta warn ya, I've never done this before. And you're taking me back to my house, right?"

"Yes. I will escort you home."

"Do you have an extra cigarette?" She asked.

Eric pulled the box out from his back pocket and slid her a stick. Susie put the cigarette into her mouth. Eric pulled the Zippo lighter from his front pocket and lit Susie's cigarette. Susie inhaled deeply, then exhaled the smoke as they both continued to walk off campus toward route 611.

"I can't believe Karen left me like that!" she yelled out as they walked on.

"I wouldn't put anything past my cousin Opie." Eric yelled back.

There was a moment of silence as the two walked side-by-side down the dark road.

"So, are you an AZA member?" she asked.

"Nope. Opie is. I don't belong to any Jewish social groups. I find the BBG girls a bit too Jappy for my taste."

Susie heard that quite clearly and was slightly jolted from the accusation. "Do you find me a bit too Jappy for your taste?" She grinned.

"I don't know. Do you think I'm a JAP?" Eric asked with a grin.

"I think far from it." Susie smiled. There was a brief silence as the two continued to smoke and walked. To Susie, the thought of hitchhiking for the first time was nerve-wracking. The silent walk was deafening. She wanted to keep the conversation going to calm nerves.

"So! Did you really shovel shit from the elephants at the circus?"

That nerve had been pinched. Eric abruptly stopped walking and faced Susie. He wanted to make sure she saw his lips.

"Hey! I don't know what Opie, or your 'best friend Karen' have told you about me!" Eric stormed. "But I never, ever want to talk about that! Understood?"

"Whooa, okay!"

"I don't want to ever hear about it! I don't want to be reminded about it! And in my presence, I don't even want you to think about it!"

"Okay! calm down! I didn't mean anything by it, jerko!"

"All right. I'm sorry." Eric apologized. They continued to walk in silence for a minute.

"Do you have any brothers or sisters? can I ask you that?"

Eric noticed that Susie was wearing a silver memento of a Vietnam POW war bracelet on her right wrist. "No. Just me. You?"

"I have two younger sisters."

Headlights slithered up from behind. Eric stuck out his thumb. The car whizzed by with no intention of stopping. Eric and Susie continued to walk on.

"So, you go to Northeast High?" asked Eric.

"Yep."

"I dated a girl that went to Northeast." Said Eric.

"Really, who?"

"Alice Cappadonna."

Susie covered her mouth with a sigh. "Oh! She was the girl that was killed in a car accident!"

"She was run over. You knew her?"

"Well, I knew of her. I didn't really know her. Seeing her around. Always saw her with the cool kids."

"Yeah. They were really cool." Eric responded sardonically.

"Wow. You went out with her?"

"For about a year."

"Were you going out with her when she was killed?"

"No. We had broken up by then."

Susie and Eric continued to walk with a moment of silence.

"Were you really going to leave me back there?" asked Susie.

"Yeah! You saw me walking. Nah!" Eric chuckled. "I was about to turn back. I really couldn't leave you alone. It's just that, Opie gets me so pissed-off."

"I had this feeling you would turn back for me." Susie smiled. "Where have you hitchhiked before?" She asked.

"Drive-in."

Susie was satisfied with Eric's answer until it processed. She stopped walking. "'Drive-in' what?"

Eric stopped walking and turned back to face her. He took a hard drag from his cigarette. "Theater." They continued to walk on.

"Why would anybody want to hitchhike to a drive-in theater?" Susie asked.

"Well, Opie and I didn't have a car at that time, and the Lincoln Drive-in was the only theater showing 'Charlotte's Web'."

Susie stopped walking for a second time. "That's a fuck'en cartoon!"

Eric shrugged as he stopped to face her. "Yeah, so?" They both proceeded to walk.

"Well, how did you hear the movie without a car?"

"You don't need a car at the drive-in. The snack bar has speakers. But the main reason Opie and I went to the Lincoln Drive-In was for their hamburgers."

"That good?"

"They were the greasiest, grossest, heaviest-tasting hamburgers in the world! Opie and I had eating contests to see who would be the first one to up-chuck."

Another car approached from behind and slowed down to a halt. Karen's head popped out of the front passenger side window. "Where ya going?" asked Karen.

"I'm surprised you came back for us, Opie," said Eric.

"I wasn't going to, but Karen insisted. She didn't want to leave Susie behind."

"I knew you wouldn't leave me stranded," Susie said to Karen.

"Yeah, I wish my own cousin was that thoughtful," Eric commented.

"I came back for you, didn't I?" asked Opie.

"No! Karen came back for Susie!" Eric replied.

Susie and Eric jumped into the back seat of the car shuffling over the eight-ounce plastic bottle of ammonia and empty coke bottles on the floor as Opie drove on.

"So, now where?" asked Opie, who was angry about missing Forest Green.

"How about bowling at Cottman Lanes?" suggested, Eric.

"Wrong!" Opie, Susie, and Karen howled out in unison.

"Why? What's wrong with Cottman Lanes?"

"We were kicked out and banned from Cottman Bowling Lanes forever," admitted Karen.

Eric leaned forward between Karen and Opie. "Why? What did Cousin Opie do?"

"Why do you always think I'm to blame when something goes wrong!" Opie pointed out as he drove.

"You're right," said Eric. "I'm sorry, cuz." Eric turned toward Karen. "So, let me ask you. What did Cousin Opie do?"

"Well, it was about week ago." Karen continued. "BBG and AZA had this all-night bowling party at Cottman Bowling Lanes. The party started Saturday night at seven-thirty and was supposed to end by noon Sunday. Well, anyway, about eight Sunday morning Opie organized a game of two-touch football with a number ten bowling ball." Opie began to laugh with a snort as Karen continued. "AZA chapter Dreyfus was against chapter Jordan between lanes seven and twenty-three. Second down, first quarter, Jordan had the bowling ball when the manager ran over and stopped the party. Of course, he pointed Opie out as the ringleader and kicked us out.

"A Touch of Class, with George Segal and Glenda Jackson is playing at the Tyson," suggested Susie. "We could still catch the nine O'clock show."

"Good idea," said Karen. "Let's go."

"I guess you would have had a better time with your old boyfriend -Brad- than with me tonight," said Opie.

"Why are you bringing this up again?" whined Karen. "Enough already!"

"Well, I don't know any reason why he has to call you if you guys broke-up."

Eric and Susie felt uncomfortable as Opie and Karen continued to argue at a moderate level, and Eric was sure that Susie couldn't see their faces to read lips. But she seemed to follow the conversation.

Back in the Oxford Circle section of the city, inside the single screen Tyson movie theater on Caster Avenue, Karen and Opie just about argued throughout the entire show. People around them were clicking their tongues and moving to other seats throughout the theater. Eric and Susie were embarrassed.

"Will you people please be quiet!" requested a man sitting in the next row in front. I'm trying to enjoy this movie!"

"I can't keep quiet!" Opie shouted back. "I have people with me who can't hear!"

"Then take them to a foreign movie with subtitles!" Responded the man.

Opie leaned forward and put his mouth up against the man's left ear. "How would you like me to take your lower lip and stretch it over your bald head?" Opie then put his two pinkies in both the man's ears and tried to lift him off his seat.

"Damn Opie! What in hell are you doing?" panicked Eric.

Susie's face was overshadowed with fear as Karen repeatedly slapped Opie on his back with her jacket pleading with him to stop and to get his fingers out of the man's ears.

"Get another seat, mister!" Opie ordered as he dropped the man back onto his chair.

The audience was out of patience as the manager accompanied by his usher with a flashlight rushed down toward Opie.

"Okay, pal!" announced the manager. "You're out of here or I call the cops!"

Out on Caster Avenue, Karen and Susie were so mad at Opie that they refused to walk with him. Eric tried to keep up with Opie who was so upset that he purposely walked a couple of paces ahead of the girls.

On the corner of Tyson Street and Castor Avenue a gang of five boys were hanging out.

"I'm so pissed, I'm gonna beat the hell out of those punks on that corner." said Opie.

"Wait a minute Opie!" Eric cautioned as he held Opie back. "There are too many of them. Susie is getting upset because of you two. Despite her hearing impairment, I like her. She's pretty. Now you asked me to come along tonight as a favor, and right now this is not the time or the place to argue. And I don't need this. So, you better cool it!"

"Yeah, you're right, little buddy."

With everybody piled back into the car, Opie put the car into reverse and stepped on the gas pedal before checking his rearview mirror. The car slammed into the parked Buick behind locking both metal bumpers together. Opie shoved the car into drive and again stepped on the gas pedal. Even with the whining of the engine and screeching of the tires, the two cars wouldn't disengage. Eric and the girls got out of the car to try to lift the tail end of Opie's car off the front bumper of the car behind. As they lifted, Opie stepped on the gas pedal a third time. The two cars unlocked. Eric and the girls jumped back in the car and Opie once again stepped on the accelerator peeling out of the parking spot before any of the neighborhood yentas could spot them.

With so much adrenaline pumping through Opie's veins, he accelerated, passing other cars traveling over fifty miles an hour down Castor Avenue. Wide-eyed Karen gripped the dashboard with white knuckles.

Plastic ammonia and glass Coca-Cola bottles tossed and rolled on the back floor against Eric's and Susie's ankles as Opie steered around the circle at Roosevelt Boulevard overpass. The driver's side door swung open. Opie stretched out of the car to close it. All three passengers in the car silently stared at him as though he was completely insane.

"It's just the door," Opie calmly announced trying to laugh off the incident. "It always does that."

"I've never seen that happen before." Eric proclaimed.

At the end of the evening, Opie and Karen waited in the car while Eric walked Susie to the front door of her house. It was the same style stone-front row house as Karen's in the middle of the block just around the corner. Susie opened the storm door then slid her house key into the lock of the main door.

"Well, it was really nice meeting you, Eric!" Susie said in a louder than normal tone.

"It was nice meeting you, too, Susie," Eric said slowly so that Susie could read his lips. "I know this wasn't a good night. You see, sometimes my cousin Opie acts like an ass. I wish there was a place where we could have gone to get to know each other better. I think you're a very attractive lady. And I would like to see you again under better circumstances."

"I would like to see you again, Eric. But do you have a car? Because I don't want to borrow my parents', and I ain't hitchhiking."

"Yeah. I got a car," Eric said with a laugh. "It ain't much, but it gets me where I have to go."

"Were you really going to turn back for me at the college?"

"To be honest, like I said, I don't think I could have left you there alone. I was just pissed. But since you asked me about circus boy, I think it's only fair if I ask you a personal question."

"Sure. I'll let you have one shot, jerko," Susie acknowledged with a smile.

"Your hearing impairment." Susie's eyebrows arose. "Is it from birth?"

"Hearing impairment?" asked Susie. "What hearing impairment? Karen told me that you have a hearing impairment!"

"No!" Eric shouted back slowly. "I don't have a hearing impairment! Opie told me that you have a hearing impairment! "

Both Susie and Eric look toward the car and found Opie and Karen pointing and laughing from behind the rolled-up car windows.

"Damn, Opie!" Eric said softly.

....

After school, Eric was tardy getting to work at the 'Steak 'N Brew' restaurant. Dashing into the utility closet, he grabbed the first long white shirt. Without unbuttoning it, and after slipping it over his head, it seemed to be a longer size than usual, and the shoulders were a little broad at the top. Plus, inside-out since the buttons were on the opposite side. Eric would have to fix it later after rushing onto the restaurant floor before Marty noticed he was late. Finding a gallon jug of ammonia on a shelf, Eric hastily unscrewed the cap and took a whiff. "Ah! There you are, God!"

On the dining floor, as Eric was refurbishing the salad bar, he could hear customers snickering from behind. Inspecting himself in front of the salad bar mirror, checking his hair and face, Eric couldn't find anything out of place or obviously wrong. Opie was busing a table when Eric walked by heading toward the kitchen. 'Hello'. Opie said. Eric ignored him as he continued walking on.

"I wanted to apologize for the way I was acting the other night, and to tell you that I'm sorry about leaving you at the Forest Green concert."

Eric stopped walking and turned to face Opie without saying a word.

"Karen and I kind of split for a while." Opie continued, "she said I need time to get my act together. Susie said that she likes you and wants to see you again. I'm also sorry about the hearing-impaired joke. But you to must admit, it did break the ice."

"Susie and I didn't think it was funny!" replied Eric as he turned and continued to stroll toward the kitchen. Opie watched Eric walk off when he noticed the long white shirt that Eric was wearing drooping past his knees over his jeans.

"What the fu." Opie said to himself. Then laughed.

In the kitchen, Eric passed Marty by the grills who was holding on to a cocktail as he conversed with the two cooks. Marty took a second hard look at Eric as he passed.

"Ah, Cochise! come here!"

Eric knew he was going to be reprimanded for coming late to work.

"What are you doing wearing the waitresses uniform?" asked Marty.

The cooks with a couple of waiters and waitresses laughed as Eric peered down to discover the long shirt, he had hastily put on was a white uniform worn by the waitresses.

"I thought it was a shirt!" Eric slowly went back into the dish room. Not wanting to be seen in public, Eric convinced the dishwasher to trade positions.

As Eric was settling in as the dishwasher washing dishes, keeping the dress on as an apron, the cooks and staff in the kitchen yelled out jeers and cheers as they listened to the news from a small radio by the grills. Somebody raised the volume.

President Ford announced that South Vietnam had surrendered to the Communist North. Americans were being evacuated by military helicopters on top of the American Embassy in Saigon. Secretary of State Kissinger had estimated that there were over fifty-six thousand Vietnamese refugees, with twenty-two thousand more fleeing by boat.

Opie walked into the dish room and dropped his bus tray of dirty dishes onto the long stainless-steel counter adjacent to the rollers leading into the stainless-steel automatic dishwasher.

"Did you hear the news, Eric! The war is over!" Announced Opie.

"Yeah. I just heard." Eric replied.

"You don't sound too enthused," said Opie as he sipped coke through the used straws from all the dirty glasses. "I thought you'd be happy to hear."

"Makes no difference to me." replied Eric. Opie took a bite out of a half-eaten porter house steak from a customer's plate. "That's gross, Opie! You know that? That's really, really, gross!"

"So, how's the fashion business?" Opie walked off laughing.

"Ah-ha! Very funny, asshole!" Eric shouted out over the noise from the dish room plus the radio in the kitchen.

Eric hit the switch that turned on the steam and the dishwasher at the same time. Within a couple of seconds, a long scream was heard coming from inside the stainless-steel dishwasher. Eric turned off the machine, then raised the stainless-steel door looking into the misty void waiting for the steam to dissipate. There inside the washer was Marty's steaming, dripping wet head. He was inspecting the food traps in the washer without first notifying Eric.

"Cochise! Don't you ever look in here before you start this thing?" Marty yelled out as he grabbed the nearest cloth towel to dry off his head.

"Well, no, sir. There usually isn't anybody in the dishwasher when I start it up!" Eric tried to explain.

"Cochise!"

"I know, sir. I'm fired."

"No, Cochise. You're not fired." Marty said calmly as he continued to dry his head with the towel. "The war is over. Let's go to the bar and have us a drink."

"Cool!"

Sitting at the bar, Marty was cooler than ever. It didn't matter to him that Eric was underage and still on the clock wearing a women's dress.

"So, I guess I'll order a Bud for the both of us?" Said Marty.

"I'll just have a vodka Collins."

"Why, what's wrong with Bud?" Asked Marty

"I figured if you're not drinking beer, why should I?" Said Eric. "Mind if I smoke?"

"Sure. That's not weed, is it?"

"No."

"Too bad."

"Marlboro?" Offered Eric pulling out the pack from his pants pocket from under the dress.

"Don't mind if I do." Said Marty slipping the cigarette out from its box and a lighter from his sport jacket pocket.

The bar was busy but not overcrowded. Everyone had their attention on the twenty-five-inch television set hanging eight feet over the back bar. Walter Conkrite was reporting in detail about the ongoing evacuation in South Vietnam.

"Were you in Vietnam?" Eric asked Marty.

"Yeah. I fought in that bloody war." Replied Marty as he inhaled the cigarette then a swallow of beer.

"What was it like?"

"You don't wanna know."

And so, there he was, Eric Blum. Sitting at the bar, eighteen-years-old, underaged in the Commonwealth of Pennsylvania. Wearing a white dress with a white headband. Sharing a drink and a cigarette with the boss like two old sailing swabs, watching a special report on television about the end of the Vietnam War. A war that ended six years too late for the Blum family.

•••••••••••••••••••••

That Sunday morning, before the restaurant opened, Eric had to help the cook clean up from the night before. Eric was washing dishes in the dish room when he heard a commotion coming from the grills.

"Cochise!" called the cook. "We got us a fire here!"

Eric peered over though the dish room doorway into the kitchen and could see the flames shooting out from one of the three grills. It was a grease fire. The cook aimlessly battled the flames with a dirty, greasy rag and a small fire extinguisher.

"How high are the flames?" asked Eric as he continued to casually wash dishes.

"They're about to touch the ceiling!"

"Okay. Let me know when they hit the ceiling!"

"They're starting to kiss it now!"

Eric slid the dishes into the dishwasher, then shuffled over to a pay phone on the kitchen wall, searched his pocket for a dime, calmly placed the dime in the phone's coin slot, then dialed the Cheltenham Volunteer Fire Department.

"Why are you using the pay phone?" asked the cook as he continued to battle the flames.

"It takes longer."

If this restaurant was going to burn down, Eric was going to give it every opportunity to do so.

"Hello, fire department? We have a fire at the Steak 'n Brew restaurant at the Cheltenham Mall. Take your time getting over here. It's not that big."

Eric hung up the receiver then sat on a chair to watch the fire as the cook tried in vain to contain the spreading flames with the dirty rag.

"Don't you think we should leave?" asked the cook.

"Are you kidding? This is entertainment!"

"Well, maybe we should leave all the windows and doors open for the fire department." The cook suggested.

"Well," said Eric, "I was thinking on the lines of ventilation. That will help it burn faster."

As much as Eric wanted to stay inside to watch the kitchen burn, the smoke and heat were getting too intense for human consumption.

Even though the boys left most of the windows and doors open for easy access, the Cheltenham volunteer fire department broke through the remaining windows and ran hoses through the dining area plowing through tables, chairs, counters, and partitions smashing everything in sight to get to the blaze in the kitchen. One fireman fought the fire with a two-man hose by himself and hit everything but the flames.

The bottom line in damages? Fire: Seven-thousand dollars. Volunteer fire department: Forty-five thousand dollars. The restaurant was closed for renovation. This was a great opportunity for Eric to leave the food service business without quitting. What could the school or his parents say if his place of employment had been incinerated?

CHAPTER 10

LYING IN THY BROTHER'S GRAVE

Prom night at Noah Webster: Eric rented a powder-blue tuxedo. His rented black patent leather shoes were so shiny he could look down to find his own reflection.

That evening, from her bedroom on the second floor of her home, Susie seductively walked down the stairs to the living room. She wore white high heels and a red gown with a slit on the left side that went as high as her mid-left thigh. Susie reminded Eric of actress Edie Adams when she posed for the Muriel cigar advertisement.

"How do I look?" she asked, surrounded by Eric, her parents, and two younger sisters.

"Wowzah! Man, oh man. Just beautiful," replied Eric as he slipped a white corsage around her right wrist.

That last week of April, the mahogany paneled cafeteria at Webster was transformed back the into a ballroom it had originally been during its days as a manor. All the lunchroom tables were removed. The room was void of any academia just for a soda bar, buffett of food, round tables, and chairs. The entire school staff was there. A disc-jockey who was set up in a corner spun records that were popular from the year 1974–75.

Eric and his date walked into the 'ballroom' fashionably late, which made for an impressionable entrance. Renée looked good in a blue gown. Her new date was sloppily dressed. His shoes were scuffed and shirttail hanging below his black sport jacket. Renée was envious at the sight of Eric and Susie.

Eric and Susie proudly walked over toward Warren and Carol at the corner of the room by the fireplace that was lit for the occasion. Warren in a nice black sport jacket, white shirt, and tie, Carol in a black two-piece tight pencil dress just mid-calf and red pumps. Carol complemented Eric on how suave he looked. Eric introduced Carol to Susie.

"Hi Miss. Schor," said Susie extending her hand to meet Carol's. "I have heard a great deal about you."

"Oh, I bet you have," Carol responded receiving Susie's hand questioning her integrity. "Well, welcome to Noah Webster."

Although there was no relationship between Carol and Eric, for some reason Carol was envious of Susie. The exquisite dirty blonde was truly beautiful and sweet. There was no reason for Carol's animosity.

"Eric," Carol announced, "why don't you make a speech to welcome everybody?"

"Okay, Carol. I think I will." Eric pretended he just noticed Warren standing by. "*Warren*! So glad to see you again!"

"Hello Eric," Warren said warmly unaware of the intended sarcasm.

"You know, *Warren*, we should go hunting."

"I've never been hunting, Eric."

"Neither have I *Warren*. But I'll be willing if you be -game-." Carol widened her eyes from Eric's hidden pun. "We'll talk more about this later. Right now, I must get this party rolling." continued Eric.

Leaving Susie with Carol and Warren, Eric strolled to the disc-jockey's table and picked up the microphone in a pompous manner all for Susie. Carol couldn't keep her eyes off her.

"Ladies and gentlemen girls and boys, and of course for those who are not too sure, welcome one and all to Noah Webster Preparatory seventh annual prom. As a senior class member, some of you may know this could be my last year here." Most of the students applauded. Eric scowled but continued. "And as Student Body President, it has been an honor to be Prom Master of Ceremonies for the past four years. So! While the punch is being spiked, and principal Swanson is in the bathroom getting stoned, everybody party on!"

The students and staff applauded as the music continued with Shining Star by Earth Wind and Fire. Eric walked back to Susie, took her by the hand, and shuffled toward the middle of the room. Susie was taken back at how well Eric could dance. The rest of the students followed suit. Renée sat on the side with her date who wouldn't move off his chair if his life depended on it.

For the duration of the prom, Eric, Susie, Warren, and Carol stuck close together at one end of the room forming a clique. As You make Me feel Brand New by The Stylistics played on, Eric noticed Renée looking melancholy next to her deadbeat date. Eric thought it was a waste of a beautiful gown on such a celebrated evening and perhaps this would be a good time to bury the hatchet.

"Susie, would you mind if I have this one dance with that girl sitting over there? She's just an old friend."

"Uh I guess not," Susie responded complexly.

Eric excused himself from Susie and walked over to Renée. Renée looked up at Eric with a blasé expression.

"Hi, Renée. Look, uh, what the hell. Let's have this dance."

Renée looked over toward Susie then glanced at her deadbeat date. Clicking her tongue in disgust, she got up from her chair and walked with Eric toward the center of the dance floor.

"Is there something I should know about?" Susie asked Carol about Eric and Renée.

"I wouldn't worry about it," replied Carol.

During the song, Eric held Renée close, then pulled back, slipping his right foot under her gown concentrating on the reflection in his patent leather shoes.

"Ah! The white ones. I always liked them. You still have taste, Renée!"

Renée was surprised when she realized what Eric was describing. Pushing Eric away, she turned and stormed off the dance floor. Eric shrugged as he walked back to Susie.

"What in the hell was that?" Susie fretfully asked.

"Oh, you know," replied Eric in a nonchalant tone as he dragged her out onto the dance floor. "She wanted to dance with me all night. But I told her that I was taken by somebody special."

Senior, Thomas Jones, one of the four black students at the school, and one of the school's star athletes walked up to Carol and Warren with his date.

"Miss Schor. Did you mail out my transcripts to Boston University today?"

"Holy shit, Thomas! I forgot!"

"Miss. Schor! How could you? They must be in the mail by tomorrow morning, or I'll miss my deadline! I won't be able to attend college this fall."

"All right, Thomas. Don't panic! I have them on top of my desk in my office upstairs. I'll get them, and mail them on my way home tonight at the post office mailbox. By six tomorrow morning, they'll be on their way before deadline."

Thomas had received a college basketball scholarship from the Police Athletic League (PAL) in Philadelphia. He was accepted to Boston University. All that was left was to confirm to B.U. his high school records.

Thomas strolled off with his date as Carol reached into her black handbag and realized that she had left her school office keys in another jacket at her apartment. At that moment Sam danced by with his date. Carol grabbed him before he passed.

"Get Eric from the dance floor! And I want you and him back here before me, pronto!"

"Why, what's up?"

"Get him!" Demanded Carol.

Sam left his date and dragged Eric and Susie from the center of the dance floor. Carol pulled Eric and Sam aside. Susie's and Sam's date were taken-in by the awareness of this emergency.

"Eric, you, and Sam must do me a very big favor. I left my office keys at my apartment. I have to get into my office to retrieve Thomas's transcripts and mail it out tonight or he won't be able to attend B.U. next fall."

"Well, what do you want us to do?" asked Eric.

"I want you two to break into my office and get them." The two boys looked astounded about the request. "Don't be so surprised. You've done this before. I want this done quietly and I want it done now! And Eric, the transcripts are on top of my desk in a manila envelope. Nowhere else. Understand, Eric? No-where-else!" Eric and Sam were out of sight, and on the second floor of the school before Carol could say G. Gordon Liddy.

Sam picked the door to Carol's office and began to snoop around for the Thomas Jones transcripts. Eric accidentally brushed against Carol's white sweater hanging off the back of the chair that dropped onto the floor. When he went to pick it up, he noticed a small palm size clear plastic bag with white powder inside lying on the floor.

"Sam, look!"

Sam stopped snooping for a moment and picked up the plastic bag. He opened it, stuck his finger in, then gave it a taste. "Yep!"

"Carol Schor?" asked Eric. "Do you think she's… ?"

"You would know more about her personal life than anybody else, Eric," said Sam as he closed the plastic bag, and replaced it back in the sweater pocket.

"Why would I know more?"

"Come on, Eric. Everybody knows about you and Carol. It's no secret."

"Well, it is to me, because I don't know what in hell you're talking about."

"No? You didn't crawl out of your tent the first night of the class camping trip?" Asked Sam.

"What? You weren't even there! Who told you that?"

"Look, somebody was talking, and I listened."

"Stern!" Said Eric.

"What you and Carol do outside of this school is none of my business. And that's the advice I'm passing along to you. Whatever Carol Schor does in her private time is her business. I just found the transcripts. Now, let's get the hell out of here. And Eric, can you keep a secret?"

"More than you. Remember?"

"For the benefit of all of us, just keep your mouth shut about what we did and found here tonight.

Meanwhile, in the girls' bathroom on the first floor, an eleventh grader-Cindy-was fixing her makeup in the mirror over the sink. Renée, standing next to her, looked dismayed as she was adjusting her gown. Cindy asked if something was wrong.

"You wouldn't believe what Eric did to me! I was dancing with him when he stuck his foot under my gown, and from the reflection of his shoe told me what color underwear I was wearing." Renée slipped her underpants off and stuffed them into her handbag. "Well, I'll show him."

Back in the ballroom/cafeteria, Sam handed Carol Thomas's transcripts then walked off with his date. Carol peeked into the envelope as Eric stood in front staring at her. Carol looked up at Eric as to ask 'Yes?' Eric gave a quick grin then looked away. Sam was right about a private life. And Eric left well enough alone.

"Is this place a loony bin or what?" asked Susie, getting a little annoyed about being kept in the dark. "What in hell is going on around here?"

"That's what I been trying to tell everybody!" Eric proclaimed. "Here's your proof Carol! Even an outsider can see this place is a nut house!"

"Excuse me," interrupted Renée. "May we finish our dance?"

"Yeah, sure. Why not?" countered Susie waving Renée and Eric along giving up figuring out what was going on.

"Thank you," Renée said to Susie with a slight grin as she grabbed Eric by the arm and dragged him out toward the center of the dance floor.

"I knew you'd come back to me Renée," Eric stated as a cocky proud rooster. "Just a matter of time."

Eric danced close to Renée, then for the second time pulled back sliding his shoe under her gown. He stopped dancing, stung, staring onto the floor.

"Something wrong?" asked Renée with a grin.

"Well, I didn't think that it could be possible."

"Cat got your tongue?'

"No." Replied Eric. "But I think my shoe has a crack in it!"

....

If not for the car radio playing disco music, the drive taking Susie home from the prom would be silent. Eric felt a bit of a coldness coming from Susie. There was tension in the air.

"I hope you had a good time at my prom. My school's a wild place. It's an insane asylum." Eric continued under his breath. Susie looking toward the oncoming road nodded slightly without a word. "What's wrong? We're not talking?" asked Eric.

"Eric, I want to say something. I didn't go to your prom to watch you dance with your ex-girlfriends or finagle a school coup d'état with your history teacher! I came to your prom to be with you. I wanted to share your joy tonight! But instead, I stood on the sideline like a cheerleader! I'm nobody's trophy, Eric! You know, I thought you were different when I first met you. I thought I finally met somebody with half a brain. But instead, I found tonight that I was with another AZA boy from Northeast Philly. It's nice to see how important you are at school Eric and well liked. But I'm very disappointed in the way I was treated."

That was the first time that any girl who was his contemporary had addressed him as an adult. And it was probably the first time that any girl had expressed really mature feelings toward him. Eric did not want to lose Susie. He had finally met somebody with legitimate feelings. More than just a girl, a real human being, a woman. Even though he didn't belong to AZA or come from Northeast Philly, Eric knew exactly what Susie was getting at.

"I'm sorry, Susie. You're right. I was so caught up in showing off in front of you, that I ignored you altogether. I'm sorry. I don't want to lose you."

"I wasn't impressed."

"I'd like to make it up to you."

"I don't know, Eric. I really don't know. I'm just tired of going out with assholes."

"Wow," Eric softly said to himself. "Susie. This is one asshole who is truly sorry and really wants another chance with you." As he drove Eric saw from the corner of his eye Susie shaking her head not wanting to give him that second chance. Eric recalled the trouble he had with Renée not giving her enough time, or with Alice who he'd smothered. He wanted to avoid a repeat performance of both those girls with Susie.

....

The following week, in the late afternoon after school, Eric was walking out from the school's cafeteria onto the stone patio heading toward the parking lot when he found Cousin Opie and his cousin John sitting on the hood of Uncle Pat's black hearse. The Stanley cup pregame featuring the Philadelphia Flyers being hosted by the Buffalo Sabers at

BRUCE BERYL FISHER

the Buffalo's Memorial Stadium in New York could be heard from the
hearse radio. Radios were not an option in hearses, but Uncle Pat had
one installed.

"You remember my first Cousin on my father's side, John O'Neal?
I got a case of coke and a twelve-ounce bottle of ammonia on the back.
Hop in Eric! We'll cruise!"

"Does Uncle Pat know that you have his car?" Eric asked.

"My parents are at a mortician's convention in Salt Lake City
this week!"

"What about my car?" Asked Eric.

"Leave it! We'll pick it up later!"

John suggested they do something mischievous with the hearse.

"I have an idea!" mentioned Eric. "Opie, can you get a white sheet?"

"Yeah. I can slip one out from my father's slab. Why?"

"Well, this is what I have in mind…"

With the car radio blasting the hockey game, Eric ended up in the
cargo bay of the hearse with his head and torso covered under the white
sheet. With no shoes or socks, his pants rolled up to his knees. His naked
feet were left exposed with a toe tag. John wore a black top hat from
Opie's father's Halloween undertaker's costume.

The first stop was the Hess gas station on Easton Road in Glenside.
A grimy, greasy looking, long-haired young gas station attendant sitting
outside the station with his chair propped up against the station wall
aloofly slid off his chair and walked over toward the black hearse.

"Yeah?" asked the attendant with a slight intolerant attitude leaning
down against the driver's side window not taking any notice of what was
lying in the back of the car.

"Ten dollars of premium, please," requested Opie.

The attendant slapped down the pump lever with the nozzle, walked
to the back of the car, pulled down the license plate, unscrewed the gas
cap, then jammed the nozzle into the fill pipe, latching the handle onto
auto feed. He casually gazed into the big rear window of the hearse fixing

260

his hair by his reflection. The attendant slowly perceived what was lying beyond his reflection in the cargo bay and lost track of the pump, which was already flowing an extra two gallons.

The attendant quickly stopped the auto-feed and withdrew the nozzle, fumbling as he screwed the gas cap back onto the car's fill pipe. The license plate sprung back into place with a 'slap'.

"I accidentally pumped in a couple extra gallons," he said to Opie in a more-humble-manor. "That will be twelve dollars."

"Twelve dollars!" Opie snapped out. "With gasoline costing as much as fifty-five cents a gallon, you want me to pay for your mistake. I only have ten bucks… Eric! can I borrow a couple of dollars from you?"

The attendant looked toward John sitting shotgun for the extra two dollars but noticed movement coming from the cargo bay. Out from under the white sheet a hand appeared with two dollars. Opie reached back, grabbed the money, and handed it off to the attendant, then stepped on the gas pedal peeling out of the station. With twelve dollars in his hand and a dumbfounded expression, the attendant was left standing watching the black hearse disappear down Easton Road.

A few miles down, the hearse pulled into a Carvel ice cream parlor parking lot. John and Opie got out of the car, opened the side doors, and tucked the sheet in tighter around Eric. A dog in the next car was barking its head off. A woman walking out of the parlor with her young son eating ice cream from a cone accidently dropped it on top of her son's head after tripping over him as she witnessed what Opie and John were tucking in. A young girl inside the store looking out the store window spit out her milkshake through her mouth and nostrils after seeing the covered corpse. A small commotion was heard from inside the store as people at tables or in line stared out at the hearse and its occupants.

Six-foot-four John wearing the black undertaker's top hat looking like Boris Karloff's Frankenstein, alongside five-foot-eight Opie resembling Peter Lorre walked into the ice cream parlor while people continued to stare keeping a social distance.

After the boys ordered three ice cream cones they returned to the car. Eric slid his hand out from under the sheet to retrieve his chocolate ice cream from John. He ate it from under the sheet but between licks, Eric raised the cone out over and above the sheet. People from outside the car and through the store windows continued to watch beside themselves. Opie and John describing the people's reactions to Eric who couldn't hold in laughter any longer imagining the events unfolding.

After a couple of hours of terror-cruising the suburban neighborhoods, driving back toward Philly on Papermill Road, Opie spotted a long-haired-hippie hitchhiker. He pulled over to pick him up. The boy jumped right into the front seat next to John.

"I'm going to Plymouth Meeting Mall," said the hitchhiker. John changed the radio station from sports to Grand Funk's American Band on W.I.F.I-FM.

"Yeah. We'll take you there," replied John.

"Gee, thanks guys for the lift! I had never ridden in a hearse before. How are the Flyers doing?"

They all discussed hockey then sang along with Grand Funk. "You know, it's kind of cold in here," said the hitchhiker.

"Yep," replied John.

Opie had the air conditioner raised to the highest setting so Eric would remain cool under the sheet.

"It's for him," added Opie as he pointed toward the back of the car.

"Oh, my," said the hitchhiker looking behind for the first time. "Is he?"

"Dead," said John.

"How did he die?"

"He was stabbed in…" said Opie

"Roslyn," John responded.

"We're taking him to…" said Opie.

"The funeral parlor," continued John.

"My...," said the hitchhiker.

"God." Replied Opie.

It was a narrow back farm road heading toward Plymouth Meeting with the four boys who continued to sing along with Grand Funk Railroad. Opie stopped singing and just three voices were heard. John stopped singing but two voices were still heard. The hitchhiker stopped singing. A single voice was heard. The hiker hesitantly turned to look behind and found Eric sitting up with a broad smile and chocolate ice cream smeared around his mouth singing and waving at him. The hitchhiker screamed. At twenty-five miles an hour, he opened the hearse door, jumped out, rolled on the ground, then ran down the road. The three boys in the hearse laughed so hard that Opie had to pull over to the narrow shoulder to avoid a head-on collision.

The hearse headed back toward Philadelphia. Stopped at a red light, Eric was sitting up in the cargo bay with the white sheet covering his legs. John scanned the radio band and stopped at the sounds of hysteria over the airwaves.

"It's over! It's over!" the sports announcer screamed until he was hoarse.

"The Philadelphia Flyers have just won their second Stanley cup against the Buffalo Sabers! Bobby Clark will be hoisting the Stanley cup on his shoulders... !"

"See, Eric," declared Opie. "If you hadn't gotten yourself fired from the Spectrum, you would've been there right now breaking up the ice!"

"I didn't get fired from the Spectrum." defended Eric.

"You got fired?" asked John.

"No, I didn't get fired."

From behind the hearse, red lights were flashing. The sound of car doors slammed closed. Four men in black leather jackets surrounded the car. A head popped down next to Opie's driver's side window. It was Plymouth Whitemarsh Township Police. Opie slid down his window.

"Driver's license and registration, please." Request the lead officer.

Eric and John were frozen in place. Opie was a bit shaken, but without protest he slid his wallet out from his back pocket and gave the officer his ID.

"What is this all about, officer?" asked Opie.

"I want all you out of this vehicle with identification." Ordered the police officer.

The boys piled out of the hearse, slid out their wallets from their back pockets, and handed over their IDs to the lead officer.

"Turn, face the vehicle, and lay your palms on top of the roof. Don't any of you move until I get back!"

Standing with their palms on the roof of the hearse, Opie stood next to John who was still wearing the undertaker's top hat. Eric -to John's right- in his bare feet with his pants legs rolled up toward his knees and a toe tag still attached to his left big toe and chocolate smeared around his mouth.

"I have a right to know what this is about, officer." Said Opie.

The lead officer stopped in his tracks, turned, and faced Opie. "Did I tell you to talk?"

"No, sir."

"Well then, that was your second mistake. Unless you want to make it a third, shut your mouth!"

The lead officer continued to walk back to his patrol car. Two more officers checked out the hearse for contraband, while a fourth guarded over his detainees. Altogether, four police cruisers with flashing lights stood guard behind the hearse.

The hearse was registered commercial. Uncle Pat had Opie take his chauffeur's driver's license test when he took his driver's exam at sixteen. Otherwise, impoundment and jailsville. In that scenario, Opie wouldn't have to worry about his parents killing him and hiding the body. Uncle Pat would just have to warm up the crematorium. And Mrs. Blum would make sure there was enough room for two.

The lead officer walked back to the hearse and returned the IDs to their rightful owners.

"Put your hands by your sides and face me."

"Do I have a right to know what this is all about?" Opie asked again.

"Well, Mr. O'Neal. You know…"

Eric could hear the crisp cracking sound of leather jacket and gun holster as the officer prepared for his all out, ball-breaking, mind-bending, nerve-wracking lecture.

"… I was on my way to work earlier this evening when I saw you guys at the gas station in Glenside. I really didn't think much about it, 'till we were getting complaints over the radio that you guys were terrorizing and scaring the daylights out of people. So, my colleagues and I began searching for you. I knew you wouldn't be hard to find. I mean, let's face It, this car sticks out like a, excuse the pun…"

"… Sore thumb?" John volunteered with a smile.

"Tombstone!" said the officer. "Did I tell you to say anything, Boris?"

"No, sir."

"'Boris'," laughed Eric. "He called you 'Boris'".

The officer stared at Eric with less than an amusing grin. Eric straightened up.

"It took us a couple of hours. But we found you," The officer continued, "I don't think what you guys are doing is funny. This is a gross joke. Personally, I take death seriously. I had buddies who were killed in the line of duty. Now, I just did a run on this vehicle, and your IDs and found you all just turned legal age of eighteen, which means I can book all of you as an adult on mischievous conduct, unlawful, and immoral use of a commercial vehicle, and disturbing the peace. Mr. O'Neal? Is this prank worth losing your chauffeur license over for the next five years?"

At this point, Eric was praying that Opie would answer correctly and keep his wisecracking mouth shut.

"No, sir," replied Opie.

"And you, chocolate boy?"

"OY!" Eric jumped slightly as the toe tag flipped over covering the top of his foot.

"You were involved in an auto accident back in January, weren't you?"

"Yes, sir."

"You destroyed county and federal property. Isn't that true?"

"Yes, sir."

"And you… Herman Munster," the officer addressed John. "You're a long way off from the South, boy. What's your relation here?"

"I'm his cousin," John said, pointing toward Opie.

"I'm not!" declared Eric, denouncing his relationship.

"Well," said the officer, "seeing you all don't have any other outstanding moving violations or warrants, tell ya what I'm going to do. Since you two are from Philadelphia, and since everybody is in a festive mood because the Flyers have just won their second Stanley cup, and I gotta tell ya, I'm a Flyers fan too, I'm…"

"I worked at the Spectrum!" Eric spouted out hoping the officer would be more lenient.

"He was fired," announced Opie.

"I wasn't fired!"

The officer just looked at Eric with a tilted head as the RCA dog listening to his master's voice. Then continued.

"… Going to let you boys go with a warning. My associates and I will be more than happy to give you a personal escort to the county line. And I don't want to see you boys or this vehicle here again in my township. Is that understood?"

With their red lights flashing, one police car in front, the hearse, and three police cars behind escorted the hearse to the Montgomery County/Philadelphia line. The four officers got out of their cars and watched as the hearse disappeared down the Road.

Once the hearse rolled deep into Philadelphia territory, with Eric sitting in the front seat next to John, Opie broke the verbal silence.

"Now what do you want to do?"

"Why don't you drive me back to Webster, so I can get my car," suggested Eric.

"Why, Eric? The night is still young! Don't let the fuzz bum you out!"

"I want to see Susie."

"Eric, she's a Northeast JAP. So is Karen. They Both are! Forget them. Here's the facts, man. We're not in their league! We don't travel in the same circles. We don't have parents who can afford to buy us new cars or have condos in Margate for the summer. We can't afford to drive them to Atlantic city every Sunday to eat at Lou's restaurant in Ventnor!"

"No, Opie, I think you're wrong. I think we can be in their league. But right now, we're just a step below. We're a couple of assholes."

"'Assholes', Eric? Is that what we are? Does Karen have to continue talking to her ex-boyfriend while she's seeing me? Look what happened at your prom! Susie didn't like it when you socialize with your friends from school.

"That's not what happened." Defended Eric. "If you can't realize that Karen had a life before you, and will after, then yeah you're an ass-hole, Opie."

"How about you, John?" asked Opie. "Does your girlfriend give you a hard time?"

"Nah. My girlfriend's back home! We get along real fine. We want to get married. She's like family already. Actually, she's my mamma's daughter from her first marriage."

Opie and Eric stopped to think for a moment to process that information.

"Okay, Eric." Opie continued. "Maybe you're right. I'll drop you off at your car. If you see Karen, tell her I said 'hi'. Maybe that will break the ice. Oh, and by the way... sometime next week, my father may have a funeral that he's personally taking charge of. One of his old high school buddies. He's dying from cancer. He is in something they call, 'hospice'."

"'Hospice'?" asked John.

"Yeah." Replied Opie. "it's an organization that watches over you while you're dying."

"The whole organization?" asks Eric.

"No. I think they send out a nurse." Opie responded.

"Oh, I'm sorry to hear that," said John.

"That's all right," replied Opie. "Anyway Eric, when that time comes, my father wants to know if you'll be one of the pallbearers. He'll pay you one-hundred-fifty dollars for the day."

"Yeah, sure. I'll have to clear it with my school to take off if it's during the week. But I think I can do it."

"Oh, just one more thing, Eric." Said Obie. "If you're going to see Susie, wipe the chocolate off your face."

....

After Opie dropped Eric off at Webster's parking lot, Eric drove the old Chevy to Northeast Philly. There were so many people lining the streets at Five Points celebrating the Flyers victory over the Buffalo Sabers, Eric couldn't make out the World War-I war memorial in the center of the intersection. As far down as he could see down Cottman Avenue, banners in black, white, and orange hanging from building windows reading 'Flyers Number One Stanley cup champs!'

Eric glanced toward his right off Cottman Avenue to find a group of people on Oxford Avenue trying to roll the Y bus. Eric drove through the countless crowds of people slapping and pounding on the Chevy with their fists. The car crawled its way to a secondary street away from the madness of the revelers.

Eric doubled parked in front of Susie's house. Susie and Karen were sitting on the front steps by the sidewalk.

"Susie!" Eric called out from his car. "Did you guys see Cottman Avenue?"

"Let's take a drive over there!" Karen suggested.

"Please, Eric! can we?" pleaded Susie.

"Are you kidding? How do you expect me to drive through that crowd of people? I nearly got here myself!" Eric announced.

After another beg and a whine from the girls, Eric thought this voyage through the bowels of a botchery could get him back into Susie's good grace. It might be well worth it.

Slowly and carefully manipulating through the festive crowd, Eric managed to drive out to Cottman Avenue. So many people surrounded the car that Eric couldn't tell if there were any cars in front or behind him. Susie was sitting out of the open window on the front passenger side. Karen sat out of the back window behind Susie as Eric drove through the abusive crowd once again pounding and slapping on the hood and roof. At Five Points off Township Line, Eric turned the car away from the crowd at the A&P supermarket parking lot where he saw two intoxicated teenage boys jogging in the direction of Five Points completely naked except for white tennis sneakers. Each one clenching onto a can of beer.

"Hey!" Eric screamed. "You two! Over here!"

The two boys could hardly run fast enough toward the puke-green Chevy. One of the boys jumped onto the hood while the other hopped onto the roof. Susie and Karen stared up in awe at the two endowed boys. At the supermarket, a man and his wife dropped a bag of groceries in disbelief as they watched the car drive by with two naked boys on top.

By this time there were well over a few thousand people in the Five Points section allowing the Chevy to cruise through as they cheered the naked boys who were gesturing toward the crowd like traveling Popes.

With her boobs bouncing under a loose orange, black, and white Flyer's sports jersey, a heavyset girl ran alongside the car tying a white, black, and orange streamer onto the car's radio antenna.

Hidden on a dark secondary street off Cottman Avenue, a police car with two policemen watched as the Pontiff-like streakers floated by above the crowd.

"Did you see that?" asked one cop to the other as the police radio echoed festive reports in the background.

"I think so."

"Yep," said the first policeman, as he started the cruiser's engine and flashing lights. "Let's roll."

The second police officer grabbed the microphone. "This is car 215 to dispatch."

"Go ahead 215." Replied the female dispatcher.

"We're on pursuit of two naked caucasian males, approximately in their late teens to early twenties, riding on top of a vehicle going east on Cottman Avenue between Algon and Oxford."

"Can you describe the vehicle, 215?" asked the dispatcher.

"Negative, there are too many people out here to get a positive description."

"Are you requesting back-up, 215?"

The dispatcher asked the question twice with no response. As the police cruiser was cautiously crawling through the crowd, one of the revelers had ripped off its antenna pulling the cable along with it.

"What the hell?" Exclaimed the first police officer feeling the thud and the cruiser's resistance from the antenna cable snapping off. The reveler danced through the street thrusting the antenna into the air like a king with his scepter. The dispatcher took the liberty to call for back up. Red lights from two police cars flashed within the dark madness of the crowd as they closed in on their prey from different directions.

Meanwhile, Susie and Karen were still hanging out of the Chevy's windows as the car drove back onto the A&P parking lot.

"Say, listen!" Eric yelled out toward the streakers. "I'm going to have to turn this car around! So, you better hold on!" The two streakers jumped off the car and ran back toward Five Points on their own.

When the Chevy returned to Five Points, Eric and the two girls followed the crowds gaze to find the streakers climbing up the rainspout toward the top of the Burlhome Baptist church steeple doing a dance for the cheering crowd as the police and firemen struggled to climb up after them.

"It's time to split!" Eric said to the girls. "The police are probably looking for this car!"

Eric double parked in front of Susie's house. The girls slid out of the car.

"I think I've had enough for the night," said Karen. "I'm going home."

"Can I give you a lift?" asked Eric.

"No, Thanks, I live around the corner."

"Opie said that he'll give you a call. Are you still mad at him?"

"It's not that I'm mad at him, Eric. Your cousin has to grow up a bit."

"Well, I can't argue with that."

Karen turned and walked down the dark street to leave Eric and Susie alone. Susie stood in the street next to the driver's side door. Eric pulled out a cigarette then dangled his arms out the window.

"I think I grew up a bit," Eric proclaimed.

"You think so?" asked Susie with a straight face.

She asked him for a cigarette, which Eric pulled out. He lit both cigarettes with his Zippo and handed Susie hers. Susie took a drag.

"So, I'm here to apologize from the prom," said Eric "You have to believe my sincerity. I fought crowds, riots, and the police just to be with you tonight."

Susie tried to hold back a grin that shined through. "I like you, Eric. I mean, I want to like you, but…"

"But what?"

"But. I don't know. I have to find myself."

"'Find yourself?' Now you sound like a typical Northeast JAP. And you accused me of being a typical AZA boy from Northeast? Well, I'm not from the Northeast, nor was I ever associated with AZA." Eric waited for a response that never came. Just a puff of smoke from her mouth. "Come here," he said.

Susie stood her ground and tried to restrain a grin. "What?" she asked defiantly.

"Come here!" Eric reached out, grabbed her by the waist and pulled her in closer toward the car. With her arms by her side holding the smoldering cigarette, Susie presented a slight smile.

"What?" she asked less defiantly.

"I'm hungry. Let's go to the Country Club Diner. My treat."

"We can't drive through that crowd. Besides, you're probably a wanted man."

"So, we'll walk to Nick's Roast Beef. It's closer."

"Walk?"

"It's around the corner!" Eric proclaimed. "You're not going to be that typical Northeast girl that refuses to walk, are you?

Susie dropped her arms on top of Eric's shoulders and sucked in her cheeks from his accusation. "I'm hungry. Park this green piece of shit, Circus Boy!"

. . . .

It took three weeks for Uncle Pat's friend to succumb to cancer. Carol marked Eric an acceptable absence from school to work as a pallbearer. She thought one- hundred-fifty dollars for a couple hours of work was worth missing one day of school. Besides, it was close to the end of the school year, and Eric was basically caught up in all his academic work.

Uncle Pat was driving the hearse leading the long procession out of the city of Philadelphia to Lafayette Hills, Conshohocken. Opie and Eric sat in the back in jump seats next to the casket, while Aunt Frieda sat in the front. Behind the hearse a black limousine with the immediate family was followed by an entourage of relatives and friends.

Driving respectfully through the township of Whitemarsh, a patrol officer on a motorcycle pulled Uncle Pat over along with his procession. The patrol officer straddled off his motorcycle and walked back to the hearse. Uncle Pat slid down his window to hear the policeman's explanation.

"Good morning, sir." Said the patrol officer.

"It's a funeral possession. How good can it be?" Uncle Pat replied.

"Driver's license and registration, please."

"May I ask what this is about, officer?" asked Uncle Pat as he surrendered his identification. Opie stared straight into the back of Aunt Frieda's head as a deer looking into headlights, while Eric stared out the left side window.

"I have a written warning that this vehicle tag number Pennsylvania THX-138 is barred and not to be seen in this township for a period of ninety days."

"Excuse me?" asked Uncle Pat, not believing his ears.

"The warning states that this vehicle was used three weeks prior dated May 27, 1975, in a noncommercial capacity, in an unlawful, immoral, and unorthodox manner."

Uncle Pat and Aunt Frieda glanced back at the boys. "I assure you, officer," Uncle Pat explained. "That this procession is for real, and I will get to the bottom of this 'immoral and unorthodox manner.'"

"Where is your destination, sir?" asked the police officer.

"Conshohocken." Uncle Pat replied, "Saint Matthews Cemetery."

"Well, until this warning is lifted, I'll have to escort you through the township."

The police officer returned Uncle Pat's ID, then hopped back onto his motorcycle. The procession followed suit.

"I'm not going to kill you, Opie," Uncle Pat said calmly as he followed the motorcycle. "I'm not even going to ask what you did with this vehicle on May 27. Even if you told me the truth, I probably wouldn't believe it."

"Were you in on this, Eric?" asked Aunt Frieda.

"Yes, Aunt Freida." Eric admitted, gazing out the window.

"Was your cousin John from New Orleans in on this when he came to visit?" asked Aunt Freida.

"Yes, mom." Replied Opie.

"We don't know what to do with you, Opie," added Aunt Frieda. "You get yourself kicked out of schools, you have detentions, suspensions. We leave you alone for one week and this! Your father and I are lost, Opie. We just don't know what to do anymore! I bet your mother knows what to do, Eric! I'm not going to let this go! I don't care what type of retarded school you attend! I'm going to tell your mother! I'm tired of shielding you! This is my family business! It's about time you took some responsibility for yourself!"

'Retarded school', Eric thought to himself. So, there you have it. Eric had always addressed his school as retarded, but to hear it from somebody else. A family member. Aunt Frieda's true sediment popping out from anger and frustration. 'A retarded school. That confirms it...' Eric thought. 'I'm a retard'.

· ·

That night, in the dimly lit living room, after receiving the phone call from Aunt Frieda, sitting on the worn green sofa, both Mr. and Mrs. Blum listened to Eric who was standing in front of them as he explained to his parents five times in his own words and in different variations of the theme what he, Cousin Opie, and John did with the hearse the night the Flyers had won their second Stanley cup. Mrs. Blum continued with her inquisition.

"Do you have a death wish?"

"No, mom."

"Well, it seems like you do! Riding around in the back of a hearse like you're dead! Where did you go?"

"I told you, mom. Glenside, Abington, Willow Grove, Roslyn, Whitemarsh."

"Tell me again what you did with the hearse?" Mr. Blum asked"

"Like I said. Just cursing round, scaring people as a joke."

"You better talk to Dr. Goldman about this death wish." Mrs. Blum added. Eric rolled his eyes. "Better yet," continued Mrs. Blum, "I'll call him myself! Was it the same hearse your brother was lying in?"

Eric never thought about that. Who would think about asking such a question? "Well, was it, Eric?"

'It had to be the same hearse', Eric thought. *'Uncle Pat bought it brand new back in '67. It was the first one he owned outright'*.

"Well, Eric? Was it?"

"I guess so, mom."

"Would you jump into your brother's grave if you and Opie thought it to be funny? You're sick, Eric! To play dead where your brother laid!"

"Yeah, I'm sick all right!" Eric lashed out. "I'm sick of you, mom! Just look around! I'm sick of living in this stuffy closed-in, remorse-filled asylum you created! And you're bringing dad down with you! Well, you're not bringing me down! You're the one who has been lying in that hearse all these years, mom! You're the one who needs help! You're very sick! How long did they lock you away in that nut house, mom? Three months, four? Because it wasn't long enough! Close the front door, lady! The dead man ain't coming home! So, get on with it!" Eric marched up the stairs to his bedroom and slammed the door closed.

"Did you hear the way he talks to his mother?" Mrs. Blum asked her husband.

"Maybe he's right," Mr. Blum quietly replied.

CHAPTER 11

TEACHER, I NEED YOU

THE NEXT MORNING, Eric was in his bedroom lying in bed when Opie called to see how Eric's parents had taken the news about their hearse adventure.

"Opie, why can't your father lease a new hearse every year like other normal morticians?"

"What?"

"Never mind. I don't want to get into it."

"Are you punished?" Opie asked.

"No, not that I know of. You?"

"No. I think my parents really gave up on me. Gosh, if I knew it was going to be that easy to get my parents off my back, I would have taken the hearse years ago. Are you doing anything tonight?" Opie asked.

"I'm afraid to ask. Why?"

"Well, my father has a friend who is managing this State Store in center city who needs some shelves stocked and is short-handed. I was wondering if you would like to make a few bucks under the table. The store closes at nine o'clock. Then afterword we can horse around downtown.

"But we're not old enough to work at a State Store. Besides, I misplaced my ID that D'Angelo had given me."

"You won't need ID. We're stocking shelves. Nobody will know. My father's friend will cover for us."

On December 5, 1933, prohibition was repealed with the ratification of the twenty-first amendment to the U.S. Constitution. On December 6, 1933, licensees were approved by the Pennsylvania Liquor Control Board (PLCB) to sell alcohol to bars and restaurants for on-premises consumption. On January 2, 1934, the Commonwealth allowed consumers to buy alcohol legally for off-premises consumption from government own stores called State Stores.

Eric found himself with Cousin Opie working at a State Store on chestnut and 8th Street downtown Philadelphia. It had been six months since he had last dressed in a white button-down shirt with black pants and shoes. Toward the end of the working evening, as Eric was opening boxes of vodka between isles, a short elderly nun sheepishly wandered toward him.

"Would you be a saint and reach me down that bottle of Cutty Sark from the top shelf, please?" she asked in a discreet soft but thick Scottish accent.

"You, sister?"

"Shh!" gestured the nun as she put her index finger against her lips. She quickly glanced around to make sure nobody was nearby. "Well, lad, it's not for me. It's for me Mother Superior. You see she's constipated, and this will help her relieve her bowels."

"Sure," said Eric. "Who am I to ask?" Eric reached up and brought down a single bottle of whiskey. "Here ya go."

"How much do me owe, and a paper bag please?"

"You can get a bag and pay for it at the register." Eric offered with a smile.

"Aye. Well," replied the nun, "I'm trying to keep a low profile, if you know what me mean."

"I sure do, but I'm not working the register. I'm just stocking shelves."

"Oh, all right," the nun responded disappointingly. "Thank you, and may God bless."

Nine at night is when all the State Stores in the state of Pennsylvania had to close. The store manager thanked the boys, paid them each $50 cash.

Opie and Eric walked east on Chestnut Street, then looking south on 8th Street they spotted the old nun laid flat out on her back drunk as a skunk holding onto a third bottle of Cutty Sark. Her habit threatening to fall off her head, and her black dress spread out like an ink stain over the sidewalk. The boys ran over by her side.

"Sister! Sister!" Eric shouted kneeling over. "I don't understand! You said this liquor was for Mother Superior!"

"Aye, it is for me Mother Superior lad, because she is constipated," the nun explained with a Scottish burped into Eric's face. "And when she turns the corner and finds me ass lying here, aye, she's going to shit!"

Eric and Opie helped the nun to a cab and sent her to the convent she claimed to belong to.

"So, what do you want to do now?" said Eric. "It's way too early to head back home."

"Well, I'm kind of hungry, let's get a bite to eat at Winston's." Suggested Opie.

The restaurant H.A Winston's & Co., was one of the 'in' places to eat and to be seen in downtown Philly. It was located on Front and Chestnut Street by the Delaware River. The restaurant was famous for its seven to ten once burgers known as the 'GourmetBurgers' on a huge poppy seed Kaiser roll, and delicious French onion soup. Like Steak 'N Brew, the decor was of an English pub. Pictures and knick-knacks on the walls and ceiling depicted a Victorian era.

When Eric and Opie arrived, Winston's was packed with young people shouting over each other competing with the piped-in music from the progressive rock radio station, W.Y.S.P-FM.

As the boys were being escorted by the hostess toward the back of the dining area, a tall thin man sitting at the bar was distracted from drinking his beer when he saw through a reflection in the mirror from the back-bar Eric squeezing by behind him. He tapped the shoulder of his short robust friend whom he was sitting beside and pointed in the direction of the back-dining area. The two union Bellies from the Spectrum grinned at the unexpected opportunity.

After dinner, filled with hamburger, onion soup and soda, Eric and Opie walked out of Winston's toward the Delaware River to see the newly renovated for the Bicentennial celebration Penn's Landing. The two Bellies followed suit out of the restaurant.

As the boys walked along Delaware Avenue by Penn's Landing, out from the shadows of one of the abandoned dark piers Eric and Opie were confronted by the two Bellies. Eric was astounded.

"Friends of yours, Eric?"

"Old friends of mine, Op."

Of all the years that Eric had been hanging around with his cousin, he had never seen Opie frightened of anybody or anything. But with intimidating looking men approaching with no verifiable cause, this was the first time he had witnessed Opie scared.

"I'm friends with Pete D'Angelo!" Eric proclaimed to the pursuers. "I don't think he would want to see any harm done to me."

"D'Angelo?" said the tall thin man as he and his short friend slowly advanced. "You've got the wrong family, pal! We work under Scarfo."

"D'Angelo?" Said the short man. "Ha! If you make it out of here alive tonight, you tell that poof fudge packer that I'm after his ass too," he chuckled. "But only figuratively!" he recoiled seriously.

"I don't work at the Spectrum anymore." Said Eric. "I don't understand why I should still be a threat to you?"

"It was the outcome." Replied the thin man. "You have changed the way management does business with us. It's not to our liking. And somebody must pay."

"So, D'Angelo is a fag!" Opie blurted out.

"Not now, Op," said Eric. "Not now. This is where we're going to have to split up."

Opie ran south on Delaware Avenue. Eric ran west over the Chestnut Street bridge across Delaware Ave toward center city where he thought he may have half a chance of survival out running and blending in with the night crowd. On Second and Chestnut, Eric thought he was safe until he glanced back to find the Bellies continuing their pursuit. Eric continued to run west on Chestnut Street pushing bystanders aside. With a full stomach from a late dinner, he was quickly becoming exhausted.

On 6th Street and Chestnut, a five-ton Ryder rental box truck stopped for a red light at the intersection blocked Eric from crossing. With the driver's protest, Eric climbed onto the box, blindly jumped off the other side landing through the rag top of a convertible car parked by the curve. Even though his body was in shock from the impact, his mind told him to keep moving. Like a madman Eric ripping away the rest of the metal frame and canvas, climbed out of the car as fast as he could. Pedestrians who were astonished to witness the boy jump through the cars roof were frozen in place and stood aside as Eric proceeded to run down the street. At the intersection of Race and Sixth street, stopping for a breath, Eric noticed blood from his chin and stomach soaking through his white shirt. He glanced behind and was amazed to see the two thugs were still pursuing him. Toward the east, Eric saw the pearly lights of the Ben Franklin Bridge strung down from the expansion cables like opaque Christmas ornaments leaping over toward New Jersey. The Bellies would never have the stamina to follow him over the bridge, Eric thought.

All exhausted, the chase continued in slow motion. Jogging up the steep incline on the south side of the bridge's pedestrian walkway felt like a twenty-six-mile marathon. At the apex of the bridge, Eric stopped to gaze behind to find the thin man flashing a gun struggling too catch-up. The fat man fifty feet behind was tired and sluggish. Not more than fifteen feet below the walkway was the bridge's road streaming with east bound traffic into New Jersey. Beside the road was the Linden Wald high-speed train line that followed the bridge to and from Camden. Beyond was the uninviting black and cold Delaware River. Exhausted, Eric struggled to decide if he should jump off the walkway to the road below or onto the Linden Wald train line. The Bellies are catching up. Out of desperation, Eric leaped off the walkway and onto the Linden Wald high-speed train tracks. He landed with such an impact on his feet that it felt like he had sprained both ankles. His face was the mask of death when he saw the Linden Wald train coming from Philadelphia heading toward 'Zaberers, Just Minutes Away', traveling too fast to stop and too close to see.

The thin man ran over to the spot where Eric had leaped. He looked over the railing and saw no sign of life but the red lights from the train heading into Camden. The short man had finally caught up with his partner and hung over the railing to catch his breath.

"We finished him now!" said the thin man.

Both men hustled back toward Philly satisfied knowing Eric couldn't had survived the jump or the train.

All the clocks and bells from the building and churches that surrounded downtown Philadelphia and Camden, New Jersey chimed to remind the people of both cities that midnight had arrived. Unbeknown to the Bellies, Eric had missed the train by a hair, and was barely holding on with both hands to an I-beam under the railway overhanging the Delaware River. Gripping as he struggled, city grease, grime, pigeon, and rat dung slapped his face. The throbbing heartbeat sound of a container ship and smoke from its stack passing beneath made it difficult for Eric to breathe. The reality of death with nothing underneath to break the fall if he should slip was overwhelming. But death was not an option. Bloody, sweaty, and with every exhausted muscle in his sore body, Eric climbed to a steel I-beam under the roadway. A slight sigh and a laugh of alleviation escaped as he laid on his bloody stomach. Too tired to move, the cool, filthy bridge beam was a temporary relief.

When he thought he had regained enough strength, Eric pulled himself up and sat on the beam as he began to throw up the hamburger, he had eaten less than an hour before. His vomit splattered on the beam and continued to drop one-hundred and thirty-five feet below into the black abyss of the Delaware River.

There is no catwalk or grating under the roadway of the Ben Franklin Bridge. Still exhausted and in internal pain he had to find a way to climb back onto the roadway, and eventually limp back toward the Philly side. He knew he could not go home to face his parents in the shape he was in. He didn't want them to panic and call the police.

Back on solid ground, Eric felt relieved at this time of night that the Ben Franklin Square Park at the foot of the bridge was void of people. In pain, Eric scrambled to a nearby pay phone. In his pants pocket he scrounged for enough change to call Carol for help. Carol would save him. She had always pulled through in the past.

It was after one in the morning when the phone at Carol's apartment rang. Luckily, she was home lounging in her bed wearing a pink robe with a towel wrapped around her hair, repainting her red toenails with tissue paper between her toes when she received the stressed call.

"Carol," Eric wheezed out.

"Eric? Are you alright?" She felt something was wrong. It was the pain in his voice.

"Teacher, I need you," Eric announced trembling.

"Eric! What happened? Where are you?"

"I'm in a phone booth by Ben Franklin Square Park. I'm in trouble, and I'm hurt, bad!"

Eric dropped the receiver as he slid down the glass on his back to the floor from exhaustion. Carol repeatedly called out his name, but there was no answer. Just the undertones from the city in the background.

"Eric, I'm coming down there to get you! Don't move! This better not be another one of your jokes! I swear to God this better not!"

Carol didn't know what to make of it. Eric was very capable of playing a joke like this to grab her attention. But she had this strong feeling she should show up at the foot of the Ben Franklin Bridge. Carol closed the nail polish bottle, jumped out of her robe, and slipped on a T-shirt and a pair of jeans. In her bare feet without taking out all the toilet paper from between her toes, she carried her clogs, grabbed her purse, and hopped into her loud VW, and as fast as she could drove to Center City Philadelphia to look for Eric.

Luckily traffic was light, and it took Carol over forty-five minutes to reach her destination. She illegally parked in front of a fire hydrant at Ben Franklin Square. In her car, Carol pulled out all but one of the tissues from between her toes. She slipped into her clogs and ran up to the only phone booth lit by its florescent bulb. The receiver was dangling down from its cradle. There were traces of blood on the glass and floor, but the trail stopped short outside the booth.

Gazing around the square, she found something or someone in the shadows of the shrubbery. It was Eric. What a mess. Helping him into her small car was no small task, especially trying not to break any of her newly polished fingernails. Carol repeatedly asked Eric what had happened. But Eric was too exhausted and in shock to reply. As they drove off, Eric shaded himself from the bright lights from the oncoming traffic. He glanced down at the car's floorboard and noticed a wad of tissue paper sticking out from Carol's right clog from between her big toe. Carol wanted to take him to a hospital. Eric refused and kept insisting not to be taken back to his parents' house. Knowing his mother as she did, Carol drove Eric to her apartment. Warren wasn't there and she figured that Eric would feel more at ease. What else could she do?

At the apartment, Eric didn't want any bright lights. Carol kept one lamp light on and lit a few incent candles, then ordered Eric to take a hot shower to relax his sore muscles and wash off the city dirt and the dried blood from his body. While he showered, Carol threw his clothes-which had an odor of garbage on vomit and smelled like a homeless person-into the small washer/dryer located in a water closet in the kitchen. The white shirt was destroyed with rips and stains from the battle of survival.

After his shower Carol handed Eric the only thing she had to offer since she was in the mist of drying her own laundry. A blue silk Japanese kimono. He stepped out into the living room wearing it. It barely fit him. The kimono stopped a few inches above his knees. At the sight, Carol unsuccessfully tried to hide the laughter behind the palm of her hand.

"You think this is funny?" he asked.

"Well."

"Funnier than 'Circus Boy?'"

"It's a pretty close second."

"You're not going to tell anybody at school, are you?"

"Honey, nobody will ever know from my lips that you were here with me at my apartment tonight."

That's all Carol needed, the school to find out she harbored one of their students at her apartment, half dressed in a Japanese kimono. How could she explain that?

Carol walked into the kitchen and boiled a pot of water and made hot chocolate. They both sat on the living room floor with their backs leaning against the two opposing sofas facing each other sipping their warm beverages.

"Want some music?" Carol asked as she got off the floor and approached the record player on a metal entertainment cart.

"Yeah. Nothing too loud, please."

Carol picked up the first of a few albums that were lying on an end table. It was The Best of Bread. She put the record on the turntable and placed the needle to the first soft song, Want to Make It with You.

Carol sat back on the floor across from Eric. Eric seemed stable by then, so Carol decided to ask a few questions.

"How did you ever get in such a mess?"

"Oh, man. Remember I told you about those goons at the Spectrum who tried to kill me? Well, they caught up with me and Opie at Winston's in Center City."

"Opie! Where is he?"

"I have no idea. The last time I saw him, he was running south on Delaware Avenue."

"He left you. That asshole! Why am I not surprised?"

"No, we split up! I hope he made it. I'm sure they were just after me.

"Do you want me to call your parents?"

"No!" Eric called out.

"Well, your parents must know where you are. It's late."

"I'll call them. I know how to handle my mother."

Eric carefully and stiffly crawled to the other side of the living room to reach the phone on the end table. His mother answered on the second ring.

"Hi, mom? I know it's late, but I'm with Carol Schor." Eric offered a fake giddy laugh to throw off any scent of suspicion his mother might have. "I know I should have called earlier, but Opie and I met Carol and her boyfriend *Warren* downtown, and before we knew it, it was after midnight. So, I'm staying over at Carol's tonight. She'll take me home tomorrow... Yes, yes, everything is fine. *Warren* is here." Carol shook her head as Eric exaggerated Warren's name. "I know I should have called earlier, but it was one of those things... Well, Opie took the subway home... Yes, I could have taken the subway with him, but I know you don't want me to take the subway at night; besides, I was tired and Carol and *Warren* insisted that it was too late to ride the subway, and Opie is still walking on thin ice at home from the hearse incident, so he thought it would be better if he went home... Yes, she will drive me home tomorrow morning. Goodnight, mom... I love you too mommy. Bye... Yes, I'll thank her for you." Eric hung up the phone.

"I didn't think that I would be the entire story," Carol said as she sipped her hot chocolate.

"Yeah, well. I'm sorry. But I'm here, so…"

"What hearse incident?" Asked Carol,

"You haven't heard? Wow! Opie and I took the hearse for a joy ride."

With the dim lights from the candles, listening to the music for a few moments. Eric and Carol stared at each other in silence when she caught Eric's toes rubbing against hers. Thinking it wasn't the most inappropriate song to play at that moment, Carol jolted off the floor, and turned off the stereo.

"So!" Said Carol. "I think we both had a very exciting evening. And tomorrow is another day."

Eric watched her as she made a makeshift bed from the living room couch with a sheet and a spare pillow, she received from her bedroom closet.

"Your shirt was destroyed. I may have an extra one." Carol walked back into her bedroom, shuffled through the dresser drawer, and pulled out a white button-down shirt, walked back into the living room and threw the shirt on the couch.

"Yeah. It's Warren's. Take it. I don't want your mother to get too suspicious when you return home without a white shirt. Besides, Warren won't mind."

"And where is the *Warren*?" Eric asked with half a smile.

"He is at his '*apartment*'. Carol knew that was coming. It was only a matter of time.

"Uh-huh! I see. Are you sure that he's at his apartment?" Eric teased.

Carol sucked in her cheeks from his accusation. "And where was Susie tonight?"

"With her girlfriends."

"Are you sure she's not at a BBG social?" Eric's only reply was a smile. "You think you'll be comfortable on the couch?"

"No. I don't think so. I'm scared of the dark."

"Well, tonight you're going to have to be a brave little boy. Goodnight."

As Carol walked toward her bedroom, Eric got up from the floor with some strenuous effort, passed her and blocked her entrance to the bedroom. They were nose-to -nose. Carol turned her head slightly, not wanting to look into his face.

"Eric?" She paused. "What do you think you're doing?"

"I was hoping you wouldn't need to ask that question," he replied in a soft voice. "I was hoping we would both know what to do."

"What-are-you-doing?" she asked more sternly.

"Can I go to bed with you?"

It was to the point. No games. No hints. No bullshit. Carol began to tremble. It was from the shock of a straight out, up-front question. Of all the years of their relationship, she never knew or thought of Eric in this matter. This was not French Creek. They were alone. No witnesses. She wasn't sure how he would react if she should reject him.

"No, Eric. I'm sorry."

"Why, I'll be gentle. Nobody will ever know."

"I'll know. And we've been through this at school, at the hospital, and French Creek. The answer is still 'no'. I can't. I won't."

"But there's nobody here. No 'risk'. Isn't that what you told me at French Creek? The only thing between us was risk."

"No. That's not what I meant."

With both hands, Eric gently ran through her hair and around her chin then softly slipped his left index finger over her mouth to rub her lips. Carol closed her eyes anticipating the inevitable. Eric took his finger away from her mouth and stared at her as he massaged her shoulders.

When Carol was going to college-she had attended a couple feminist and women's ERA (Equal Right Amendments) meetings. They taught her that, in case of rape, if you can't fightback, stay calm and let it take its course.

"Eric," Carol said as softly and as non-confrontational as possible. "I'm going to dry your clothes, then I'm driving you home."

"At this hour?"

"At this hour."

"No. Don't take me home!" Eric pleaded. "Please! I don't ever want to go home. I want to stay with you. I want a life with you. I want to be with you for always. We'll make it work, Carol! I'll get a job. I have connections. I know some people. I can make a phone call and *Warren* will disappear." Carol's eyes widen in dismay. "I love you, Carol."

"No Eric. You're in lust with me."

"I'm madly in love with you!" Eric proclaimed. "I always have been. If there was a choice between you or Alice, I would have pushed her off that curve myself."

"We can't be together." Carol proclaimed. "You can't be with me! You just can't. I don't love you in this way. It won't be fair for both of us if only one person is in love with the other. What kind of life would that be for you?"

"A life with you. I would be with you. That's the kind of life I want." Said Eric.

"It wouldn't be fair for me." Replied Carol. "I'm in love with somebody else."

Eric's eyes began to fill with tears. "You can learn to love me. We can grow together, Carol. I never want to go back home. I can't go back home now. Please don't take me home. Let me stay with you. I'll behave. I promise."

"Then, get over to that sofa. And go to sleep." Carol slowly turned the doorknob behind her and slipped inside the bedroom, closing the door, locking, and leaving Eric alone in the living room. Eric leaned his back against the closed bedroom door. Carol leaning her head on the other side could still feel his presence.

"I never wanted to hurt you," Eric said through his tears. "All I ever wanted to do was to love you. Just love you." Carol turned and leaned her back on the other side listening to Eric sob softly. Her own eyes began to cloud up as she slid onto her bed staring at the phone by the night table. It hit a nerve when Eric mentioned that Warren might not be at his apartment. Carol dialed Warren's number.

"Hi, Warren… Yeah, I know it's late. Did I wake you?" Eric put his ear against the bedroom door. "No, nothing is wrong… I know… I was out earlier. Eric had an accident, so I came to his rescue…Yeah, you know that, Eric Blum." She chuckled. "Lately I seem to be his knight in shining armor. I'll explain later… Yeah, he's all right. I drove him home to his mother's. I miss you. I love you too… No! You don't have to come over tonight. I'm really tired besides, it's late…Yes! I'm sure. No, not tonight… Goodnight. I love you too."

• •

The following Monday morning. Nobody from school knew that Eric had spent a night at Carol's apartment. She couldn't afford any more rumors about the two of them. She wasn't worried. She knew Eric wouldn't say anything. After that close encounter the previous weekend, the child she had met four years earlier had died. She found it difficult to face him. Carol decided from this point on to keep her distance. All morning she had been trying not to pay too much attention to Eric.

"Okay, let's talk about current events," Carol announced to the class.

"I heard that Mayor Rizzo is going to announce an energy conservation plan for the city," Mark Stern called out. "I read in the Evening Bulletin last night that the mayor will stop using oil on his hair." The class laughed.

"Now what I heard, Carol," announced Mick Maze, "is that the mayor has so much oil on his hair, the United States Government wants to take over his head."

As the class laughed on, Tony dropped his desktop down.

"I thought you were over that!" Carol said.

"Oh, you have to let me have one more!" Tony replied with a smile.

As the period bell rang out, all the students jolted out of their seats to rush out of the room except for Eric who was still sitting at his desk in the back of the class chewing the last of his double-decker peanut-butter and jelly sandwich. Carol sat at her desk preparing for her next class.

"Opie called me last night. He made it."

"That's good to hear. That Opie made it," Carol replied as she concentrated on her paperwork.

"I couldn't help but notice how concerned you were about my wellbeing this past weekend. We also had a golden opportunity." Announced Eric.

"Eric!"

"What's the problem, Carol? Nothing happened between us!"

Eric carefully peeled out of his seat and approached her with some stiffness. A line of freshman students for next period stopped by the classroom threshold.

"Can we come in?" one asked.

"Yes! come in, sit down, and shut up!" Carol squawked back. "We have to talk," she said to Eric in a single breath. "We have to talk right now!"

Carol popped out of her chair, grabbed Eric by his wrist, and rushed out of the room brushing students in the hallway. Carol continued to toe Eric through the reception area, the cafeteria, and outside the school onto the stone patio where they could be alone.

"This has got to stop right now! Do you hear me? Now! My job is online every time we have a private talk! We've been through this cat-and-mouse game for the past four years! It was cute at first, but this past weekend you went way over and far beyond your bounds…"

"But Carol…"

"No! Don't but me! And shut up! I've had it, Eric! I can't fight you on this subject any longer! I don't like you in that way! You have got to stop this game with me and know your limits!"

"It's not a game." Eric said softly. "I'm madly in love you,"

"Shut up!" Carol glanced around to see if anybody was nearby. "Just shut up! Oh God, Eric! I thought you were going to rape me the other night!"

"I wasn't going to rape you…"

"Shut the fuck up! This is your problem! You don't know when to shut-the-fuck-up!" Carol paused as Eric stared silently onto the ground. "Look, Eric. This year we've been getting too close. I think we have to back off like, for the entire summer! Susie is a beautiful girl. She's your age. You two can grow old together. And if Susie turns out not to be the one, well, in a few days, you'll be out of here. You'll go to college. You'll meet another girl. You'll forget all about me, I know you will."

Eric looked up at Carol's face. "I'm leaving?" he asked in surprise. "I'm actually leaving this place?"

Carol recoiled and thought about what she had just announced. "I wasn't supposed to tell you yet. You're getting out of here. You proved yourself this year. I've known about it for the past month."

"Why didn't you tell me?"

"Don't you think I wanted to! But I was afraid that if you knew, you would start to slack off. And I was sworn of secrecy… Oh come on, Eric! You knew the whole time. That's what you kept saying this whole year. 'This year will be my last'."

"Yeah, but to hear it from somebody else of authority! It's time to celebrate! A farewell event. We'll do something that the school will never forget. I'll have to think about it."

"Eric! I just went over this with you!" She grabbed him by the ears and pulled him in closer. "We-are-not-an-item!"

"Yeah, yeah. Do you know why Cousin Opie was kicked out of Bishop McDevitt this past year?"

Carol let go of Eric's ears. "Why the fuck do I care?"

"Because he was going to put 'ex-lax' in the school's milk. Now I got this idea."

"Eric, you're not listening to me!"

"If I could melt it down," Eric continued.

"Look," she interrupted him. "I don't know what's on your mind, but I still have to work here next year. So, I can't get involved!"

Carol started to walk toward the building when Eric pulled her back.

"Just listen to me, Carol. For the last four years we've been pulling off the greatest stunts that could be pulled off in a private school. We weren't as good as Cousin Opie, but we wrote the book! Carol, let me make the plans before you say no."

"No!"

"I have to get to my next class." said Eric as he raced back toward the building. "I'll talk to you about it later!"

"Oh, and that's another thing, Eric!" Carol shouted after him. "I don't want you calling my apartment anymore!"

Carol glanced up at the second floor and saw a couple of students watching from an open window. "Uh-oh!"

CHAPTER 12

'CONGRATULATIONS'

FOR THE FOLLOWING two days, Eric tried to explain to Carol his idea for a final prank at the school. She didn't take him seriously, so Carol let him babble as she looked on with amusement.

Then, it was graduation day. Seven graduates, including Eric Blum, Mark Stern and Thomas Jones whose transcripts reached Boston University on time, took their place in line on stage in Curtis Hall at Curtis Arboretum Park in Cheltenham Township. The entire student body and staff were there to witness the ceremonies along with parents, local political dignitaries, and guests. Mr. Swanson was Master of ceremonies.

After speeches of encouragement and felicitations from local dignitaries, the turning of the tassels commenced. Eric stood third in line and was apprehensive if his tassel would be turned. Carol walked behind Swanson handing out the diplomas.

Swanson approached Eric and stared at him straight in the eye like a marine drill sergeant. Eric stared back as he swallowed. Swanson slowly turned his tassel. They both gave up a grin accompanied by a handshake. Carol handed Eric the diploma with a broad smile.

"Congratulations Eric," she whispered.

Clasping her hand. "Five-thirty tomorrow morning," Eric whispered back "I will pick you up from your apartment. I have a plan."

Carol lost her smile and quickly pulled her hand away from his as she moved along to the next student. There was no way he was going to drag her ass out of bed at five-thirty in the morning for some sort of school coup.

Mr. Swanson walked over to the lectern to recite a few words of praise to the graduates and then introduce Eric as the exiting student body president. Eric walked up to the lectern while guests and students applauded.

Eric took a slip of paper with an outline of his speech from his back pocket under his graduation gown and placed it on the lectern. Before commencing, he quickly glanced around the room and saw his parents sitting with the rest of the guest. His father with an approving grin, his mother had tears of joy streaking down her cheeks.

"Ladies and gentlemen, student body, faculty, and guests. As we are all aware, another school year has ended. Some of you will be returning in the fall, others will not. For all those who will not be returning a farewell speech is appropriate. A farewell speech usually consists of past accomplishments and failures and fragments of nostalgic moments that can only be revisited and remembered by photographs or by vivid mental pictures.

"As a species of reason, we never seem satisfied with the present. We find ourselves reminiscing about the good old days or we're excited about an event of tomorrow, but we're never happy about, now. I'm no exception.

As I stand here delivering my final Student Council speech, I can't help but think back to the four years as Student Body President. If there were any way to go back of course I would govern my office differently. How different is not important now. What has happened has. We cannot change the past, but we can surely change the future. This is what I say to the grads., at this point in our lives, it is not too late to say that we cannot move forward."

The hall applauded. Eric waited until they subsided. "Since everything in life is subjected to change, no matter what we decide to do with our lives or where we decide to go from this day forward, we will always be learning. I have learned firsthand this past school year that life can be short lived for a handful of people. I have learned this past school year about the workforce. I have found that in most cases, employees are not looking for young people with brains. They're looking for older people with experience. If this trend keeps up, there won't be enough older people around with experience, just a lot of young people with brains. Then what will this world be like? Perhaps we'll think twice about dumping untreated chemicals and nuclear waste into our drinking water, rivers, and streams. Perhaps automobile manufacturers will think twice about letting their latest model roll off the assembly line, only to be recalled by the outcome of a fatality from a manufacture's defect. Or perhaps…" Eric stopped for a moment to compose himself. "… A young congress will think twice about getting into a war they had no intentions of winning."

He paused again to permit a cloud of tear clear from his eye. "Maybe, just maybe, if we had won that war, if we had gotten out a few short years earlier, I know my brother would be sitting among us here today listening to my high school graduation speech."

As he paused to let the choke in his throat dissipate, Eric looked toward the audience to find his parents shedding tears. To his surprise just a few rows behind, Uncle Pat and Aunt Frieda. Aunt Frieda's eyes clouded with tears, giving a grin and a nod of approval.

"Experience is not to be taken lightly. It is for the most part the important ingredient for every employer's formula. To my fellow graduates, good luck, goodbye, and thank you." Eric received a standing ovation as he took his seat with the graduates.

At the reception, Eric was surrounded by his parents, Aunt, and Uncle.

"Your speech was one of the best I heard today, Eric." Declared Aunt Frieda as she hugged him. "I'm very proud of you. I also want to apologize for calling your school retarded. I was angry and didn't mean it to come out the way it did."

"Well, it did come out that way, Aunt Frieda." Responded Eric. "And out of anger comes the truth. But by you? I was surprised. What you said I heard all through my school years. But it was said, and it's in the past. And now, we'll move on."

Carol walked over to Eric and his family. She said hello to his parents and shook hands. Mrs. Blum then introduced her to Aunt Frieda and Uncle Pat.

"I'm sure you know their son, Opie." said Mrs. Blum.

"Oh!" Carol responded with a jolt of false enthusiasm. "Yes. I have met Cousin Opie several times throughout the years. What a fine young man. You must be very proud of him."

All stood in a moment of deadpan silence aware of the truth. Carol turned her attention toward Eric.

"That was a fine speech, Eric." Carol handed him a pocket-sized hardcover book entitled *The Prophet* by Kahlil Gibran. "This is for you. I want you to have it. It was great seeing you all," Carol said to his immediate family. "It was good to finally meet you Mr. and Mrs. O'Neal."

As Carol walked away to mingle with the rest of the students and their parents, Eric opened the book to the first blank page where Carol inscribed a passage:

'My Dearest Eric,

For without words in friendship, all thoughts, all desires, all expectations are born, and shared with joy that is unclaimed.'

Eric thought about the passage for a moment, then tucked the book into his back pocket. He gazed over the room to find Carol conversing with a couple of the other parents. Eric excused himself from his family and walked over toward her.

"Carol!" he announced. "Thanks for the book. Quite profound. Five-thirty, tomorrow morning."

·····················

A legal school year in Pennsylvania is counted as 180 days. Graduation for Noah Webster Preparatory was on the 179th day. By law in the Commonwealth of Pennsylvania, the graduates had to attend one more day to make it complete.

On that 180th school day, at five-thirty in the morning, Carol was startled out of a deep sleep by the sound of somebody hammering away at her apartment door. Sliding out of bed next to Warren, slipping into a T-shirt and a pair of sweatpants, she opened the door and was confronted by a wide-eyed, wide-awake, Eric Blum.

"Eric!" She announced, holding her head still half asleep. "What in hell are you doing here?"

"You're not dressed! come on, let's go!"

"Who is it, Carol?" asked a male voice from in the dark apartment.

"It's Eric!" She shouted back.

"Eric?" asked the voice.

"Who's that?" Eric asked Carol.

"Who do you think?"

"Carol, we don't have time to play house. Get dressed!" Eric demanded.

"For what?"

"For our farewell party!"

"Eric! Go home!"

"I can't go home. I just sneaked out of the house. Besides, by the time I get home, it will be time for school!"

"Then hang out on the school's parking lot or go to Mister Donut!" Carol slammed the door closed.

"Screw you! I'll do it myself!" Eric said after her.

Eric marched back to the apartment complex parking lot, jumped into the aquamarine Chevy, and turned on the ignition. As he pulled the car into reverse and was about to roll out of the parking spot, Carol ran after him adorned in a pink robe. She tapped on his passenger side window. Eric leaned over to roll the window down.

"Eric, what in hell are you doing?"

"I have a plan. I am not leaving this school without a bang! Hey, how come you're not wearing that cute Kimono?"

"Eric, it's five fuck'en thirty in the fuck'en morning."

"I know, and we're late!"

"I don't know what you have in mind, but I'm not going to let you go through with it!"

"With you or without, I'm leaving!" Eric put the car into drive.

"Wait!" Carol announced. "Give me twenty minutes to get dressed."

"You got five minutes to get dressed!"

"Fifteen!"

"Ten!"

Carol scurried back to her apartment and rushed into the bedroom to get dressed. Warren was still in bed waiting for her.

"What was that all about?" He asked.

"Eric is planning on doing something crazy to the school, and I have to stop him."

"Like what?"

"I don't know. Can you pick me up after school this afternoon?"

"Yeah, I think so. You know, if I didn't know any better, the way you two carry on, one might think you're having an affair with one of your students." Jested Warren.

"Oh, come on Warren! Not you, too, pleeeease!"

"I'm only kidding, honey." Warren smiled.

"I knew that." Carol confirmed with a kiss on his forehead as she rushed to finish getting dressed.

It was about six-thirty in the morning as the sun was beginning to rise when Eric drove the Chevy onto the school's empty parking lot with Carol alongside.

"Now what?" Carol asked.

"Now we wait."

"For what?"

"The milk truck."

"I can't believe I'm here," Carol said looking into her handheld mirror as she finished applying makeup. "What milk truck?"

"The milk truck that delivers the school's milk every morning."

"Why are we waiting for the milk truck?"

"Do I have to go over the plan one more time with you? All right, yesterday I hid all the school's toilet paper above the drop ceilings."

"I don't want to hear this," Carol announced as she closed the mirror and put it back into her pocketbook.

"I bought a few extra boxes of Ex-Lax, and I took a couple of hypodermic needles from the science room." Eric explained.

Carol put her hands over her ears. "I don't want to hear this!" She said again.

"When I got home last night as a test, I melted down the Ex-Lax on a portable burner—the one I have in the back seat that I borrowed from Cousin Opie."

Carol snapped her head to glance at the back seat where she found the portable hotplate with its chocolate contents all set up to be melted.

"Eric, stop! This is insane!"

"No, it isn't Carol," Eric calmly explained. "All we have to do is wait for the milkman to deliver the milk onto the steps of the school. We take the milk crate, drive to the park next door, and inject the cartons with

299

the melted diluted Ex-Lax. We then drive the crate back to the front steps of the school where Mr. Swanson picks it up and carries it off to the school's refrigerator."

"I'm leaving!" Carol said as she opened the car door, but Eric pulled her back in.

"You can't leave now! I already explained my master plan to you. You know too much. Like Pete D'Angelo taught me… if two people want to keep a secret, one must die. Don't make me kill you, Carol! Besides, it's too early in the morning and I drove you here. Where are you gonna go?"

"I'm going to tell Swanson when he gets in this morning," she threatened.

"You do, and I'm going to tell Biff the science teacher that it was you who put the thumbtacks on his chair during the PTA meeting."

"Oh, he was being an asshole that night! Look what you're doing! You got a clean break out of here. Can't you just make this your last day?"

"What is a last day of high school without a fond farewell? Look Carol, nobody is going to get hurt."

"I still can't believe I'm here," she said.

The milk truck crawled up the school's driveway. Eric and Carol ducked below the Chevy's dashboard hitting their heads on the way down. They were so close to each other that Carol felt the warm air from Eric's nostrils. There was not enough space for Carol to pull back. Millimeters apart, their lips were just about to touch. Eric slowly moved closer. After delivering its cargo on the school's front steps, the milk truck drove back down the driveway. Carol suddenly pulled away from Eric's potential lip contact.

"Come on! Let's get the milk!" She said as she threw open the car door and darted across the parking lot toward the front door of the school. She wasn't getting into Eric's practical joke. She just wanted out of that car and away from a potentially dangerous situation with Eric.

At the front door to the school, Eric grabbed hold of one side of the milk crate as Carol stood by and watched.

"Come on! What in hell are you waiting for?" he hollered.

"I'm not doing this, Eric," she announced calmly. Carol turned to walk back toward the parking lot.

"Oh, Jesus!" Eric yelled out as he chased after her. "What do you mean you're not doing this? Where are you gonna go at seven in the morning?"

"I'll walk to Mister Donut."

"That's about a mile from here! How are you going to get back home after school? You think I'm going to drive you after you deserted me?"

Carol stopped walking to face him. "I'll call Warren. He'll pick me up." she teased.

Carol continued to walk on. Eric jumped back to the crate as mad as hell and carried it to the car by himself.

"Yeah, well, I know where you can find him!" He called back as he watched her walk toward the highway. "I heard him in your apartment when I came to pick you up this morning!" Eric tossed the crate of milk into the back seat of his car next to the portable burner. After jumping back into the driver's seat, he drove off the school's parking lot passing Carol on the way. "Are you going to tell him?" He yelled out after her as the Chevy floated by. "Are you going to tell Swanson?" Carol continued to walk in silence. "It doesn't matter! I graduated anyway, bitch! You know, Tony Burns was right! You're fuck'en' possessed!" Eric stepped on the gas pedal and peeled down the highway.

Carol was so mad at him for addressing her in that manner, she held a tight upper lip as she continued to walk in silence. But the silence was deafening.

"I should have left you at the bottom of that bridge!" She shouted back. By then Eric was too far-gone to hear her.

In a vacant parking lot of the church next door to the school, in the back seat of the Chevy, Eric lit the propane tank for the portable burners with his 'Zippo' lighter, then placed a small pot with its chocolate purgative contents over the burners. He reflected as he waited for the chocolate laxative to melt.

"Let her tell him. I don't care. I graduated anyway! I don't understand her! I know she likes me. There isn't anybody who could change my mind about the fact that she wanted to kiss me this morning. Nobody!"

Eric filled the hypodermic needles with the melted laxative and carefully injected it into the pint-sized cardboard milk cartons between the folds.

After the inoculations, Eric drove back to the school. Principal Swanson's car was already parked in its spot. Eric dropped the crate on the front doorstep, rang the bell, then ran off. Swanson opened the front door and lifted the crate off the steps. He noticed the tail end of Eric's car rolling off the school's parking lot toward the highway. Thinking nothing of it, Swanson took the crate of tainted milk, and placed it in the school's refrigerator.

....

At lunchtime, Eric held onto a pint of milk as he sat alone in the corner of the cafeteria observing everybody eating lunch and drinking their milk. Since one pint was never enough, most of the students drank two cartons.

After about twenty minutes, some of the students who had drank the milk got up from their seats to use the bathrooms on the first floor. Soon, all the students who had consumed the milk stood impatiently waiting in line for their turn to use the bathrooms. A student was heard calling out from inside one of the toilet stalls.

"Holy shit! No toilet paper!"

At that moment, Eric lost it. He ran through the French doors of the cafeteria to the stone patio laughing all the way running full speed toward the park next door. On his way he passed students with bare rears hanging off dripping from the edge of the stone patio not willing to wait their turn for a toilet. Renée - who did not have any milk- was standing on the patio surrounded by the pandemonium, wondering what all the hoopla was about. She spotted Eric running out from the school toward the park laughing hysterically. Then she spotted Carol laughing, running out from the French doors of the cafeteria after Eric. As sick as this stunt may have seemed, the scene was just too funny.

At the park, Eric was doubled over in laughter as he fell and rolled onto the grass. He paused at the sight of Carol running toward him with tears of laughter. They laughed like lunatics as they rolled on the grass together. Surrealism set in when Carol realized that she was on top of Eric with their lips locked. Eric was holding her tight, not wanting to let go. With a slight struggle, Carol broke free from his embrace and without a word she pulled up like a zombie. Solemnly without a word she walked back toward the school.

"Yeah sure!" Eric yelled out after her. "Walk away! You had your chance when I spent the night at your apartment!"

Carol abruptly stopped walking as though she had slammed into a brick wall. The wall was Renée who had followed them both to the park and had seen and heard everything. Carol and Renée stared at each other for a moment. Carol silently brushed by her as she resumed walking toward the school. Eric and Renée were confronted with each other. Renée glared at Eric in shock at what she had just witnessed. Eric, still lounging on the ground surrendered a defiant grin. As Renée turned to walk back. Eric sang out a verse from the rock group The Left Banke.

"Just walk away Renée. You won't see me follow you back home."

Without turning to face Eric, Renée stopped for a moment then proceeded to walk on.

•••••••••••••••••••••

In the dark room on the second floor of the school, Dr. Goldman sat behind his desk smoking his pipe across from Eric who was sitting in that comfy leather armchair.

"So, what's this I hear about you playing dead in the back of a hearse?"

"My mother, no doubt." Said Eric.

"No doubt." Replied Goldman.

"It was a joke! It happened three weeks ago! Didn't you ever play a practical joke when you were a kid?"

"Not like that."

"Well, if you had access to a hearse, would you?"

"Not exactly." Explained Goldman. "I would have added an open casket to lie in." Eric and Goldman laughed.

Goldman picked up an eleven-by-fourteen-inch manila envelope from his desk and tossed it toward Eric. His face became stone serious as he continued to smoke his pipe.

"What's this?" asked Eric, receiving the envelope.

Without saying another word, Goldman watched Eric turn the envelope over to read the address. It was mailed to Goldman's residence. The return address was from the 'FRD, Federal Research Division (Customize Research and Analytical Services, Library of Congress)'. Eric reached into the envelope that had been previously opened by Goldman, pulled out the report, and read it out loud.

"August 16, 1969. At approximately zero-eight-forty-five, a squad of ten American Army soldiers from the first Brigade, fifth Infantry Division marched point outside the town of Fan Theyit?"

"Phan Thiet." Goldman corrected.

"Phan Thiet." Eric continued. "In Central Vietnam at the Annamese highlands. The squad encountered hostel North Vietcong guerrillas in a rice patty. Sergeant William Strong radioed air support. Two F-4 Phantom jet fighters dispatched from the aircraft carrier Constellation (CV-64) off the coast assisted the request. One of the F-4 Phantoms fired an AIM-7 Sparrow air to ground missile. Because of poor ground visibility due to the morning mist, the missile was aimed and impacted thirty-five yards short of its target. Sergeant William Tim Strong, Privates - Elliot Blum," Eric looked up at Goldman then continued to read. 'Steve McPhee, and corporal-Clarence Johnston, were struck by the in-coming American missile."

"Where did you get this?" Asked Eric.

"I have colleagues who have practices at the Pentagon who owed me a couple of favors." Said Goldman. "So, I inquired. Your mother will have closure now that she will know the truth."

Eric slipped the report back into its envelope, tore it in half, then into quarters, and threw it back onto Goldman's desk.

"What are you doing?" Asked Goldman. "I had to jump through a few hoops to get that information. That was official! This is how your brother was killed! This is what your mother has been waiting for!"

"My mother will never know that my brother was killed under 'friendly fire'. This will not be closure. This will reopen the wound. After stopped writing letters for the past three years, she will begin all over again for the rest of her life to find out any significant reason or cause for 'friendly fire'. I can't do that to her again. I won't. I want you to throw it away. Burn it! I will be the only one in my family who will know for sure how my brother died in Vietnam."

Goldman paused for a moment as he sat back in his chair blowing more smoke from his pipe observing Eric. "And how do you feel about that?" He asked. "Is there closure with you?"

"I feel no difference. I never thought of that term closure. My brother remains dead whether I know the truth or not."

"I think I understand," said Goldman. "So, let's close it right here and now! Let us move on in life. What are your plans for your future?"

"I have an appointment with a guidance counselor at the Philadelphia community college next Tuesday."

"Any ideas what you want to study?"

"I don't know yet. But even though I don't know what I want to do for the rest of my life right now, I think I got myself together." Eric stood up from his chair to shake Goldman's hand. "Have a good life, Doc. Thanks for inquiring about my brother." Eric walked toward the door.

"Eric! Do you remember the beginning of the school year when we first met? With all my credentials you asked me what I was doing at this 'one-horse school'? I said that perhaps we both could find the answer together?"

"Yeah?"

"The answer is very clear. Call it divine intervention if you wish, but I think I was sent here to help get you out and to move on. Help comes in mysterious and roundabout ways." Eric smiled as he was about to leave the room. "Blum!" Goldman called out for a second time. Eric stopped short of the threshold. "You still want to see me? I mean during the summer at my house?"

"Who's going to pay for that?" Eric inquired.

"Well, I think we can work something out."

"I think it's time for me to work out my own problems. I'm old enough. Like you just said, it's time to move on. Thanks for everything, Doc."

Goldman took the pipe out of his mouth and smiled as he blew out a puff of smoke. "That's what shrinks are for Eric. Have a good and prosperous life. Oh, and Eric, please. The next time I get a distressing phone call from your mother about you being driven in the back of a hearse, let it be for at least seventy years from now."

Eric smiled then pointed at the torn-up envelope on Goldman's desk.

Goldman picked up one quarter of the torn envelope and with the lighter from his desktop, lit it. Eric left the room nodding. Goldman patted the flames out with his left palm, tossed it into the trashcan by the desk, then closed his notebook and manila folder. "Another case accomplished." he said to himself with a pleasant smile as he sat back in his leather chair, putting the pipe against his lips, with smoke spilling out.

•••••••••••••••••••••

Principal Swanson and Carol were in the first-floor classroom over-looking the parking lot discussing the latest problem that had plagued Noah Webster Preparatory during the lunch hour. Swanson paced the room, while Carol took the chair closest to the window watching students bid their farewells out in the parking lot as they climbed on board the short yellow school bus. Swanson glanced over at the parking lot and spotted Sam and Aaron about to hop into Eric's car. He vaguely remembered seeing the back of Eric's car leaving the driveway before school had started that morning. It then dawned on him.

"It was milk! Milk! Milk! Carol, do you think that? No, it can't be. He couldn't have!" Swanson faced Carol. "Could he?"

Carol continued to glance out the window to hide a mischievous grin.

....

Meanwhile out in the parking lot. "Well, Stern. Take care of yourself," Eric said before Mark slid into his mother's canary yellow Ford Torino.

"I will, Blum. We'll keep in touch."

"Sure," Eric replied wearily.

Eric hopped into the old Chevy with Sam sitting shotgun and Aaron in the back seat. Eric turned on the ignition, pulled the green car into reverse, and for the last time slid the car out of the Noah Webster Preparatory parking spot. Before leaving the school's property, Eric spotted Renée about to climb on board the short yellow school bus. Not knowing if he would ever see her again -although Eric had no committed feelings toward her- he felt ill at ease to leave Renée hinging about the scene she had witnessed at the park. If there was going to be time to straighten out what truly went on between him and Carol, it would have to be now. Eric called out from his car window.

"Hey, Renée!"

Renée stopped short before climbing into the bus and turned to face Eric with an impatient stance. Eric waited for a verbal response from her that never came.

"Come on, Eric," said Sam. "She ain't worth it."

Eric waited for another beat. "Never mind!" he said to Renée as he stepped on the accelerator. Renée watched the car roll off the school property disappearing down the road toward Philadelphia.

Before Renée climbed on board the bus, she looked back toward the school where Carol was sitting on the edge of the stone patio waiting for Warren to pick her up. Even though there was less than fifty yards between them, Carol could feel the betrayal and hostility within Renée.

"Let's go, young lady," announced the bus driver. "It's getting late. And we gotta go!"

Renée climbed on board that short yellow school bus. The door swung close behind her, then proceeded to roll off the school's property.

CHAPTER 13

POSTSCRIPT

THAT LAST DAY of school in June of 1975 was the last time Eric Blum and Carol Schor had seen or spoken with each other.

The following fall in 1975, Eric Blum minored in Early American History at the Philadelphia Community College. He graduated with a BA in journalism from Temple University in 1980. In 1991 he was employed by a cable news network as a foreign correspondent. Eric Blum resides somewhere in France, married with two daughters and a son.

Carol and Warren were married in 1977. They have two daughters and reside in a small farmhouse in Buckingham, Pennsylvania outside the town of New Hope.

After being convicted of drug trafficking, Cousin Opie O'Neal spent five years in the 1980's at a Guatemalan prison. After his release, some years later he was elected Mayor of a small town in Upstate New York.

Early Saturday morning of March 14, 2015, two cocaine drug addicts broke into Noah Webster Preparatory looking to steal valuable items to support their habit. To hide their tracks, they set the building a blaze. The 170-year-old English Tutor with its black slate roof, wooden frames and everything in between were burned to the stone walls. Up in smoke went the rally point for the dreamers of the future, and the memories of those from the past who received the extra push they needed to succeed in society.

Today people pass by an overgrown lot that once supported an institution who did not always agree with the teaching philosophies of public schools or the excess medicating of children or the excuses of ADD or ADHD but had accepted and was encouraged to the fact that some people just think outside the box no matter what color or size school bus they travel on.

END